Advance Praise f

“The push and pull relationship between these two powerful women does more than flesh out truths about foster care; it shows the raw honesty in the fundamental human endeavors of creating a family and finding a home—a place that is not just shelter, but rather a place where one belongs. The entwined stories of Melissa and Patrice, told openly and without guile, are ultimately the story of us all.”

- *Faye J. Crosby, Distinguished Professor Emerita of Psychology, University of California Santa Cruz*

“I found myself in tears at the many poignant, heartbreaking, and complex situations that both Melissa and Patrice experienced. Anyone who has been at either end of the fostering system, or is interested in experiencing how life within this system feels, will be captivated by this intimate diary.”

- *Terry Grove, Educator and Former Foster Parent*

“This gritty true story of two women navigating a myriad of emotional and lifestyle complexities on their way to forming a ‘perfectly flawed family’ reinforces our faith in the durability of all families.”

- *Virginia Scott, Family Therapist, Founder of the internationally acclaimed Family Wellness Program, and Author of* Raising a Loving Family

MELISSA COME BACK

By
Patrice Keet
and
Melissa LaHommedieu

ISBN 978-1-63988-816-0

Published by *atmosphere press*

Cover design by Bridget A. Lyons

Some names in this memoir have been changed to protect individuals' privacy.

atmospherepress.com

To those who speak up for children

"Melissa come back."

A coax? A hoax?
A dare? A prayer?
A taunt? A flaunt?
A plea on bended knee?
An offer? A proffer?
A command? A reprimand?
A hand held out,
Or a demand in a shout?
Yelled out the window,
Or whispered down low?
Words suspended in air.
Out of need? Or love and care?

Melissa, what do you hear?
What do you reckon?
Words dismissed? Some sadly never spoken.

\- *Patrice Keet*

PART I

1
Patrice

The banquet hall's floor-to-ceiling windows begged for my attention. So, instead of concentrating on the keynote speaker, I was staring out at sailboats on the Monterey Bay when a seemingly innocuous sentence sent me reeling.

I'd been thinking about my long and complicated history with CASA, short for Court Appointed Special Advocates, the event's sponsor. My husband, Bob, and I had attended the annual fundraiser for this Santa Cruz County foster care support agency at least ten times. This particular incarnation, the 2014 one, culminated in a thirty-something woman on the podium telling her story—an abusive birth family, a childhood in foster care, a teenage pregnancy, her own children being taken away from her. While I should have been shocked by these details, it was this line that stunned me: "When I was nine and living with a family in Santa Cruz, Kristin, my CASA advocate, was the one adult I could always count on."

I spun my head back towards the stage and focused on the speaker. Blonde hair, blue eyes, about the right age. A family in Santa Cruz. An advocate named Kristin. The woman's last name was unfamiliar, but her first name wasn't. I grabbed Bob's arm and watched the blood drain from his face. "Is that *our* Melissa?" he said.

How had I not recognized her voice? There was no mistaking it. "Oh my God!" was all I could get out before I collapsed into him.

For nearly a year and a half, Melissa had been part of our family, but it had been over twenty years since she left us with holes in our hearts.

2
Melissa

"Please come with me," my fourth-grade teacher said. "You're going to miss Spelling today and spend the period talking to a nice lady." I already knew what I would be talking about: the same thing all those other adults had wanted to talk about.

When we got to the office, a pretty middle-aged woman with curly red hair was standing at the door. She had smiling eyes—the kind that instantly make you feel warm and comforted. "This is Patrice Keet, the school counselor," my teacher said, before she left the two of us alone.

It was the fall of 1993. I was nine years old and had just transferred to Capitola Elementary—the third school I'd attended in the year and a half since I'd been removed from my family home. During that time, I'd talked to social workers, psychologists, detectives, counselors, and every other kind of professional out there. I had learned that asking questions about who someone was or why I was meeting them was pointless; I was never given a straight answer. So, I just showed up at these meetings and did what they asked.

When I met Patrice, I was living with a temporary foster family. I don't recall their names, but I remember that they owned a flower shop in Capitola, California. They were fair people, in it for the right reasons. The man had all-white hair. He worked on boats and listened to classical music. There were several other kids that lived in their home, and I couldn't differentiate between the biological children and the foster children, which was a good thing. In the homes where I could make that distinction, it was usually because I was treated poorly compared to the family's "real" children.

I lived with this couple for four months—a significantly longer time than it was supposed to be, since their house was considered a "temporary placement." My stay had been extended several times. Apparently, finding me a permanent placement wasn't easy.

The meeting with Patrice didn't strike me as significant at the time, since I wasn't in a dire situation for a change. There wasn't anything I needed to withhold or anything I really needed to discuss—unlike in my previous foster homes, where abuse was all around me, and I never knew if I should reveal everything or nothing at all. I answered the questions like I always did, then I shrugged the whole thing off and went about my business. I walked home that day especially aware of the salty breeze coming off the ocean and the seagulls sailing on the currents of air.

3
Patrice

"Are you ready to meet Melissa?" Shirley asked through my half-opened door.

In addition to my private psychotherapy practice, I worked two days a week at an elementary school in Capitola, a beach-front village about five miles from our house in Santa Cruz. Shirley, a fourth-grade teacher, had told me a bit about this girl who had been in her classroom since the start of school a month before. "She lives in a foster home nearby," Shirley had said. "I guess she's been in a number of them before this one, and I'm learning that she's had a lot of trauma in her life." She went on to tell me that Melissa was very smart, but that she had a chip on her shoulder which pushed kids away and showed up as anger in the classroom. "I think she could use your help," Shirley had said.

The picture of Melissa I'd created in my mind was of a child weighed down with worries. The bright-eyed nine-year-old who entered my office was the opposite of that. She bounded in as if she had arrived at a birthday party. Her wide smile showed teeth so perfect she could have been on a dental office poster. I was struck by how stocky and muscular she was in her faded blue t-shirt and cut-off jeans, and her energy knocked me off balance.

She looked around the office, then walked over to the sand tray set up near the stuffed animals and kids' games. "Hey, my counselor has a sand thing like this," she said, as she picked up a miniature plastic bunk bed. "But yours is even cooler." Before I could say a word, she spun around and planted herself in the chair by my desk. "So, what do you want to know about me? And what should I call you?" She leaned forward and spread her hands on the desktop, her elbows jutting out to the sides.

"Some people call me Mrs. Keet, but Patrice is fine. I like that better." I smiled at her over my glasses. I was surprised by her confident presence. "Why don't we start with how things are going for you here." As she held my gaze, I looked at her more carefully. She had shoulder-length blonde hair that framed her wide and lightly freckled face. Her clear blue eyes reminded me of the huckleberries I picked in Upstate New York as a child. What was really startling was that she could have stepped out of one of my own family's photos—that's how much she resembled my children, Ellie and Colin.

Melissa told me that her new class was "sort of okay," except for some snooty girls who wouldn't play with her. "Maybe it's because I'm new or because they know I'm a foster kid. I did push one of them against the jungle gym, but she deserved it." She said she really liked her teacher but added something like, "She expects me to do every bit of homework and not talk in class. That's a pain." I asked her what was hard about those rules. "Well, I'm pretty smart, and I already know all the stuff she shows us. I talk a lot because it's fun to make the other kids laugh."

When I asked her how she ended up coming to Capitola Elementary, she told me she'd moved in with a new foster family in our district over the summer. She didn't hesitate in laying out her grievances: There were way too many kids there, and she had to share a room with two girls who always took her stuff and made fun of her. "The parents are okay. Not the worst I've had. At least I can get a snack once in a while instead of being locked out of the kitchen." She scowled and continued. "Every house has its own stupid rules, *and* they always have mean kids." She then told me she was thinking this family might adopt her since she couldn't go back to her own mother, but she wasn't sure because they already had too many of their own kids.

She got up from her chair and ambled over to the corner. She seemed to know just what she was after as she picked up a snow-white polar bear nearly as long as her arm. Sitting back down, she held it close and nestled her face against its back as she mumbled, "I was taken away from my mom because of what my stepfather did to me. But he's in jail now." Her voice got louder when she said she was glad he was out of the picture, but she didn't think it was fair that she had to live in foster homes while her little sisters still got to live with her mom. "I've lived in a bunch of places in the past couple of years."

When she said this, I had a sudden impulse to reach out and pluck her off the merry-go-round of foster homes. I hardly knew this girl, yet I felt strangely protective of her. I could picture a blur of household chaos with kids stepping on one another and Melissa getting lost in the shuffle. The thought of a crowded foster home where she had to vie for attention and affection at the end of the school day made me feel sick. I'd never had such a personal, visceral reaction to a child in my dozen years of being a marriage and family therapist. I stood up to stretch, then sat back down. "Um, please tell me more—about your family."

She talked about her older brother, Daniel, who had also been taken away from their birth home, and she grinned when she described how cute her two little sisters were. Then, she said words that made my breath catch: "Someday, I'll have a family I can call my own." I couldn't help but picture the family Bob and I had created. Our children, Ellie, a seventeen-year-old who had just moved to the University of California at Santa

Cruz campus a couple of miles from our house, and Colin, a thirteen-year-old in middle school, were growing into wonderful human beings. Recently, my widowed father, Richard, had come to live with us as well, and, as a fivesome, we laughed a lot. At family dinners, we shared the events of our days and discussed everything from interesting medical cases to city politics. When our busy schedules allowed, we lounged in front of the fireplace reading or played board games on the back deck. We argued like any family, but everyone was anchored and safe in the harbor we'd created. I imagined Melissa hadn't ever known a family like ours.

She crossed her arms over her chest, pursed her lips, and gave a quick, sharp nod as she continued. "I'll have a room of my own, all the food I want, and maybe even a pet. Yeah, a cat or a dog. I'll be special, not just another foster kid getting in trouble in a new house."

I leaned back in my chair and gripped its arms. "All the food you want and a pet...yeah, that sounds good. I really hope you will, since you have such a good idea of what you want." I wasn't sure what else to say because my mind was swirling. As if on cue, Melissa asked me about my job at the school. I shook my head and willed myself back into the conversation. Before I knew it, the recess bell rang.

"Is it okay if I go out to the yard now? I only get a little time to play." I nodded and gestured to the door. "But can I come back tomorrow? You're easy to talk to." She cocked her head and gave me a big smile.

"You can come back and see me anytime," I said, stumbling over my words.

She knelt down in front of the dollhouse and moved some furniture around. Then she stood up and carefully replaced the stuffed bear on the table. She lingered over the sand tray for a few moments, then turned and dashed out, yelling, "Bye!"

On my way over to close the door, I noticed that Melissa

had arranged all of the figurines—the adults and the children—around the dining room table.

4
Melissa

I wasn't abused by my biological father. In fact, he might as well have been a saint in my mind. My dad was a paranoid schizophrenic. Because of his diagnosis, he had every excuse to do us harm. But he wasn't the one who filled my childhood with shame.

My mother, Paula, was very young when my parents got together, and they separated in 1984, before I was a year old. Still, I remember my dad being around a lot when I was little. At times, he lived with his mother, and, when he did, I spent many comfortable weekends at their house. Other times, he lived in psychiatric centers or halfway houses. I didn't see him when he was suffering from a bout of mental illness. When I did see him, our relationship was really wonderful. I never fantasized about my mom and dad getting back together like other kids did. They'd never been married. To me, things had always been the way they were, and I was okay with that.

The nurturing male figure in my life should have been my stepfather, Victor. He was the one I saw day in and day out. He was the breadwinner. He had some good qualities to him; he was kind and attentive to my half-sisters, his blood children. But my older brother, Daniel, and I were treated quite differently.

As is common with sexual predators, I later learned, Victor had two distinct sides to his personality. One was very kind and loving. The other was dark and sinister. I have a lot of memories from the three different homes we lived in together. None of those memories are good. The earliest is from a one-bedroom single-wide trailer in Prunedale, California, a rural community about ten minutes from Salinas. My mom, Daniel, and I all slept on the same queen-sized mattress there, laid out on the floor. Victor was in the Navy then, so he wasn't always around. When he was, he slept with us, too. In this memory, I'm two-and-a-half years old. I'm lying down on the bed, face up, with my legs spread-eagled to the sides. I have matches in my vagina, and they have to be removed. I get the sense that I'm in trouble. But rather than being afraid, I'm angry because my mother is right next to me, and, instead of taking the matches out of me herself, she's having Victor do it.

I don't know if he put the matches there or if I did, but I know I was blamed for it.

I assume the abuse started when I was about a year old, because, by the age of two or three, I already knew not to say anything about what was happening. I was already angry. Somehow, I had learned that this was something I didn't like but couldn't say anything about.

Early on, most of the abuse consisted of his touching me and masturbating in front of me. I know now that those behaviors are generally precursors to more serious abuse. When predators want to have an ongoing in-house thing, they develop it over years. They start with touching you inappropriately and revealing themselves to you. Then they move onto fondling you and forcing you to watch sexual acts. And it keeps going from there.

What I remember most were his eyes. They looked at me as if to say, "No, no, Melissa." From just that look, I knew what would happen if I said anything to anyone: I'd be beaten. Or worse yet, he'd beat Daniel and make me watch. By the time I was four or five, he'd say things like: "You know to be quiet now. Your mom's going to be angry with you if you wake her up now." Or "If you get too loud, it's your own fault. You know you'll get in trouble."

Victor never left marks on me. He was hell-bent on keeping the abuse secret.

5

Patrice

The leaves on the gingko tree outside my office were a golden yellow I hadn't noticed before. The sun glinting off the parked school buses had an odd intensity. Even the sound of the lunch carts being rolled down the carpeted corridor outside my door caught my attention.

My desk was piled high with forms that needed to be completed, reviewed, or passed along, but I felt too wired to take on those tasks. My mind kept sliding back to my meeting with Melissa. I still saw her hugging the stuffed polar bear and telling me about the family she dreamed of. What she wanted seemed like every child's birthright, but she'd never had anything like it. Mixed in with my sadness about her situation was a warm feeling of connectedness to her. She reminded me of myself at her age. Even though I grew up in a two-parent family, I was lonely as a child. I sometimes felt isolated within my family, and, as much as I loved my parents and my sweet younger sister, Kathy, I always wanted to have more people around. People fascinated me. I wanted to know what made them tick, what their hopes and dreams were. I remember begging to invite the World Book Encyclopedia salesman into the house. I knew his books contained worlds much bigger than the small town I lived in. I was determined to experience them someday. Like Melissa, I had no problem talking to strangers. I, too, was desperate to connect with adults other than my parents—ones who didn't live in a house where the windows had been painted shut. In theory, my parents had sealed them off to protect against Saranac Lake, NY's bitter winter cold. I'd always wondered, though, if it had really been their way of keeping to themselves.

Since it was a lovely day, I decided to head out to the playground and observe two students I'd been coaching on appropriate recess behavior. As I made my way toward the metal climbing structure, I was nearly swept off my feet by a push from behind. A pair of arms tightly encircled my waist. "Hey, can I come and see you again tomorrow? Please, please?" I turned to find Melissa clinging to me. I wanted to give her a hug right back, but I settled for telling her that I'd really like that and would check with her teacher. She grabbed my hand and pulled me over to a dark-haired girl about her size. After introducing me, Melissa hopped up and down while she described my office to her friend. "And I'm going to see her again tomorrow," she added. Then she broke loose and ran off to join a group of kids playing dodgeball.

When I came back in from the playground, I felt ready to explode, like those crystals that burst into dinosaurs when submerged in water. Maybe Melissa, too, had felt a special connection between us. I found myself hoping that I wouldn't end up being another in the string of adults who had disappointed her. I wandered around my office until a car horn in the parking lot outside startled me, and I realized I'd been staring at the dollhouse in the corner. Back at my desk, I glanced down at the notes I'd scribbled after my meeting with Melissa. They left me wanting to know so much more. What did this little girl love to do? How would she decorate a room of her own? And, most importantly, how had she held onto her bright spirit through so much trauma?

I needed to talk to someone. My first thought was Gayle, the principal, who was also a friend of mine outside of work. I walked down the hall, knocked on her partly closed door, then stuck my head around it to see if she was there.

"Hey, come on in," she said, gesturing towards a seat.

I had too much energy coursing through me to sit down, so I leaned against her desk and recounted my experience with Melissa. "Gayle, I don't know what came over me, but about ten minutes into hearing her story, I was overtaken with the idea that I wanted her to become *my* foster daughter." I leaned forward. Gayle's eyes got wider, but she tilted her head, encouraging me to go on. I told her that I knew how strange it must sound, but that the idea had blossomed into a fully played-out scenario in which the girl moved from her current placement to our home and was adopted by us. "I'm pretty sure she's not happy where she is. What if Bob and I could make her life better?"

Gayle suggested that I slow down and offered me a cup of tea. While she got up to get it, she asked if being foster parents was something Bob and I had previously thought about doing. It was an innocent question, but one that triggered a tangled mess of emotions. I was transported back to a conversation I'd had with Bob on a lakefront dock in Upstate New York. We were eighteen years old at the time, lying on his family's dock on Lake Colby—just a short boat ride from the beach where we'd first met two summers before.

"Hey, have you ever read *Cheaper by the Dozen*?" I asked Bob.

"Is it a book about raising chickens?" I heard him chuckle.

"No, silly, it's about kids. This really cool and quirky dad sets up the family house like a school, with new words posted on the kitchen walls and constellation maps in the bathroom." I went on to explain how, in the book, the two parents and twelve kids go to museums, amusement parks, zoos, and all kinds of other places as one big gang. "It would just be so fun to have more people around all the time. I'd never be lonely."

"How could you ever be lonely with all the friends you

have?"

He was right. I did have a lot of friends. I talked to them every night, with the telephone cord pulled from the hall through the door to my room. Yet, I was still lonely a lot of the time—especially during the long upstate winters when I was stuck in a house filled with cigarette smoke, TV noise, and my mother's occasional depression. She didn't have a driver's license, so she rarely left our home space, except to work part-time as a night nurse at a hospital where she was much liked. My mother had an amazing memory and sense of humor so staying home as much as she did must have been difficult for her. When I was twelve, I started working at my dad's store—in part because I saw it as an opportunity to experience more people, more energy, more life.

"Unlike you, I never see anyone from my high school outside of class," Bob continued. "My only friends are up here in Saranac Lake—and I only see them during the summer." He'd told me this before. Bob grew up in New York City where he spent his free time studying, playing bridge with his parents, and taking the subway to other neighborhoods to go to museums or stores. He was proud of being independent, but I always detected a bit of sadness in his voice when he talked about his life there, and I knew he envied my connections in town.

"I just...I just think it would be so much fun to have a houseful of kids. Maybe even twelve!" I leaned my body over his muscled chest and traced his cheekbones with my finger. "It would be like having a summer camp at home."

"That'd be a handful! We'd have to have good jobs. And a big house. I guess we'd better start thinking of names." He rubbed the small of my back under the blanket. "After all, we only have four years 'til we're out of college."

"Okay—let's make a list. You go first." We rattled off far more than twelve names before we dozed off in each other's arms.

In that moment, no one would have been able to convince me that I'd only have two kids. My eighteen-year-old heart would have broken if I'd known that the decision wouldn't be mine to make. But shortly after I'd given birth to Colin, I'd had a prolapsed uterus. My obstetrician strongly advised me not to have any more children, and Bob, a doctor himself, concurred. My dream of a dozen kids evaporated. This had led to talk about both adoption and fostering, although we'd never gone so far as to take steps towards either process.

I was thinking about all of this when Gayle asked her question, but I decided she didn't need to know the details. I settled for saying that we'd casually discussed the idea. "But, Gayle, this is something completely different—maybe not even rational," I was quick to add. "I don't know. What I do know is that I'm drowning in feelings. You know I've been in the therapy business for a long time. I've never had a reaction like this."

After I stopped rambling, Gayle gently said, "There's a lot to think about before going any further, Patrice—starting with a longer conversation with her teacher and her social worker." She got up and laid a hand on my shoulder. "I'm here for you to talk things through anytime you want to do that."

6
Melissa

Our home was not the kind of place where milk and cookies waited for us on the table when we got back from school. Most of the time, no one even knew if we'd gone to school at all—let alone sat around waiting for us to return.

In 1989, we moved to Salinas. Since our apartment was less than a mile away from Frank Paul Elementary, we didn't have bus service. My mother didn't have a car, and Victor needed his to get to work, so Daniel and I—who, at ages six and five respectively, were inseparable—walked to school on our own. Most days we made it there. The free breakfasts of Fruit Loops, whole milk, and orange juice in mini cartons were the big draw, since there often wasn't anything to eat at home. The lunches were less appealing, so about half the time we left school after breakfast and spent our days somewhere else. We tried to stay out as late as we could every day. Since Victor worked swing shifts or graveyards at a refrigerator warehouse in town, we knew that if we got home after he'd left, we'd be safe.

My mom was always home, though. For a lot of the time we lived there, she was pregnant or had a newborn baby. In every memory I have of her, she's lying on the couch. I know she must have cooked sometimes, but I can't picture a time where we sat down to eat as a family. I had to forage for food, and I distinctly remember eating raw hamburger meat straight from the fridge, sometimes with a little salt and pepper on top. I know I ate Top Ramen noodles a lot. Sometimes, I'd stand on a chair to boil water for them, but I ate them dry just as often.

I have one vivid memory from our time at school there. I was in kindergarten, and Daniel was in first grade, although he looked a lot older. He was at least four or five inches taller than I was back then. He was always chunky, and he had the softest curly hair, with blonde ringlets that fell around his face.

Daniel's teacher had yelled at him. I was so pissed off at her and so protective of Daniel that I decided that we should leave. During recess, we formulated a scheme to run off. "Wait until they blow the whistle," I said. "Everyone will start walking in, and the yard duties will follow. We'll hang over here, and then we'll run out and hide behind the slide." There wasn't much space behind the slide, but there was an open gate that parents used to bring their kids in through the back entrance. Someone had to have seen us running through it, but we managed to get out anyway. Past the fence, there was a trench where water ran off from the nearby agricultural fields. The only place to hide was inside the trench, so we headed there.

In the process, we found these tubes that led back up into the fields. When I discovered that some of them were big enough for me to crawl into, we realized that we'd found an amazing playground. "We're not going home now!" I said to Daniel. From there, we discovered a condemned house that had homeless people living in it. It had to have been "a trap house"—you know, a drug den—at some point. But, to us, it looked like the best fort ever.

At one point, my foot slid and got stuck in the mud. I pulled and pulled on it but couldn't get it out because of the suction. Daniel grabbed my foot to help me, and together we yanked on it until I yelled, "Ow!" A piece of glass—or something sharp—had cut my ankle open. While I washed the mud off my foot with the nasty water from the culvert, I realized we had to get home. I could barely hobble down the road. I don't think I was frightened or freaked out about my ankle bleeding. I was scared because I knew I was going to get spanked for skipping school. "Mom's going to yell at us," I said to Daniel. She didn't actually care that we were missing school; she was afraid the truancy officer would come after her. We both knew she'd tell Victor as soon as he got home, and we'd get punished. That's how it worked.

When I lived with my birth family, no one ever read a book to me. I couldn't read, and I know I couldn't tell time on an analog clock either. My grandmother's house on the other side of town was the farthest away from home I'd ever been.

7
Patrice

Was I really imagining adding a child to our lives? On the heels of that thought came my worry that the hole left in my daily life after Ellie's recent departure for college would never be filled. I looked at my well-worn Moleskin datebook, seeing days filled with Colin's activities, trips out of town, and dinner parties. I started making a list—my favorite activity when I feel stressed. I tried to calculate how much extra childcare Melissa would require as I mentally plugged her into our calendar. Instead of scaring me, the process excited me.

My talk with Gayle had helped me put words to my powerful feelings. The idea of making Melissa part of our family was developing a life of its own, and I was bursting with excitement to talk with Bob about it. I called him at his office and caught him between patients. "Hey, honey. Are you sitting down? I just had a meeting here at school with the most adorable nine-year-old girl."

Bob was used to my bursts of enthusiasm for novel experiences. For decades, he'd been the rock of stability and pragmatism that balanced my spontaneous nature. Still, I could picture his handsome features contorting a little as I first described Melissa and then blurted out, "What would you think of having another kid in our family? I mean, on a foster basis."

He didn't say anything for so long that I was worried that we'd been disconnected. "Uh, seriously?" He coughed into the phone. "Did I hear you right—a foster kid?" I was about to start speed talking, but he stopped me and said he'd need to hear a whole lot more. "I'm happy to talk about this over dinner tonight, okay?"

That evening, Colin and my father had planned a boys' pizza and movie night, so Bob and I had the house to ourselves. Although I'd prepared a simple pasta meal, it occurred to me that maybe the good china and candles might be in order, since I had a lot of explaining to do. Bob was extraordinarily flexible and open to new ideas, but this one was orders of magnitude greater than anything I had previously sprung on him. When we were both settled at the dining room table, Bob poured some of the chardonnay I'd brought home. "Okay, give me your pitch. I'm all ears."

I told him what I knew. My voice quavered when I explained that she'd been molested by her stepfather who had since been put in prison. "Bob, I felt like a lightning bolt hit me when she told me about the fantasy life she envisions: a family to call her own and a place where she could have her own room and maybe a pet. 'Somewhere I can feel special,' is what she said. Even as she was talking with me, the image of our big house was looming in my mind." Bob and I often talked about how lucky we were to live in abundance and how important it was to share that. "We have the space. We have the resources. And, well, here's a kid who needs a stable, loving home. We still have a lot to give, don't we?"

He sat there silently for a few moments. Then he refilled both of our glasses and took a big slug from his own. "I don't know." He gestured down the hall toward the kids' bedrooms. "Where would we put her? And that's just for starters. Would she change schools? How would we handle all her activities? Oh, and what about *our* lives, anyway?" He kept clenching and unclenching his hands.

"Honey, this *would* be our life. An amazing little girl who needs us. Remember how we talked about having a dozen children when we fell in love?" I was stunned at the speed with which Bob had jumped into logistics and did my best to answer his questions. As I set down a steaming plate of pasta in front of him, he brought up the tougher ones: "What do you think our kids would say? How hard is it to become a foster family? What about her own family? Does she still see them?"

Now *I* needed a huge breath. I pictured the kids as being cautious and protective, but supportive. "Ellie's not living here anymore, really." She had moved up to the University of California at Santa Cruz campus when she'd started college a few months earlier. "And Colin is so busy with his own life that he might not even notice another person in the house," I joked. As far as his questions about fostering and Melissa's family, I had to admit that I didn't know much.

He dove into the big, ugly questions too. "What if it doesn't work out? What if she turns out to be too much of a handful? Could we get out of it once we started?" I just let these hang in the air. I never thought about things not working out.

As we did the dishes, Bob said he'd consider meeting Melissa on a casual basis, a "just come meet my family" kind of thing. He was adamant when he said, "No promises—not even a whisper of the idea to her or anyone else until we talk it over with the kids, okay?"

Later that night, as Bob and I got ready for bed, he said, "If we're at all serious about this, it seems like our next step is to contact Melissa's social worker to see how we'd proceed." I rested my head against his chest as I thanked him for being so open and generous. The last vision I had before drifting off to sleep was a picture of Melissa, all dressed up, going to see *The Nutcracker* with me—something I wished I could have done with my own mother.

8
Melissa

By the time we'd moved from Prunedale to Salinas, I was regularly performing oral sex on him. I was six years old.

Everyone always asks me, "How often?" The answer is I don't know. I just remember that it was a normal thing for me. Victor was out of the Navy by then, so he was living with us full-time. I don't think I had to deal with him every night, but I know I felt fear every night. I had trouble sleeping. I would lie awake in my bunk bed, tangled up with my body-sized Raggedy Ann doll, listening for footsteps on the stairs and wondering if the footsteps would come into my room. If my door opened, I pretended to be asleep, hoping he would go away, hoping he would leave me alone. Sleep for me was like an escape, a reprieve from the world, so my biggest fear was that I'd drift off, and he'd awaken me. I didn't want to fall asleep until I knew I could be completely transported to a better place.

I don't have many detailed memories of the nights when he came into my room. In order to get through these kinds of experiences, you have to completely disassociate. You float above your own body, watching these things happen to somebody else. You have absolutely no emotional connection to what's going on—there's no pain, there's no sadness, there's no sympathy for that girl you're watching. You're completely cut off.

There is one event that I remember clearly, though. I was

six or seven years old. Victor attempted to penetrate me—the first time anally, the second vaginally. I say "attempted," because, just prior to being taken into foster care, I was subjected to examinations aimed at corroborating or disproving my story. They found scar tissue in my vagina and anus, but they couldn't say for certain whether or not the abuse I described had taken place. I know it hurt. I know I cried, "Ow, this hurts!" and I know my screams got louder and louder because of the pain. He stopped because he was afraid to wake up my mom who was almost always downstairs, asleep on the couch.

I distinctly remember feeling anger from that point on. As much as I hated what I had been forced to do before that, none of it had ever caused me severe physical pain, and none of it had caused me to cry. The one time I did cry, Victor didn't like it. I think it made him feel more like the monster he really was. While this wasn't the first time I had cried with him, it was the first time I couldn't hide it and the first time I couldn't keep my screams inside of me. Until then, I'd been able to maintain a separation between the man who was my caregiver—the man who loved me and bought me things—and this other man. But now that physical pain was involved, everything shifted.

I began behaving in ways that sent up red flags. For instance, I remember masturbating in front of people, out on the lawn behind our trailer. My mother said, "Well now, Melissa, you just don't do that," and I felt ashamed. But she didn't do anything about it. She either didn't recognize that my actions were obvious signs of abuse, or her own childhood experiences had been so similar that she thought my behavior was "normal."

I think my father's family began to take notice, however. My mother and Victor were happy to get rid of Daniel and me when they could, since, by then, they had two more little kids—my stepsisters—to take care of. So, when my dad was well and staying with our grandmother, we spent weekends over there.

His family started asking, "Is somebody doing something to you?" and, "Does Victor hurt you?" I know that, at some point, my dad found out something that sent him into a psychotic episode. He was removed from my grandmother's house in a fit of anger, and I didn't see him for weeks afterward. That further reinforced my need to keep my mouth shut.

The questioning was traumatic. It had been firmly ingrained in me to never say a word to anybody. If I did, someone else was going to get hurt. "He'll murder Daniel," I thought. I knew Victor was abusing my brother too, and I didn't want anything I did to make Daniel's life any worse.

"Your mom isn't going to want you anymore," Victor had said. "You'll get sent away." He used so much intimidation—sheer, cruel intimidation.

9
Patrice

As a counselor, I regularly talked with mental health professionals involved with children at our school. This made it easy for me to get the number of Melissa's social worker, Joe. I introduced myself and told him about my meeting with Melissa.

"I'm really surprised to hear from you," he said, "because Melissa was just placed with the new family a few months ago." He said he'd assumed that she liked the family and was doing fine both there and at school. I told him that, while she didn't seem to be in a crisis, I wondered if there could be a more optimal placement for her—in particular, one where there was a better chance of her being adopted.

"Well, we're always looking for 'optimal placements,' as we call them, but, as you might know, they're really hard to find, especially for older kids." He went on to talk about their waiting list of children who needed homes. This felt like the perfect opening for me to tell him about the connection I'd felt with Melissa and the strong pull I felt to help her. Finally, I managed to blurt out that my husband and I were interested in fostering her. "Wow, really? You have no idea how seldom I hear those words," he replied. He said he was overdue for a home visit with Melissa and would plan to do one as soon as his schedule allowed. Then, he added that she was a wonderful kid but not the easiest child to place, since she still had strong emotional ties to her birth family. Joe told me she'd tried to run away from foster homes in the past, but even that information didn't slow me down. Since we were expressing interest in becoming a foster family, he wanted to do a brief interview right then, over the phone. "Do you have time now?"

"Sure," I stuttered, feeling my stomach lurch. He could say no to me. I flashed back to being twelve years old, to a night when I'd asked my mother, once again, if I could have a couple of girlfriends over for a sleepover. "You know, the two I had over a few weeks ago to play Monopoly, Sarah and Vicky. You met them."

She shook her head and threw up her hands. "I don't see why you always have to go and fill our house with other people's kids. I'm tired." Was I setting myself up for more rejection now, doing a foster parenting interview with absolutely no preparation? I took a deep breath. I wanted to keep this moving. "It's as good a time as any."

"So, what's your house like? Let's start with whether you have enough space for a foster child."

That was an easy one. We'd lived in our house for five years. In my typical obsessive fashion, I had dedicated myself to finding just the right spot for our family. I'd made up a questionnaire for Bob, Ellie, and Colin, asking them to define the most important features of a neighborhood and house. When we finally identified the neighborhood we wanted, I wrote to every homeowner there to see if they wanted to sell.

The rambling California ranch house whose owners said "yes" didn't give us that love-at-first sight feeling. Its outdated kitchen and wood-paneled living room gave it an air of sprawling funkiness. But Bob and I both brightened up when we walked through an archway into the large family room. This was a space that revealed a world of possibilities. An expansive glass wall ran the length of the combination dining room and family room, and the lush, tree-covered ravine beyond the deck felt like an extension of that space. A built-in trampoline sat on a lower deck. I saw room to spread out, room to play in, and, most of all, room to include other people. We made an offer that day and moved in a month later.

"Oh, yes, we have lots of space. She could have her own bedroom and bathroom," I told Joe eagerly.

"Okay. So, tell me a little bit about you and your husband. And, who else is in your household?" He seemed to be going down a checklist.

"Well, my husband, Bob, and I were high school sweethearts. We met when we were sixteen, and we've been married for twenty-three years now." I explained that I was a licensed marriage and family therapist, in practice for ten years at that point, as well as a part-time school counselor. He knew my name as a part of the community of therapists in our town. I told him that Bob specialized in geriatrics, and Joe remembered that he had taken his mother to see Bob before she moved out of the area. I breathed a sigh of relief hoping we might have a head start with the process. We were a known quantity.

When he heard that our family also included my seventy-seven-year-old father, Richard, he said, "So you know something about having extra people around, it sounds like?"

I could have written a master's thesis on the subject. When we moved to California from New York in 1974, we didn't know anyone and felt a bit like orphans. Our survival strategy had been to create a new family among our group of friends. We were no strangers to a somewhat communal lifestyle, and we thrived in that environment. "We love opening our home to family and friends, and it's always worked out well."

"Alright, so how long have you been thinking about fostering a child? And have you been to one of our agency's orientations on fostering?"

"Um, no, we haven't." I shifted in my chair. As a fairly impulsive person, orientations weren't really my style. But I sensed that this was important, so I chose my words carefully. "Fostering is a very new idea for us, but we've thought about adopting a child over the years."

When he asked how parenting our own teens was going, I thought about how much I missed Ellie and still loved being around Colin. Parenting was a role I cherished, and it was one that seemed to fit me like a made-to-order garment. I thought I'd done a great job with my kids so far, but I knew that my bubble of self-confidence hadn't been tested by Ellie and Colin, who'd been deemed "exceptionally easy" by all of our friends. "They're fun and interesting people to be around," I said to Joe. "They're doing well in school, they have friends, and they're nice. No complaints."

That evening, as Bob and I sat out on our deck looking at constellations through the redwood branches on the hillside, I explained the next steps Joe had outlined: attend a foster parent orientation meeting, complete a CPR training, and undergo a home study that included a home safety inspection, fingerprinting, and background checks of all adults. Finally, we'd have to show income verification to prove that we could afford to take in an additional child. Bob reached for my hand and said, "I'm excited to meet this Melissa, since you're so taken with her."

10
Melissa

When I was six, my mother called me into the bathroom to join her as she relaxed in the tub. Paula didn't interrogate me; she started to share some of her own stories. "When I was a little girl, sometimes people would do bad things to me that I didn't like," she said. She didn't "out" the man who did these things to her, although I later learned that it was her father—my grandfather, who had been involved in my life for as long as I could remember.

I was dumbstruck by my mother's revelation. I'd thought I was the only person in the world having the experience I was having. I'd thought I was the only person who had *ever* had this experience. And I knew in my gut that what was happening to me was wrong. When my mother shared her story, I felt like a crushing weight had been lifted, and it was safe to talk. If this had happened to her, maybe she understood that I wasn't supposed to tell. And, if neither of us was supposed to tell, but she had said something—well, then I could say something too, right? It was like some kind of weird kid logic, but it made sense to me. So, I told her what had been happening. I remember feeling incredibly embarrassed, giggling as I spoke because I felt so awkward talking about penises with my mother.

Her reaction frightened me. She'd been washing her hair in the tub while we were talking, but, once I told her, she jumped out of the water and left the bathroom with suds still in her hair. I didn't know where she was going, and that same old dread came rushing back. "What did I do? What's going to happen now, and what's going to happen to *me*?" I knew Victor would be coming home at some point, and I made sure to keep myself awake until he did.

I was sitting up in my room when I heard him open the front door. "How *could* you?" I heard. "Don't even try to lie to me, how *could* you?" There was a full-blown argument going on downstairs, and, oh man, I *knew* I was the cause of it. I knew they were talking about me. I was in my room, on the top bunk. My heart was racing, pounding so hard I heard it beating in my ears. I snuck down from the bunk and slid out the door. I walked straight down the hall and hid at the top of the stairs, behind a wall where I could hear them, but they wouldn't be able to see me if I needed to run back to my room. Their tone shifted from anger to sadness, and I heard him pleading and apologizing. "No way!" I remember thinking. "He admitted it!" Then I heard him coming up the stairs. I sprinted back down the hall to my room, climbed onto my bunk bed, and threw the blankets over me. There was no way anyone would have believed that I was sleeping, since I was panting in panic. But I laid there with my eyes closed anyway, keeping as still as possible, pretending as best I could. I heard them come to the doorway and held my breath. Then, there was a whisper: "Don't you dare!" and steps walking away—away from my room, away from me.

After that, I have absolutely no idea what happened. There are gaps. Huge gaps.

11
Patrice

As Bob was getting ready for work the next morning, I pounced on him again. "Hey, honey, any interesting dreams last night or, um, thoughts about our conversation about Melissa?"

He paused for a moment while tying his tie and said that questions had swum around his brain as he'd stared out at the moon for much of the night. He said he felt overwhelmed by the idea of a foster child, but that his nagging feelings of guilt about our big house and significant resources were powerful. "You know how much joy I've gotten from raising our kids," he mused almost under his breath. As he combed his hair, he turned towards the bed, where I was still under the covers. "So, I guess I ended up thinking, well, why not talk more about it and even pass the idea by Ellie and Colin?"

I tossed the duvet off and leapt out of the bed. "Does that mean you want me to figure out a time for us to get together with them?"

"Yep, let's at least go that far for the moment." I nearly knocked him off balance with my hug and then smothered him with kisses.

The next evening, Bob and I arrived at our favorite Italian restaurant ahead of the kids. As we were settling into our places in the corner, Colin came in, having gotten a ride with a friend's father after soccer practice. I looked at him in his team jersey and felt a familiar pang of regret; he was growing up much faster than I wanted him to. The scrawny towhead

I'd raised was now almost as tall as I was, and his freckles had given way to high cheekbones and a strong chin. It wouldn't be long before he'd have girls falling all over him. At thirteen, he already seemed to have a full-blown life of his own, complete with a handful of exceptionally close friends who headquartered at our house.

All I'd told Ellie on the phone was that we had something we wanted to talk to both her and Colin about. My scholarly and serious daughter walked in carrying her familiar accessory: a thick book. My heart leapt like it always did when I set eyes on her. I missed her every day. She was witty and smart, and she always kept us on our toes with her knowledge and thoughtful perspectives. Because she had skipped eighth grade, she'd gone to college a year early. She, too, was growing up too fast. As she came closer, I saw that her face was flushed. "What's wrong?" were the first words out of her mouth as she sat down next to me.

I remember Bob reaching over the large round table and taking her hand. "Honey, everything's fine. I'm sorry for our secrecy."

Ellie's face reddened further as she fought back tears. "I've been so worried about you guys since Mom called. I thought one of you might be seriously ill." I moved closer to her on the banquette seat we shared and inhaled her familiar smell. I felt like we didn't have time for any of the usual pleasantries because Ellie was so upset. "Sweetie, I should have known you'd worry. I'm sorry, too." I stroked the back of her hair and saw her shoulders relax. I'd been practicing what to say to the kids all day, but, in that moment, all of my careful wording went out the window, and I just blurted out my story, ending with: "So, Dad and I are bouncing around the idea of taking her in as a foster child."

Colin's eyes went wide. "Wow, I didn't expect that."

Ellie scrunched up her face and looked sideways at me.

"You just met her, and you got this idea? And now you want to know what we think? Really, Mom?"

I looked over at Bob as a signal for him to take over, but, just then, our drinks arrived. As the waiter stepped away, Ellie and Colin started talking over each other, throwing out questions about how and when this process might happen. "How much do you know about her background?" Ellie asked. "She might be a real handful. I mean, I've heard you talk randomly about adopting another child, but I never thought you were serious." She barely paused before blurting out, "Do you think Grandpa Richard could handle something new like this?"

After gulping a sip of wine, Bob said, "We plan to talk with Richard, but we wanted to know your reactions first."

Ellie startled me by saying, "It's a pretty wild idea that needs some serious thought." She must have seen my reaction, because her face softened. "Although, I can imagine you guys doing it. Mom, it seems like you both still have a lot of love to give a child—and probably the energy for it, too. I mean, you've been great parents."

I took a deep breath, inhaling her words. Tears came to my eyes as I said, "Thanks, honey. You've made it easy."

Colin furrowed his brow, leaned across the table toward me, and started asking a bunch of questions in quick succession: "What room would she have? Could my friends still come and stay over all the time? Where would she go to school?" and "Would I be her babysitter?" He shook his head from side to side and tapped his fingers on the wooden table. I ran my hands through my hair and turned to Bob. I was glad that he and I had already talked about these things.

We took turns answering Colin's questions and trying to reassure him that we would work to keep his life like it was. He leaned back and turned to Bob. "Well, it would be pretty weird being someone's older brother, even for a short time. But I guess I could learn to boss her around." He gave Ellie a poke and a wink. With each nod of their heads and every playful comment, I grew more and more hopeful that both kids were on board with the idea.

As we left the restaurant, I floated the idea of bringing Melissa up to campus to meet Ellie. "First things first," Bob said. "I still have to spend time with her, and she hasn't been over to our house yet to meet Colin or Richard."

Colin gave me a familiar smile, put his arm around my shoulder, and said, "Yeah, Mom, I want to meet this kid that might become my other sister."

12
Melissa

In my next memory, I'm seven years old and at my aunt Jenny's house, in a room where a bunch of us kids were coloring. My cousins were giving me crap about not being able to color inside the lines when they brought it up. They knew. Everyone knew. It's why I was there. I had almost forgotten about what had happened until then. But it all came back to me in slow-motion, like in a dream where you try to run away from something, but your body feels so heavy you can't escape. "Oh God, this isn't over," I thought. Boy was I right about that.

I think my father's family may have been the ones to report the abuse. I doubt my mother did.

I don't remember being physically taken away from my family. I don't remember being placed into protective custody. I don't remember the sequence of events that landed me at my aunt Jenny's house. I do remember my aunt being present during the medical examination. I felt awkward, and I wanted her to leave, but I didn't want to hurt her feelings by asking her to. There were both rectal and vaginal exams with cameras. I could see my insides on the TV, which was really embarrassing for me. It wasn't just the physical exposure that made me feel ashamed; it was like they were exposing this *entity*—this evil being that I lived with or that lived in me. Now, it was out there in the world for everyone to see. And they were examining it, poking it, prodding it, and inspecting it so they could know all about it. In my own way, I understood that there was doubt around my story. I understood that they were corroborating what I said and building a case against Victor. But it still made me angry. So, on top of the fear and shame I already felt, I was mad. "Who would make this stuff up?" I wondered. "Who would live through these things and tell these stories by choice? How dare you!" I thought. "I should have never told you."

There wasn't a cave dark enough for me to hide in. I remember thinking that what I was going through was so foreign and so intimidating that I would have preferred to endure the abuse that I had grown accustomed to. At least I knew how to cope with that.

13
Patrice

We hadn't set up any plan for how we'd identify each other, so I was relieved when Melissa's CASA Advocate, Kristin, waved me over to her table in the corner of the coffee shop. CASA stands for Court Appointed Special Advocates, and Kristin's role made her one of the gatekeepers whose approval we needed to bring Melissa into our family. I didn't want her to see me as an intrusive or eccentric school counselor who hadn't thought about the seriousness of being a foster parent.

It turned out that Kristin wasn't the least bit scary. On the contrary, she was a lovely woman—tall and graceful, with wavy hair, hazel eyes, and an impish smile that drew me to her. She looked to be around my age, which would have put her in her mid-forties. "I'm so very pleased to meet you," she said, holding my hands in a warm handshake. "I take it you've been smitten with Melissa. She does that to people."

I could feel my cheeks getting warm and nodded my head in agreement, although hearing the word "smitten" made me feel like a teenager with a crush. "I haven't stopped thinking about her since I met her last week," I said, before launching into yet another version of my meeting with Melissa.

Kristin and I spent the next hour talking about everything from the members of my family to why Bob and I wanted to be foster parents. She also took the time to explain how the foster care system worked, describing the many different motivations that propelled people into fostering. Some made a business of it, getting a monthly payment for each child under their roof, and, in some cases, a larger amount if the child is determined to have special needs. Some families or individuals foster children because they are good-hearted and have space, time, and energy for parenting. And some, like us, fall in love with a child, and the stars align when need intersects with opportunity. We eventually learned that the social services agencies in our small city, like thousands of others across the US, were on a perpetual search for foster families. Many foster families were licensed only as short-term placements because they had no intention of adopting, but the goal of the foster care system is to place all dependent children in permanent, safe, stable, loving homes—with an emphasis on the *permanent* part.

Kristin was more than willing to answer my questions about Melissa, saying that she was kind, great with little kids, and full of potential. "I should warn you, though," she added, "Melissa's pretty headstrong, and she still feels a powerful draw to her birth family. Following rules and backing down when it's called for are hard for her." While I took note of her words, nothing she said changed my mind about Melissa. We weren't like those other foster homes she'd been in. We were different. I refrained from telling her that I thought Bob and I had the "secret sauce" of parenting.

Before leaving, we made plans for Kristin to bring Melissa over to our house to meet the rest of my family. We both thought that it was important to make the visit casual with no hint of our real agenda.

By the time I walked outside into the October sun, I felt ten pounds lighter. I'd found someone who knew Melissa well and loved her. And I was feeling even more confident about the path we were on.

14
Melissa

The night of the confrontation in the Salinas apartment was the last time I saw my stepfather. I was seven years old and deathly afraid of meeting him in court. Luckily, I never had to. He took a plea that avoided a trial. Still, there had been a lot of prepping just in case—a lot of sessions with lawyers, doctors, and psychologists. I couldn't tell any of the adults apart. I completely disassociated from all of it.

Daniel was taken away too, although I don't think I realized that until later.

I later found out that Victor got six years and served three. He's been free ever since. On Megan's Law, the California sex offender website, he's listed as a "transient" in Monterey County. My mother and grandmother stay in contact with him; I don't.

Throughout the process, I never cried in front of people. I remember crying by myself every night. But never in public. I didn't just lay emotions out there for people to see. "They're mine," I thought. "They're the only things I have control over, and you don't get to see them. You can make me undress, and you can investigate my body, and you can ask me questions, but you don't get to see these. These are mine."

15

Patrice

My friend Laura and I dodged bicyclists, moms with strollers, and wetsuit-clad surfers as we took a rare walk together along West Cliff Drive. The three-mile multi-use path has always been the go-to strolling spot in Santa Cruz, thanks to its stellar views of the Pacific Ocean. On one side of the path sit multi-million-dollar mansions; on the other, undulating kelp beds shelter sea otters. As we approached the iconic lighthouse that sits just off the path, we stopped to lean on the metal railing overlooking Steamer's Lane. Below us, surfers jockeyed for position, paddling out past the rocky point before spinning quickly on their boards to catch some of the best waves on the west coast. We weren't alone there. To our left was a man holding a camera with a foot-long lens. To our right, a few wide-eyed tourists were pointing and gasping.

Seeing the excitement of the small crowd reminded me of how easy it was for me to take all of our city's marvels for granted. From where we stood, I could see the wharf and the Beach Boardwalk—two places we'd have to take Melissa right away. I started making a mental list of all the other sites we could visit—the butterfly grove, the tide pools at Natural Bridges State Park, the arboretum up on the UC Santa Cruz campus. When Laura suggested we sit down on the grassy field next to the lighthouse, I launched into a condensed version of the steps we'd gone through so far to bring Melissa into our home. The process had gone so quickly that I hadn't even had the chance to share it with her. Laura listened with her usual attentiveness until I took a breath and asked her, "So, what do you think after hearing all this?"

She took her time before asking me if I thought there was any relationship between this strong desire to bring a child into our family and Ellie having left for college only two months before. I admitted that it had occurred to me. "But this idea feels so powerful," I added. "It feels so right, like something Bob and I were *meant* to do." Laura and I shared a therapy suite and many of the same values. We often talked about economic injustice—its roots, solutions, and where we fit into it. Already that day, we'd passed several homeless people who were rolled up in sleeping bags on the benches beside West Cliff Drive. "I know we can't take on the problems of the world, but this little girl needs a permanent home, and, God knows, we have the room and the resources."

She put an arm over my shoulder. "I get all that, and you guys are some of the most open and generous people I know. But I worry that you haven't given yourself enough time or space to grieve Ellie's departure."

I took my eyes off the breaking waves and looked at her. "You know that I thought about following her to college and living in that cramped dorm room with her, don't you?" She chuckled as she stood and extended a hand to help me up.

On the walk back, Laura noted how Ellie shared so many of our interests—being outdoors, reading, science, debating ideas. "I can only imagine how hard it is that she skipped a year of high school and went to college early," she said, and I could feel my shoulders tightening up. She was right. I did miss Ellie terribly—not just as a daughter, but also as a companion. In so many ways she was solid—emotionally, intellectually, and temperamentally—and she seemed to know herself from a young age. I was more emotionally needy and mercurial. She kept her needs to herself like her dad did. A slideshow of good times with her flashed through my mind: skiing in Tahoe, taking her to Paris, hiking in the Adirondack Mountains. But missing her didn't mean I couldn't get on with my life, and that life might include bringing another kind of daughter into it.

By the time we got back to the parking lot, my whole body ached. I sat in my car alone, staring at the ocean. I hated the feelings that welled up—sadness and loneliness. Ellie was moving on, like she was supposed to. So why did I feel so empty? I pushed these feelings about Ellie away by making a list of the to-dos necessary to bring Melissa into our home. I didn't want to wallow for fear that I would sink into a depression. I didn't wallow; I moved forward.

I stared at my list until I realized I could immediately check off one of the tasks on the way home. I put on my seat belt, started the car, and headed to the police station to get fingerprinted.

16
Melissa

After I was taken away from my family in 1991, I was placed into my aunt Jenny's care. Aunt Jenny had been in my life off and on before I came to stay with her and her husband, but I didn't really know her well. At first, we lived in an apartment on Sunny Hills Drive in Watsonville, a small agricultural city between Salinas and Santa Cruz. It was down the street from my paternal grandmother's townhouse, where my brother Daniel had been placed. While we were in that apartment, I got to see Daniel a lot. It was almost like we were still living together, and having him close by made me think my life might go back to normal. But, after a short time there, we moved to a rural area of Aromas, about five miles away.

Then, a few months later, Jenny's husband was transferred, and we all moved to a two-bedroom condo in Colorado. Jenny and her husband had the master bedroom on the second floor. My cousin Lisa had the other bedroom, and her brother, Brian, slept in the loft. That left me sleeping in the basement, with its concrete floor and small, high windows. I remember feeling scared and lonely down there, looking around at file boxes full of old papers and waiting for a little bit of light to creep in. No one ever came down there to check on me.

From the moment I moved in, Jenny told me over and over again that she loved me like I was her own child. I didn't believe her at first, in part because there had always been a rivalry between Jenny and my mother, Paula, that overflowed onto my cousin Lisa and me. I wasn't allowed to do things that Lisa did. For example, I was placed in choir at school. The minute Jenny found out, she had me pulled out and placed in an art class. "Singing is for Lisa," she said. "That's Lisa's thing, not yours." By keeping me from singing altogether, she could ensure that Lisa would always be better at it. Similarly, Jenny often said, "Long hair is so beautiful, little girls should have long hair, like Lisa's." Then she chopped off my hair and forced me to wear it in this short boyish cut. "You can't have long hair; your hair is stringy, and it tangles—not like Lisa's." It was an insignificant thing, but the message I heard was that my hair wasn't as good as Lisa's, and that *I* wasn't as good as Lisa. In fact, I shouldn't even try to be.

"Don't you worry, Miss Melissa. You're family, and I love you. I love you like my own daughter, and this is your home now," Jenny said, again and again. But I kept getting into trouble for violating rules I didn't know existed. I took my dinner plate to the sink without asking permission and was scolded for getting up from the table. I woke up early one day to wander around the neighborhood like I always had at my mother's house, and Aunt Jenny put me to bed without allowing me to eat. Every weekend morning, her birth children, still in their pajamas, piled into bed with her to snuggle. I was allowed to do that too, but not until after the three of them had had their "family time." I was a part of the family, yes; but I was on a lower level of the hierarchy. For the first time in my life, I felt jealousy.

Still, after about a year and a half with Jenny, I came to believe that she loved me. After all, I had grown up in a home where there were two distinct "levels" of children: Victor's kids, who weren't being abused, and Daniel and I, who were. I believed that my birth family loved me, despite the differences in treatment, so I supposed that Jenny must love me too.

Then, suddenly, just a few days before my ninth birthday,

I was told I was being sent away to a foster home. There was no build-up, no discussion, and no explanation. Aunt Jenny wouldn't even tell me what a foster home was. One day I was living with her, and the next day I was on an airplane back to California—just like that. I was heartbroken. I felt rejected and worthless. I really had believed that she loved me like she loved her own kids; sending me away shattered that belief. I remember our goodbye at the airport. Jenny cried and embraced me with emotion while she shoved a pink-spotted bag of birthday presents into my hands. I didn't say a word. I didn't cry. I disassociated, like I had done with Victor—a strategy I would use more and more over the years to come. I waved to her and walked away with the social worker who had been sent to claim me.

I had no idea where I was going next.

17
Patrice

I easily spotted my father's impish smile and slightly stooped shoulders in the crowd of passengers exiting his plane. I threw my arms around him and held him in a tight bear hug. It was a foggy day in mid-October of 1993, and I had just navigated my way over the winding mountain highway that connects Santa Cruz with the bustling Silicon Valley city of San Jose. I felt a warmth extend through my whole body at the thought of having my dad back. He'd been staying with my sister, Kathy, in Saranac Lake for four months.

My father was a charming and easygoing seventy-seven-year-old who almost always had a twinkle in his eye. Two years earlier, just after my mother died, he had moved in with us. This change offered him an unexpected new lease on life. He sought to fulfill a long-held dream of "living the California lifestyle"—one he'd hatched while being based in Los Angeles as a Naval officer in World War II.

I settled him into my car and listened to news of his trip back east as I drove. When there was a pause in our conversation, I said I had some news for him as well, and I told him that we were thinking about fostering a little girl.

"What? What's that mean?" He turned to me with a puzzled look. I understood his confusion. After all, I couldn't remember having met anyone who was raised by a non-parent relative until I moved to California and started graduate school when I was thirty. We certainly knew plenty of dysfunctional families in our small town, but, back in those days, they mostly toughed it out without getting anyone else involved. "Did you say you might take in someone else's child?"

"Yep, Dad, that's what we're thinking of doing."

"But why would you do that? You already have your own kids." This wasn't the first time I'd heard questions like this. Some of our closest friends had asked, "Don't you guys have enough on your plates?" and, "Geez, just when your own kids are getting out of your hair, you want to sign up for *more* parenting?" I took a deep breath. I had hoped my father knew me better, but I launched into an abbreviated version of what led Melissa to be placed in foster care, carefully avoiding the word "abuse."

"But why would you take a stranger into your house?" He was looking at me through squinting eyes. "How much are you going to get paid? I mean, what are you going to get out of it?"

"Oh, Dad, we wouldn't be doing it for money. You know how much I love kids. Remember all my years of babysitting? And the day care center I founded my first summer out of college? And the fact that I got a teaching degree?" I was surprised that my interest in this role didn't seem obvious to him. "I mean, I became a family counselor, after all. Kids have always been a big part of my life. Besides, we have so much—love, time, resources. We've been blessed with abundance. We just...well, we want to share that."

My father had lived through the Depression, and I knew he saw the world from a place of scarcity. Even though he had been half-owner of a modest family grocery store and my mother had worked part-time as a nurse, we'd never had money for vacations or luxuries. I'd always felt like we were okay financially but giving money to charity either wasn't in their nature or within their means.

"You know how we like to have other people around, Dad. This girl needs a stable home where she can blossom. I fell in love with her when I met her, and I'm pretty darn sure you will, too." I reached over and patted his wrinkled hand.

He smiled the smile that I knew was meant to be supportive. "I've always trusted your judgment." There was a sadness in his voice when he added, "I'd just hate to see you or Bob hurt."

18
Melissa

There was something very shadowy about the foster home I moved into in 1992, right after I was sent away from Jenny's. The darkness there was similar to what I had gotten used to living with Victor and my mom. I remember thinking that something wasn't right.

The house was a 1970s ranch house in Aromas with horrible carpets—rust-colored in the living room, olive green in the playroom. Three girls were living there already, and the home was run like a military academy. There were locks all over the place—on the fridge, on the pantry, on the cupboards—and there were rules for everything. Nobody got to eat until it was the designated time to eat. Nobody got to go outside until they'd accrued enough points to go outside. When I first moved in, I thought I'd earn lots of points and get all the privileges. It didn't take long for me to realize how skewed their system was. I earned some snacks that I knew I deserved, but they didn't give them to me. So, I rebelled like the stubborn kid I was. I started doing little things that I knew I could get away with that would make their lives difficult—things like sneaking food.

I remember going to Manresa State Beach with them once. It was a rare excursion, so I was looking forward to it, even though, at age eight, I didn't know how to swim. I didn't know anything about waves either. At some point, while I was running around near the waterline, I turned my back on the ocean and a sneaker wave knocked me over. I was terrified; it seemed to come out of nowhere, and it carried more force than I ever imagined water could have. I was left face down on the beach, soaking wet and panting. I clutched at the sand that was disappearing under my fingers, feeling like I was fighting for my life. After what seemed like an eternity, the wave receded, and I got up. When I walked back to where the rest of the group was, they just pointed at me and laughed.

Shortly after I moved in, another little girl showed up, bringing the total number of children up to five. Once I was no longer the new kid, I could get away with more. But this little girl was horrible. She was small and blonde and had a very memorable mouth. It was tiny and stuffed with awkwardly sized, overlapping teeth. This combination somehow gave her a demonic look. Worse than her look was her behavior: she taunted me, she pulled my hair, and she punched me in the stomach. One day, I was walking in one of the fields surrounding the house, and I found her sitting down in the grass, holding a rabbit. She had a push pin clasped between her fingers—the kind with the little colored ball at the top—and I watched her pull it out of the rabbit's foot. I turned and ran back to the house as fast as I could.

I had to share a room with this girl. I tried to steer clear of her, but she would seek me out.

When I lived there, I had this sparkly pink address book that I treasured. My aunt had sent it with me when she shipped me away, and it contained contact information for all my relatives. I took this address book with me everywhere I went. I knew it would be important when I eventually tried to run away—not just because it was dear to me, but also because it contained the phone numbers I'd need to call once I'd escaped. That cruel little girl saw how attached I was to my address book and, about five months into my stay at that home, she took it from our room. She ripped out pages and scribbled out numbers with dark-colored magic markers. I was crushed. My lifeline to everything I knew and loved had been destroyed.

I needed help protecting myself from her, so I made an alliance with another girl in the house, Rochelle. She was fifteen, about six years older than I was at that point, and the family had formally adopted her. We got to be close. She even showed me how to dog paddle once, when we went to some other family's backyard pool one afternoon. She'd been scared by the scene at the beach and wanted to help me out. Later, on another trip to that pool, I was able to mimic her actions and teach myself to swim. I never took lessons in anything in my life, so I had gotten really good at watching and learning.

Over time, Rochelle told me what was really going on under the surface at that home: the foster father was sexually abusing Rochelle and had raped her roommate, a seventeen-year-old girl, at knifepoint. The foster mother knew about the abuse and was protecting her husband. That was the darkness that I'd sensed. It made me shudder, and I worried that I might be next.

Rochelle and I wanted to get even with the pint-sized psychopath, which, in retrospect, was so stupid; she was such a troubled little girl. One night, we put as many disgusting things as we could find—things like worms and perfume bottles and maple syrup—into her bed. We made the bed up neatly so that she'd never suspect anything and would crawl right into it. She did, and then she freaked out. "Who did this?" she yelled at the top of her lungs. I could hear Rochelle laughing through the wall, and I started giggling. The little girl came at me with a vengeance. We had an all-out punching and kicking and scratching fight which ended when I threw her off me. She hit the wall with a thump loud enough to awaken everyone. The father burst in and picked me up by my hair, which, at the time, I wore in this palm tree-style ponytail. In a fury, he dragged me into the hall, shoved me into Rochelle's room, and locked the door.

I went out the window and ran like hell.

Of course, I got caught. The foster dad picked me up on the road. He had hate in his eyes, and I knew I was in trouble. The next morning, when my social worker arrived, I felt like I had to puff up my chest to defend myself. I needed to get out of this situation without revealing what Rochelle had told me about the abuse, and I didn't know how I was going to do that. Acting tough seemed like the best option, although I was scared to death. "If you make me stay here, I'm going to keep running away!" I shouted at the foster parents and the social worker in an explosion of anger, hatred, and fear. I didn't want that man to touch me; I already knew how that felt. I needed out.

19
Patrice

When the bell rang, I climbed off the ladder and scurried to the front door. I was hanging up Halloween decorations, and I'd forgotten that I had a long string of paper skulls still draped around my neck.

"This is quite a welcome," Kristin said with a laugh. She turned to Melissa, who had a charming smile on her face. "You remember Melissa from Capitola Elementary, don't you? We're on our way to go roller skating, and I wanted to stop in and say hello."

As I welcomed Kristin and Melissa, Colin, Ellie, and Bob came in from the garage. They were covered from head to toe in sawdust, and Bob's hands showed signs of wood stain on them. "No, these aren't their Halloween costumes, just a woodworking project," I explained.

"Hi, you must be Kristin," Bob said, taking a small step towards her. Then he focused on Melissa. "And you are?" Melissa stepped forward and introduced herself without hesitation. I realized I'd been breathing shallowly since I had answered the door. I had a lot riding on this blind date and had been worrying all day about how it would play out. "I'm Bob, and these are my assistants, Ellie and Colin," he said, putting his dirty arms around our two kids. "We've been refinishing a bookcase for Ellie's college dorm room."

"I'm so glad you stopped by," I said, trying to seem relaxed. Then I turned to Ellie and Colin. "You guys want to show our guests around while I get some treats for us?" Ellie brushed herself off and asked Melissa if she liked trampolines. After that, they were off and running.

When Colin challenged Ellie and Melissa to a game of pool, the threesome headed for the family room, leaving space for Bob and me to talk with Kristin. Bob asked her how she thought Melissa was doing in her current home, and she summarized a lot of what she and I had talked about over coffee. "She seems awfully animated," Kristin said. "Not that Melissa is shy or anything, but she seems really comfortable here."

"Can we find another time soon for us to spend more time with her? Take her somewhere maybe?" Bob asked. I turned and beamed at his eagerness and reminded him that we'd been invited to an afternoon birthday party for one of our friends a few days later. I suggested that Melissa go along with us. As we hashed out the details, Melissa came bounding out to the deck with Ellie and Colin trailing behind.

"Wow, this house is gigantic," Melissa said, elongating the word to match her outstretched arms. She pivoted toward Bob. "Bob, can I see where you build things?" He proudly led her to the garage off the kitchen where he spent a lot of his spare time. I could hear her admiring his wall of tools and large table saw through the open doors. "That really looks like fun. I'd like to do that sometime," she said when she returned.

"Well, not today, girl," Kristin said, moving towards her. "We've got a roller-skating date. Time to say goodbye." Kristin took my hand in hers and winked. Melissa was already giving Ellie and Colin hugs, and I heard her thank them for teaching her how to play pool and showing her their rooms.

"I'll see you at school the day after tomorrow." I patted her on the back. "And I'll want to hear how roller skating went."

As Bob, the kids, and I sat around the kitchen table eating a hastily made lunch, I could feel my heartbeat in my throat. Here I was, Master of Ceremonies. I'd met this darling girl, felt a compelling urge to bring her into our family, and started a ball rolling that was gathering speed by the day. Would this be the moment when my idea crashed into a wall of reality—where someone told me "No"? Would the kids say something like, "Fine, we've met her, now cool it with this wacky idea"? I sat looking expectantly from one to the other as I nervously swished my tuna salad around on my plate. Bob was looking at me with the smile that I'd seen many times over the years, the one that meant he was on board with me. He winked and nodded.

I don't know how the conversation went after that. Ellie remembers telling us that she liked Melissa and was impressed how comfortable she seemed. But she also recalls telling us to watch out for ourselves and not get hurt. She worried that we'd get invested in Melissa, give it our all, and then she wouldn't stay in our family for some reason, and we'd get hurt. All Colin remembers is saying that he didn't care, as long as his life didn't change that much. I know I was feeling like a steam engine, rolling forward towards my goal, and I know that when I get like that, there's not much that can deter me.

Jumping into deep water is, and has always been, my style.

20

Melissa

According to my biological family, if I kept running away, I'd get to come home. I had court-mandated visits with my mother and grandmother—once a week, at first—during which they would always say, "You can always run away—just come to a phone and call us." I thought they wanted me back home where they could keep me safe. When I was older, I realized that my safety had nothing to do with it. They just wanted me with them.

At some point, my mother's visits were reduced to once a month. I was never told why, and I had always assumed it was because I had done something wrong. In retrospect, I suspect that her visits were limited because she was still in contact with Victor, and she probably wasn't showing up to her mandatory drug testing and counseling appointments. I know that a few years later, she married a man who had been accused of child sexual abuse. At that point, a social worker explained to me that this choice had further limited her visitation rights. Still, I thought I would never really be safe until I was with her again. My stepfather was in jail for having abused me, and, in my mind, Paula had never done anything wrong. The court might have thought she neglected me, but my young judgment disagreed. She was at the center of all my happy family fantasies, and I still desperately wanted the life I imagined we would have when we reunited.

After three more attempts at running away, I ended up

telling my counselor about the abuse in that household. Until that point, I had been afraid to do so, mostly because I had promised Rochelle that I wouldn't talk to anyone about it. She was protecting me from my roommate, and we had a connection. But I was scared, and I had to get out of there. The foster father lost his license, and all the girls were removed from the house. Criminal charges were never brought against him, however, and I remember feeling really angry about that. "Why isn't he in jail?" I wondered. "My stepdad's in jail, why didn't *this guy* go to jail? I guess the foster care system just doesn't want that kind of publicity," I thought.

I don't remember where I went to live after that house. According to my social worker, I was in a string of different placements, each for less than a month, and some as few as two or three nights. None of them were anything like the home I dreamed of.

21
Patrice

A few days after Melissa's social worker, Joe, had done our home inspection, he called to tell me that all the boxes were checked. We'd been cleared to foster Melissa. "So, what are you and Bob thinking?" he asked. "Are you still ready to jump in with both feet?" I told him that I hadn't once doubted our decision–with a level of certainty and conviction that still amazes me to this day.

"Great. The only thing left, then, is for you to have a look at her file."

I felt my chest tighten up, and I clutched the receiver like I was wringing its neck. "I have to read her file, really?" He'd brought up this topic so quickly. "I've been meeting with her at the school, she's been to our house twice and to a party with us down at the soccer fields. I've talked with Kristin, and I really feel like I know enough about Melissa and her past at this point." I didn't want to read her file, and it looked like I was going to have to try to explain why. "I just have this idea that I'd like for her to have a fresh start here. I know her past is part of her, but I guess I don't want to be prejudiced by other people's experiences." As I said this, I had a sinking feeling in my stomach that we could lose our chance to bring Melissa into our family if we didn't do what he asked. In the most agreeable voice I could muster, I added, "Maybe Bob could go down and read some of it? It's okay if just one of us reads it, right?"

As I heard him shuffling papers and sighing, I held my breath. After what seemed like minutes, he cleared his throat. "Uh, um, I guess that could work."

"And then, after that happens, how soon could she move in?" I wanted to stop talking about the file and get back to her future. "Because we are ready to be her foster parents."

"I'd say it could happen by the end of this week. How would the weekend be?" And that was it. Melissa would be moving in, and I managed to get out of this task that I wanted nothing to do with.

One day after work, Bob went to Joe's office and read through the part of her file that was open to foster families. "Holy shit, she's been through more than you can imagine," Bob said when he returned. He sat down heavily on the couch. "I mean, wow. When she was only..."

"Whoa, hold on." I stood in front of him and stuck my hands out. "I can see from your face how upsetting it was, but I think I've heard as much about her past as I want to hear. That's why I asked you to go down there." I took another deep breath and eased onto the couch next to him. "I want to be able to preserve a clear space in my head where Melissa can start over without my clinical judgments getting in the way of being a mother to her." In reality, I think I was too scared to face the details of Melissa's past.

"Okay, I get it, when you put it that way." For the thousandth time, I realized that Bob would hear me and protect me. I went back to grabbing plates and utensils for dinner, thinking about how, in a few days, I'd go back to putting out five place settings once again.

It never occurred to me that ignoring Melissa's past might come back to haunt me.

22
Melissa

I later found out that the same day I met Patrice, she contacted Bob to tell him about me. From what I was told, the ball started rolling very quickly. I think only ten days elapsed between that first meeting and the day I moved into the Keets' home. Typically, there are a few more meetings first—some "get-to-know-you" type things. I knew this because when I was placed on the adoption list, I had met several potential families. They don't just pick out a kid from a window and say, "I want that one, give me that one!" or flip through a magazine and place their order online. There's a process. And in this case, it moved more rapidly than usual.

In my next memory of Patrice, we were at some sort of event. I was wearing a dress. We were standing out in a grassy field, and there were chairs and tables set up. That's all I remember. And then I was living at the Keets'.

I don't remember moving my things. Since I had grown used to being taken from one home and plopped into a new one, this just seemed like another move. In my memory, I was not with them, and then I was with them, and then, before I knew it, I had been with them for some time. I guess kids' memories are like that—unpredictable and jumpy.

It wasn't until many years later, after I left the Keets' home, that I connected the two events—meeting Patrice at school and coming to live with her and Bob. As perceptive as I was, I never realized the cause-and-effect pieces in play. "We just fell in love with you and knew you had a place in our lives," Patrice told me, when we met again over twenty years later.

23
Patrice

On October 20, 1993, I'd spent most of the day cleaning, making a cake, and buzzing around the house like a tornado looking for a place to touch down. Joe was scheduled to bring Melissa and her belongings over, and I wanted everything to be perfect. Around one o'clock, Bob and I heard a car pull into the driveway. We dashed to the front door to look out the diamond-shaped window. I remember turning to Bob, whose eyes were wide. "Well, Sweetie, here goes a new chapter. Ready?"

Melissa and Joe came up the sidewalk with their arms full. I opened the door and enveloped Melissa in a bear hug, causing a stuffed penguin and a small blanket to fall from her load. She laughed and flashed a beautiful open smile. Bob helped unburden Joe as I showed Melissa down the hall to her new room. Cut flowers from my garden stood in a colorful ceramic vase on her desk. "Honey, I'm so happy you're here. Shall we put your things on the bed for now, and I can help you get settled in a bit?"

"Okay, sure," she said, dropping a pink, hard-shelled suitcase and a black plastic garbage bag of clothes and stuffed animals onto the bed. She turned toward the big open window and spread her arms out in front of her, like a monarch butterfly about to take flight. "I can put some books here." She pointed to the white bookcase covering half of a wall, then to the four-foot-long wooden desk under the window. "And set up my dollhouse and maybe do homework there. And make a home for my stuffed animals in the corner." She pranced around the room on tiptoes and touched every surface as if to determine it was real.

Joe appeared in the door with a grocery bag of plastic toys, followed by Bob balancing a cardboard box labeled "dollhouse." "Well, Missy, here you are," Joe said, looking around smiling. "Any questions for me before I leave you with these nice people?"

Melissa shrugged her shoulders and nodded. "Nope. You know, this is my very own room."

Joe patted her on the back, swept his other hand out in front of himself, and made a little bow. "I know, all yours. Have fun settling in, and I'll see you next week when I come by for a visit."

Melissa peeked in all the other bedrooms, as if checking to see if they'd changed since Ellie and Colin had given her the grand tour the week before. Then she ran back to us and asked, "Is it okay if I go explore the back decks and jump on the trampoline, please, please?" Bob and I watched from the French doors in the dining room as Melissa stepped down to a lower deck and lifted the top of our hot tub to look inside. She scampered around the railings and peered down into the tree-lined ravine that bordered our house. After she jumped on the trampoline for a few minutes, she lay down with her hands entwined behind her head and stared up at the towering redwoods.

That evening, we had the first of what I hoped would be many years' worth of family dinners. Richard, Bob, Colin, Melissa, and I sat around our expandable oak table. We raised our glasses to toast our new family member, and she glowed in the light of our attention. After dinner, Colin helped serve the German chocolate cake I'd made. The guys did the dishes while I helped Melissa unpack her clothes and get ready for bed. The day before, I'd added a few of my kids' books to the shelves in her room. "May I tuck you in and read you a couple of stories?" I asked her.

She looked at me blankly and then furrowed her brow. "Uh, sure, if you want to. Yeah, that would be good. I mean, if you have time." I came back when she was dressed for bed. I smiled when I saw her nestled with her stuffed penguin tight in her arm under a batik quilt I'd made during one of my sewing sprees. That night, as a crisp fall breeze blew in through the window, we began our shared journey to *The Secret Garden.* Other literary lands would follow.

A couple of nights later, during our family dinner, Colin quizzed Melissa about school. "So, are the kids being nice to the new girl? I remember we always made a fuss when somebody joined our class. I think you have the same teacher I had for fourth grade. Doesn't she, Mom?"

Bob and I had decided to have Melissa change schools right away so she could get used to her new situation before the Thanksgiving break. The Monday after she arrived, Melissa and I had strolled through our neighborhood to get her registered at Brook Knoll Elementary, which was a ten-minute walk away. I knew many of the teachers at the school, and Colin had really liked it there. Melissa was friendly to the people in the office; she'd clearly learned how to deal with school staff. Her teacher had posted a "Welcome Melissa" sign on the classroom door, and, by the time I closed that door behind me, Melissa was already chatting away with the girl in the seat next to hers.

I didn't get a chance to answer Colin's question, because Melissa was off and running—telling us about how much fun recess was and bragging that nobody had been mean to her yet. "That's good," my father said. "Otherwise, I'd have to have a talk with them."

Melissa chuckled and poked his arm. "You wouldn't really

do that, would you?"

"Watch out for a couple of those yard duty ladies," Colin chimed in. "They want you to follow all the rules. Seriously, though, I hope you like your teacher as much as I did. I can help you with math sometime. That is, if you need it. And maybe we can go over and shoot some baskets at the school." Melissa's eyes widened as she took another large helping of lasagna and beamed at him.

That night, in the hot tub, I leaned into Bob and whispered, "Well, keep your fingers crossed that this cozy family feeling keeps up."

24
Melissa

The Keets owned a beautiful house on Cress Drive, high in the hills above Santa Cruz. There were a lot of trees on the property, and I think I spent all my spare time in them. There was one tree, in particular, that I remember climbing to read books, draw, and write. I'd be up there in the branches at all hours with some type of pad in my hand.

My room at the Keets' was sunny and bright, with a poster of Jonathan Taylor Thomas above the bed and a fishbowl on my desk. I won a goldfish at the Santa Cruz County Fair, and somehow the little guy managed to survive in there for almost a year. On the nightstand was an alarm clock—the first I'd ever owned. "You're going to wake yourself up here," Patrice had said to me.

I didn't spend much time in my room because there was a very comfortable common area with couches and a fireplace. There was a pool table in the living room, and large French doors led out to a patio. Adjacent to the patio was a three-tiered deck with a hot tub and a built-in trampoline, where I spent a lot of time trying to jump as high as the tree branches that surrounded me.

The house had a very small kitchen with a dining area just outside of it. The walls were painted a deep burgundy color with some hunter green accents. There was a window by the sink, and I seem to remember something unusual about how they stored the dishes. They hung them from racks and just let them drip dry. I always thought that seemed exotic.

For some reason, I remember this one very typical night. Bob and Patrice were cooking dinner together. Colin was home. Bob was cutting tomatoes and seasoning them with salt and pepper, and Patrice and I were mixing up some sort of vinaigrette. While I was whisking it up, I remember thinking, "We're putting mustard in the dressing? Gross!" We all gathered at the table, and I even remember where I was sitting—on the long side, with a view towards the window. We each talked about the day, what we had done, what we had experienced. There was more than enough food to go around, and I know there was bread there because I loved bread. Patrice would always say, "That's enough, Melissa. Eat the rest of your food, and then you can have some more bread," and that's exactly what she said that night. That's probably one of my favorite memories. It's just comforting, not at all profound.

I felt welcomed in their home; I knew I wasn't a paycheck. That had defined my role in other homes, where parents fostered as many kids as they could to maximize the support money. I was aware from the start that the Keets were wealthy. At first, I was uncomfortable with that, because I had never been around money. Then, I was shocked by how wealth changed a lot of day-to-day realities. "We can go to the movies *and* out to dinner in the same night?" I thought. "It's okay to finish the last of the orange juice because you can just go out and buy some more? They don't have to make what's in the refrigerator last all week?" There were times as a child that I was hungry, so eating what I wanted, when I wanted, was an entirely new concept. Previously, I had been embarrassed to go to school in some of my clothes. Sometimes I had holes in my shoes, or I wore jackets that were much too thin to protect me against the winter weather. Other times, I felt out of place in hand-me-down clothes that didn't fit me or outfits I didn't like.

With Bob and Patrice, I got to go shopping. I got to choose t-shirts that I liked and pants that were my size.

25
Patrice

In the first few months that Melissa lived with us, I made a point of taking her to all those Santa Cruz sites I'd listed in my head on that day I walked with Laura. We started with a visit to the wharf the day after our big welcoming party, the one where we introduced her to all our friends. We'd ridden the Giant Dipper, the Boardwalk's 1924 roller coaster, at least three times, and we went to a different beach almost every weekend. When I found out she'd never been to a museum, we decided to take her to the Exploratorium, a huge educational science complex in San Francisco.

On a Saturday in late April 1994, six months after Melissa had moved in with us, Bob and I drove up scenic coastal highway Route 1 with Colin and Melissa in the back seat. The sandy beaches tucked along the coastline provided enticing picnic spots. We chose one and spread our blanket alongside a sand dune. Bob and I laid out our lunch while the kids chased seagulls and tossed a football around. It made me smile to watch how Colin engaged so easily with Melissa.

Later, over the magnetic wave exhibit nestled in a dark alcove of the Exploratorium, Colin had me to himself. Bob and Melissa were off checking out the light and sound displays. "Hey, Mom, when do you think Melissa will become a Keet?" he asked. I realized he could have been talking about the process of adoption, but I had an inkling that he meant something else.

"What do you mean, 'a Keet?' And what's a Keet, anyway?"

He responded without missing a beat. "Well, she wouldn't play with Barbie dolls, and she wouldn't eat meat. And she'd hurry up and do things fast like we all do rather than take forever to put on her shoes or comb her hair." While his answer was a humorous distillation of some of our family's behaviors, he was right that, in deeper and more nuanced ways, Melissa didn't yet "fit" into our family. His observations barely scratched the surface of the vast cultural differences between us. I agreed that playing with Barbies hadn't been something Ellie had done but explained that every child is different. But I didn't want to get into just how radically different Melissa's life had been than his or reveal details of her history and background. I figured that it was her story to tell, if, and when, she was ready. But I also knew Colin was a key player in integrating Melissa into the family. I wanted Melissa to be one of our children. Having him think of her as another sister was crucial to that.

A couple of months later, Colin came to me and said, "Mom, we have a problem with Melissa. She keeps bragging about how smart she is when she's around me and my friends, and it embarrasses me. Besides, I want her to make her own friends and that's not going to help."

I remember putting my arm around him and telling him something like, "Well, I know bragging can be annoying, but I think it's new for Melissa to feel that way about herself. She hasn't had very much encouragement in her life. I think this is a stage she's going through while she builds up her confidence." He looked at me askance at first, then he smiled and gave me a high five.

26
Melissa

Only now can I fully appreciate how far apart our worlds were. My trip to Chinatown with Patrice is just one of the many times I felt like I'd landed on another planet when I landed at the Keets' house.

I'm not sure what we were doing in that part of San Francisco—probably going out to lunch. We pulled up to the curb in Patrice's gray Volvo. I was sitting in the back, and Patrice got out to put coins in what I found out was a parking meter. I had never seen one before. My window was open, so I was looking right through the opening at Patrice. Behind her, there was a store with chickens hanging upside-down in the window. I was supposed to be getting my things together to get out of the car, but I was too freaked out. I think I was probably embarrassed. At that age, I don't even know if I had put it together that the chicken on my plate came from the same animals as the ones I was seeing in the window. I remember their dangling bodies reminding me of the horror movies I'd seen. Victor had taken Daniel and me to a lot of them—*Puppetmaster, Chuckie*, all of those—when we were five and six years old. And then there were people—lots of them, and they looked strange to me. I don't think I'd ever seen Asian people in Aromas or Salinas or Watsonville, and there were definitely no Asian kids in any of my schools. I remember Patrice saying, "It's okay. This is a new place and we're going to be going together." I know I held her hand the whole time. I also know I didn't say anything about what I was feeling. Fear was another of those "bad" emotions that you just don't express.

27
Patrice

"Hey, we're going to take you to the Grand Canyon," I told Melissa not long after that talk with Colin. "What do you think about that? It's a beautiful place in the spring."

She scrunched up her face and asked, "It's really far away, isn't it? And what about Colin; he's coming, too, right?"

I told her we'd be taking a plane and that the flight would only be a couple of hours long. Colin had daily soccer practice, so he would be staying home with Richard. I also explained to her that she'd be meeting Lee and Nancy, Bob's brother and sister-in-law, whom we'd talked about often. Despite her reservations, Melissa was ecstatic to get out of school for a couple of days. She spent the plane rides to Phoenix and Flagstaff coloring and looking out the window. I couldn't imagine what could go wrong, as we had world-class scenery, excellent meals, and relaxing time with family members we loved ahead of us.

After meeting us at the airport, Lee and Nancy drove us to the majestic adobe lodge they'd chosen on the outskirts of Sedona, a city known for Native American arts and crafts, New Age healing practices, and striking red rock views.

"Do I get this room all to myself?" Melissa asked as she flopped down on a queen-sized bed. It had a view of the valley's awe-inspiring sandstone cliffs, rising just behind the swimming pool.

"Sure do. We'll be right through here though," Bob said,

opening the door that connected her room with our bedroom, a larger space with woven Navajo blankets on the walls.

Early the next morning, we packed lunches for our day trip to the South Rim of the Grand Canyon. We drove close to two hours through ponderosa pine forest to get to the first of the many scenic viewpoints that allow visitors a glimpse down towards the Colorado River below. As we headed north, clear skies gave way to thin sheets of stratus clouds that looked like line drawings above the horizon. A light snow had fallen overnight, adding to the mystique of the vista.

After we bundled into our jackets, we stepped out of the car. Within seconds, Melissa slipped on a patch of ice hidden beneath a thin layer of snow. She broke through the ice and got her clothes muddy and wet. She quickly brushed herself off, then dashed away from us to the roped-off viewing area at the lip of the canyon. We watched stunned from the parking lot as she ducked under the rope barrier. "Bob!" I shouted, as I registered the fact that there was nothing between her and a several thousand-foot precipice. Just as we started running her way, I screamed, "Melissa, come back!" Just then I saw a ranger grab her. I could hear people around us gasping, and I think one older couple even shrieked. My whole body was trembling as I caught up to the ranger. I thanked him profusely and threw my arms tightly around Melissa. She pulled away from me and shook herself off. Bob reached for her hand, knelt in front of her, and then gently held her shoulders. I could hear him tell her that we loved her and wanted her to be safe—and that she needed to be careful, obey signs, and stay with us. From the corner of my eye, I watched as she turned away and shrugged her shoulders. I stepped a little closer and heard her bark at Bob, "What's the big deal? I was *fine*." From that moment on, I held her hand whenever we were out of the car.

After a picnic lunch, we took a short hike and then drove

back to the lodge in Sedona. I was still a little shaken up, and I sat in the back seat of the car, lost in thought. I wondered what Melissa's teen years might bring. Ellie had never disobeyed a sign in her life, and although Colin was a daredevil on his skateboard, he wouldn't duck a rope at a National Park. Later that night, as I lay in bed thinking about the day, it dawned on me that Melissa had never been to a National Park before. There were so many things I took for granted, so many things that I expected she'd know.

When we got back to the lodge, Nancy and I cut up vegetables for dinner in the small kitchenette while Bob sat in our suite calling patients. Melissa made her way outside to the patio where Lee was tending the barbeque. I glanced out the large sliding glass door and saw them lost in what looked like a deep conversation.

Later that night, after Bob had put Melissa to bed, the four of us sat out on Lee and Nancy's patio. "I have to say, that was a pretty strange conversation I had with Melissa," Lee said, as he sipped his espresso. "I'm going to tell you about it because I think you should know what's on her mind." I felt a little lurch in my stomach, as though my body knew I wouldn't like what he had to share. "Basically, she told me that she wanted to go back and live with her mother and sisters. 'And I will,' she said."

"What? You're kidding, right?" Bob said, running his hand through his hair.

"No. She was in the middle of asking me to talk to you about it when Nancy came out to check on my cooking. Melissa told me she 'likes you guys and all' but really belongs back in her own home." He paused for a moment, obviously trying to remember her exact words. "She said, 'Things are all better there now with my stepdad gone, and I'll be able to see my brother, Daniel, a lot more—maybe even live with him.' Then came the kicker. She said, 'I just don't fit in with Bob and Patrice.'" Bob took my hand as Lee went on. "I told her that I'd watched you both be wonderful parents. Her answer to that was, 'Sure. But Colin and Ellie are their own kids. I'm different.'"

About a month later, I received a call from a man named Dale who told me he was the CASA Advocate for Melissa's brother, Daniel. After a few pleasantries, he got right down to his agenda. "I'd love to get Melissa and Daniel together. He's living in Watsonville with a terrific foster mom, but he really misses his sister. They've been close all their lives, and both of them went through hell in their childhood home."

Alarm bells of fear went off in my head. Watsonville? Nope, I wanted to keep her as far away as I could from there. Spending time with her family? Nope, again. She was surviving because she'd escaped their neglect and abuse. I understood that Daniel was important to Melissa, but I was terrified that he'd get in the way of Melissa's bonding with us—something that wasn't happening the way I'd expected. I was working as hard as I could to make a new life for Melissa, and, still, she felt out of reach.

"I know," I said. "But we're trying really hard to be Melissa's family now, Dale." I wished I could just hang up on him. "I need a little time to think about this and talk it over with my husband. How about if you call me back in a couple of weeks?" I could hear his disappointment in the way he told me that I really *should* think about it. I was shaking when I put down the receiver.

About a month later, Dale called again. He pressed his point by saying that, in her other foster homes, Melissa had been able to see Daniel often. I'd done a lot of thinking about how important my own sister, Kathy, was to me, and realized that it wasn't fair or realistic for me to try to keep Melissa in a cocoon, hidden away from her closest relative. Still, I was apprehensive, and I didn't want to be the person who drove her back to Watsonville.

Dale was exuberant when I told him that Bob would take Melissa to see her brother the following weekend. They could visit while Bob ran some errands. "Great news. Yes, this is just the right thing." He gave me Daniel's foster mom's name and number to arrange the meeting. "Please let me know how it goes, okay?" he added, before hanging up.

Bob and Melissa took off after breakfast the next Saturday morning, talking and laughing about a song they'd heard on the radio as they walked out the door. Four or five hours later, Melissa stormed into the house with puffy red eyes clutching her new stuffed otter and a shell necklace tight to her chest. She grabbed one of the warm cookies I'd just pulled out of the oven. "I'm going to my room, and I want to be alone," she announced.

Bob motioned for me to follow him upstairs. He sprawled out on the bed and rubbed his temples with his palms. "It was terrible. Things were fine when I left Melissa with Daniel. But when I came back to get her, I almost had to pull her away. She totally fell apart. She was crying and saying she didn't want to leave and didn't want to go with me." He was almost in tears himself as he told me that when they got in the car, Melissa announced that she wanted to live with Daniel and would figure out how to do it someday soon. She also said that she wanted to go back to her mother's house. Bob swallowed and went on. "The cutting blow was when she yelled, 'I don't want a new family!' I felt like all the air was kicked out of me." He shook his head and lowered his chin. "I didn't know what to say, so I let her talk on and on. I'm not sure I can go through that again."

I sat down next to him on the bed and stroked his head. "I'm sure this will pass." I started to say, "I knew this would happen," but stopped myself. She just needed to have more experiences with us—and more time.

28
Melissa

I have a vivid memory of being with Patrice one night when she was getting ready to go out. I remember her having a wide variety of accessories—hats, scarves, jewelry—and I always loved digging around in the drawers where they were organized. That night, I was asking questions about various necklaces and earrings. "Where did this come from?" I'd ask, dangling a pendant in front of Patrice. And "Which one of these is your favorite?" I'd inquire while laying out three different bracelets. I recall that Patrice was in her undergarments, in the process of getting dressed, and yet, I felt completely comfortable having a conversation with her. Looking back at this scene now, I realize that I hadn't had that kind of intimacy since I'd been taken away from my mother.

We spent a lot of time reading together, and that was completely new to me. No one in my biological family read books, and, since I barely went to school when I lived with them, I couldn't read. When I lived with Aunt Jenny and went to school regularly, I had to catch up on everything I had missed—reading, counting, listening skills, how to participate in a classroom. I was still struggling with kindergarten-level books when I was in second grade, so reading for fun was not a part of my life then. But by the time I was living with the Keets, I had caught up, and I was proud to be a good reader. I even developed a love of reading, which Patrice reinforced. We would just sit on the couch together, sharing a blanket. Sometimes we read separate books, but other times I read to her—*Down by the Seashore* and *Matilda* were my favorites. She wanted to know what I thought about the characters. She wanted to hear what I had to say. I felt more like an equal and less like the dumb kid who had been such a burden at all my other houses.

Patrice showed affection through praise, and this was totally new to me as well. "Great job with the dishes," she said, after I finished one of my chores. I was also praised for qualities I didn't even know I had. "You are *so* smart!" I was constantly told. At first, I didn't know what to make of this. Was it real? Was it sarcasm? In my biological family, I had been praised for being beautiful or thin or dainty, or for having bright blue eyes and a big smile. Their traditional gender values were reflected in how they reacted to me. At the Keets', I won praise for being talented, showing creativity, and "thinking outside of the box." While I was totally uncomfortable with these statements at first, over time, I started to like hearing them.

Above all, the Keets showed me another way to live. All of my foster homes had seemed worse than my birth home, so I had begun to assume that life consisted of being taken from one bad situation to another, year after year. At the Keets', I saw that a home could be happy and healthy. Life could actually get better.

29
Patrice

As the summer of 1994 approached, I lay awake at night thinking about everything we'd do on our annual vacation back to Saranac Lake—my hometown and the town where Bob and I had met. I was disappointed that Ellie's job was keeping her in Santa Cruz for the summer, but the fun of introducing Melissa to this place would help distract me from Ellie's absence. I was excited to organize canoe trips with overflowing picnic baskets, eat sumptuous meals with both of our extended families, and cuddle on the screened-in porch during dramatic thunderstorms.

In the days leading up to the trip, Melissa and I poured over photography books of the area. She was full of questions: "Will I get sick on the plane? Are there a lot of bears at the camp? What if I get lost in the woods?" I hugged her close and told her that we would take good care of her, there and everywhere.

It was a hot and humid late July afternoon when we arrived. Lee and Nancy, Bob's brother and sister-in-law whom Melissa had met on our Grand Canyon trip, greeted us with cold drinks and beach towels, and we all bee-lined for the inviting lake. By dinnertime, Melissa had checked out the rack of canoes and kayaks, and she'd run her fingers over the spruce ribs and cedar hull of what looked like a wide canoe but was actually a handmade guide boat. Bob explained to her that these specially designed boats were made in the Adirondacks for taking city folk on hunting and fishing expeditions. She spotted a wall of fishing rods, and Bob beamed when she asked if he would teach her to fish. After swimming, Melissa peeked into each of the six bedrooms and was surprised when she got to choose her own. She darted back and forth between the lake-facing, beadboard-paneled room and a smaller, green-carpeted room with a birch log bunk bed. “I like looking out at the forest, and I want to be near you in this big house,” she said, tossing her suitcase onto the lower bunk of the smaller room. That evening, she nudged the whole family into taking a sunset swim. I smiled as I toweled off, thinking about how she was already getting the hang of lake life.

My daily routine in Saranac Lake always involved an early morning swim. The day we arrived, I’d told Melissa that she’d be welcome to join me, and I was thrilled when she asked me to wake her up the next morning. We bundled ourselves up in beach towels embroidered with the names of the highest Adirondack peaks and quietly left the house. The mist was clearing as we headed to the water. We had the placid lake to ourselves. After diving in, we climbed back up the metal ladder and made a game of inching ourselves down the wooden boat ramp until we hit the slimy boards at the bottom and shot into the lake. Melissa suggested that we race to the floating raft offshore. After our sprint, we climbed up onto it and waited for a loon family to glide by. At first, Melissa was distressed by their strange and haunting calls, but she soon learned to recognize and even appreciate them. By the end of the trip, she could identify the different markings of the males and females and even gauge the age of the babies.

One of my favorite parts of the typical vacation day was dinnertime. Meals were always restaurant quality, since Nancy was an exceptional cook. The table was set with fine china, linens, and crystal, and the non-stop conversations and debates resembled table tennis tournaments. I loved them;

they were classy versions of the scenes I remembered from *Cheaper by the Dozen.*

A few days into the trip, Melissa had had her fill of these events. "Are you kidding me, another fancy dinner with everybody showing off what books they've read? Can you just make me a peanut butter and jelly sandwich and let me go sit by the lake?" I was setting the table for sixteen and wanted her to be part of the group. "I don't even know what all of you are talking about most of the time. And everyone asks me dumb questions. How am I supposed to know what I want to be when I grow up? I just want to watch TV, and there isn't even one here. That's so weird."

"How about having dinner with us and you can sneak off with your dessert afterwards? Deal?"

She huffed loudly. "If I have to. And I'm not going on another 'short' hike that ends up taking ten hours tomorrow—just to see the same mountains we looked at the day before."

"Come on, I thought you had a good time on St. Regis Mountain today. And it was only three hours." I rustled her hair. "And you like canoeing, right?"

There were plenty of moments during those two weeks when I felt like I was dragging her into our activities. But then I'd see her wandering on the lakeshore looking for ducklings or swimming her powerful freestyle out to the dock and back, and I'd think that she was really happy, that she was starting to get into the magic of the place. That made my heart sing.

Just before we left, I noticed that she'd placed a piece of birch bark on the dresser in the bedroom she'd used. The words "Melissa's Room" were scrawled on the papery white surface.

30
Melissa

After spending most of a school year with the Keets, I had gotten accustomed to the fact that they lived a different type of lifestyle than I was used to. There was a lot of flying and traveling that just happened, as though going to faraway places was normal. I had only been on an airplane once before moving in with Bob and Patrice, when my aunt Jenny shipped me back to California from Colorado. But that was a short flight, and I wasn't going on a vacation.

This was a long flight; we were going all the way to the other side of the country, to New York. Of course, I thought New York was New York City, and I expected to see skyscrapers, bad drivers, and great fashion. We did see the tall buildings of the Manhattan skyline from the airplane, but we landed in Upstate New York, surrounded by gigantic trees. At the time, I had no idea that so much of New York was rural and woodsy. I remember feeling like I was in that Disney movie *Pocahontas,* where the first settlers were totally blown away by experiencing these huge eastern forests for the first time.

Every place has its own essence, I think, and I remember immediately loving the essence of Saranac Lake. We stayed in an enormous old house with multiple stories. It was right on the water, and there was a tree root path that made steps in the hillside leading down to the dock by the lake. Lee and Nancy lived there, but I think the house belonged to the whole family. It sure seemed like the whole family was there, because

I spent so much of the first two days meeting people and figuring out who everyone was. We all ate lunch together, went out on the lake together, and even played Scrabble and charades around the fire together in the evenings. It was called "family time," and I know I'd never experienced anything like it before.

In my biological family, we never even ate meals together, much less hung out as a group because we wanted to. Any kind of family gathering that had to happen—for a required birthday celebration or a graduation, for instance—always felt strained. Or feigned. No one wanted to be there, but we had to make a show of it for someone. These people seemed like they actually wanted to be together. And I was included.

I also remember feeling so free paddling around in a kayak. I'd never been in a one-person boat like that before. I'd never even been on a lake. And here I was, allowed to take a kayak out by myself, out to the middle of this big blue bowl where I could just sit and look at the huge dome of the sky and the amazing trees surrounding the water.

One afternoon, I was out in one of the kayaks when I heard Patrice screaming from on shore. I looked over, and she was jumping and waving her arms around frantically. "Am I in trouble?" I thought. "I must have done something wrong again."

As I paddled in closer, Patrice yelled, "Come in, come in! Get off the water!" When I got to shore, she said, "You can't be out on the water in a thunderstorm. If lightning hits, it's going to strike the first thing on the water, and that'll be you." I didn't know it was dangerous to be on a lake in a storm. I didn't even know it was storming. I remember feeling relieved that I wasn't in trouble, and I know I apologized. But I also remember walking back to the house thinking how different this had been from the Manresa Beach incident with the Aromas family. It was clear that this person wanted to protect me.

Foster kids don't have photo albums that organize all the highlights from their childhoods, but I do have some snapshots in my head of different scenes from our travels. I call them "unintentional memories," because they're not the big things that I feel like I *should* remember; they're just moments. Like wearing Bob's heavy woolen pea coat on a ferry boat from Seattle to one of the islands in the sound. Collecting ten pounds of rocks from the Washington seashore. Buying a new Speedo-style purple bathing suit in a San Diego gift shop so I could swim in the hotel pool. I created so many first-time memories with the Keets.

31
Patrice

Despite some of the tensions we'd experienced, we came out of our summer vacation with Melissa feeling a sense of accomplishment and hopefulness that she would become a permanent member of our family. The two weeks in Saranac Lake could have been a lot more difficult. Melissa was farther from home than she'd ever been, and she'd been thrust into a totally new environment. Bob and I really enjoyed having another child with whom to share our love of mountains and lakes, and, in a lot of ways, Melissa had really thrived. After that, Bob and I went from occasionally talking about adopting her to discussing the idea more seriously. She'd been living with us for almost a year, and we wanted to give her a more solid sense of security.

"You know, I think some of Melissa's behavioral issues would improve if she knew she had a permanent place with us," Bob said one evening as we lay in bed. Late into the night, we'd ponder how unsettling it must be for her to wonder if we were going to keep her, and we wondered if her backtalk and occasional angry outbursts were the result of deep insecurity. She'd once told us she thought she'd be shuffled from home to home until she reached the age of eighteen. Bob and I both knew that she deserved better, and we really thought that we were the right family for her. I decided it was time to start investigating the adoption process.

Joe wasn't available, so I called Kristin and asked her to

take a walk on the beach with me. The ocean fog had lifted by mid-afternoon at Seacliff State Beach in nearby Aptos when I pulled into the parking lot. I scanned the lot for her, taking in the view of the Monterey Bay and the concrete freighter—the SS Palo Alto—that had been intentionally grounded there in 1929 to be part of a tourist attraction. Kristin was already standing on the worn wooden steps that led down to the area's longest stretch of sandy beach.

As we walked, Kristin said she wished the dilapidated ship and fishing pier in our sights still held the dance floor, café, and fifty-four-foot heated swimming pool that had been there in the early 1930s. Thinking about the Boardwalk, where we'd recently gone to indulge Melissa's skee-ball obsession, I said, "I wonder if people around here were more relaxed back then."

"Maybe," Kristin replied. "Lots of people are working hard just to stay afloat here in Santa Cruz County these days—especially the folks we see through CASA. I'm not sure how they make ends meet most of the time." As we passed fishermen with their big surfcasting rods dug into the sand, I thought about how Melissa had talked about the food rationing that happened in some of her foster homes.

While I took off my sweater, I told Kristin that Bob and I wanted to take the steps needed to adopt Melissa. I went on to say that she'd been doing a bit better in school and following directions more since our successful summer vacation. "Of course, she hasn't bonded with us as fast as I would've hoped. Sometimes I'm not even sure what I mean by that, but it's a feeling that's missing." I told her that Bob and I both felt like Melissa always had one foot out the door. "She drops comments that make me realize how tied she feels to her birth family." I bit my lip. Maybe my years of family counseling should have prepared me for what I was experiencing, but I had to admit the truth. "I just don't know what to do about that."

Kristin tilted her head back then nodded. She looked out over the water and told me that she was thrilled that Melissa had found a wonderful family like ours. "You're right that she still feels huge emotional ties to her biological family, especially to her brother." She looked over at me. "She'd really like to be in a home with him, and I assume that's not going to happen with you guys."

"Yep. That's not something we could manage now."

As we walked, she slowed down her pace and reached for my hand. Then she looked directly into my eyes and said, "You know, you might still be in the honeymoon phase with Melissa." In her typical no-nonsense tone of voice, she continued. "I'm not trying to discourage you, but she's got a lot of baggage."

"Yeah, I know that, but we think giving her a permanent home will give her the security to unpack some of that baggage and move forward." I stopped by a pile of kelp covered with sand and fished a mussel shell out of the rope-like strands. I wondered what she meant by "not trying to discourage" me. Her comments sure felt discouraging. Wasn't her stated goal to find Melissa a permanent home? I ran my thumb over the peeling black scales of the shell. Mentioning the "honeymoon" and her baggage rubbed me the wrong way. I was a grown-up, and a mental health professional besides. I knew all about relationship honeymoons and baggage.

By the time we got back to our cars, I'd solidified my decision. Kristin just didn't realize how much we loved Melissa and how committed we were to her. We'd just love her through the challenges that might come up. That would be enough, wouldn't it?

32
Melissa

In every new house, there's a "honeymoon stage." That's the period of time when everybody is afraid of offending the new foster kid—and vice versa—so everyone in the home is on their best behavior. As a child, I knew all about this phase, and I knew how to milk it to get what I wanted.

In my mind, the honeymoon stage was as close as my life would ever get to *The Brady Bunch*. As a foster child, you idealize everything you don't have and everything you once had but lost. That was particularly true for me because I'd been forcibly removed from my birth home. Even though I had grown up in an unhealthy environment, my family was still my family, and it wasn't my choice to leave them. So, I had created a whole scenario in my mind: Someday, I'd go back to live with my biological family, and it would be just like an episode of *The Brady Bunch*. In the meantime, I'd do everything I could to prolong the honeymoon stages in all my homes. To do that, any type of irritation or misunderstanding had to be kept totally bottled up. At some point, that bottled up emotion would just burst out—usually over something stupid, and usually when I butted heads with another strong personality in the household. In the Keets' house, Patrice was that strong personality.

A few days before school started, we went to the mall to go clothes shopping. It was near the end of the honeymoon stage. I was nine going on ten, and I wanted a bra. A training bra, to be specific—one of those cute little ones made from two triangles of fabric that doesn't really do anything. So, I said to Patrice, "I'd like to have some undershirts, can I get some undershirts?" I deliberately called them "undershirts" because I was too embarrassed to ask for a bra.

"Sure, go ahead and pick out some undershirts," Patrice replied. I came back with two bras, each with little pink ribbons on the straps. Patrice said, "What are those? You said you wanted undershirts."

"Yeah, these *are* undershirts." I knew what I was doing. She knew what I was doing too.

"No, they are not. Those are bras."

"Undershirts, bras, same thing."

"They aren't the same; you know they're not the same. You said you wanted undershirts. If you wanted bras, you should have said you wanted bras. Not undershirts. Which do you want?" I just stood there, staring at the tile floor. I couldn't look at her. "Which is it that you want," she repeated, "bras or undershirts?"

"I want these." I was still clinging to the clear plastic hangers that held the training bras.

"Then why did you say you wanted undershirts?"

I kept looking down. There were diamonds on the floor tiles, mostly black ones alternating with white ones, but there were some gray ones thrown in there too. "I don't know."

"You told me you wanted one thing, but really you wanted something else. That sounds like lying."

Patrice doesn't like being lied to. I knew that even then. But I didn't think I was lying to her, because I didn't feel like I had done something wrong. To me, as a child, a lie was a malicious thing, something that injures someone. When you tell a person she's pretty, even though you don't believe it, that's not really a lie. Technically it is, but nobody gets mad at you for it. I had survived on those kinds of lies. Telling them didn't make me a liar and being called one really hurt my feelings. I got in trouble for something I didn't deserve to get in trouble for. I hadn't tried to steal the bras, after all.

I didn't want to show that I felt hurt and angry. Those were the "bad kinds" of feelings, the ones I was supposed to hide. So, I just kept quiet. We left without buying anything.

33
Patrice

Through the kitchen window, I saw Kristin park in our driveway. The passenger door flew open, and Melissa leapt out carrying a big grocery bag. As she pushed the door closed, she waved at Kristin with one hand and hugged the bag to her chest with the other.

When I heard her in the hall, I hollered, "Welcome back, honey. How did your visit go?" Melissa stormed into the kitchen where I was preparing vegetable tagine for dinner, a recipe that takes concentration to make well. As I was adding the Moroccan spices, she planted herself right in front of me so I had to back up against the refrigerator. She leaned forward and scowled. "How come I can't live with my mother when my little sisters are still there? That's just not fair." I took a deep breath. Part of me wanted to say something like, "You know darn well that the courts took you away for your own safety." At the same time, another part of me ached for her and her loss, even though her home had been far from ideal. After all, home is the place where most kids grow up—ideally, with the people whose job it is to take care of them.

"Honey, I know it's hard being away from them, but we're trying to make a good home for you here." I wanted to reach out and pull her close, but I didn't dare.

Before I could say any more, Melissa shouted, "Oh yeah? Well, you're not my family, and *you* are definitely *not* my mother. You'll never be." She spun around and ran out to the trampoline. I put my wooden spoon down with a sigh of resignation and turned off the burner. Then, I made my way to the dining room table and sat down where I could watch Melissa without being noticed. She was sitting cross-legged in the middle of the trampoline with her head down. I could see her rifling through her bag and flinging candy bars, lollipops, and large packets of M&Ms onto the canvas. "Oh, God," I thought. "Another battle we'll have to go through."

Every time she came back from seeing her mother, Paula, there'd be something to contend with. It was always a snippy attitude and ramped-up defiance. Often, it was also clothes that were two sizes too small for her or some broken gadget that had once been useful. Once, I watched her twisting and turning a Mickey Mouse clock her mother had given her. One ear was broken off, and the face had a crack running down the cheek. She wound it up, set it down, and waited for the hands to move. She did this a few more times before the corners of her mouth turned down. Finally, she held the clock to her chest like she was cradling a baby, and tears streamed down her face. After each visit, Melissa would continue to embrace these ill-suited treasures, knowing that they represented her mother's love to her. The overfilled bags of candy were today's offerings, and they would be harder to manage.

After she'd eaten at least four candy bars, she repacked the bag and scampered across the trampoline to set it on the deck. She rolled around and bounced up onto her feet with her arms flapping like a freed bird. I watched for a few minutes as she did a routine of flips. Neither of us mentioned the outburst when she came in panting to grab a glass of water.

That evening, after I got Melissa settled in bed, I called Kristin. I told her once again how hard Melissa's re-entry was after the visits. "What can I do? She comes back and is so undone. I think it's getting worse, and I'd so hoped that things would get better." Kristin told me that Paula had cried during the meeting that day, something that happened with regularity. I'd learned that Paula and Vera, Melissa's grandmother, would frequently say things like, "You don't belong in that family. You belong with us. Melissa, come back. When you do, everyone will be so happy to see you. These people don't really care about you." This was all said as if Melissa had a choice, as if she were punishing them by not hightailing it back to their house.

"When she's not blowing up at me over some little thing, she's passively acting out by not doing what she's supposed to," I told Kristin. Melissa's sweet smile often reminded me of the thin coat on the surface of a pot of oatmeal just before it bubbles over. She'd be charming one minute and bursting with vitriol the next.

"You have to keep plugging away, gaining her trust, letting her know that you're there for her no matter what—even when she pushes back," Kristin said.

I knew this, but Melissa's angry outbursts would often catch me off guard. What seemed to me like a simple request, like, "Would you please clean up your mess in the bathroom?" would often prompt an edgy response. "What do you want?" she'd yell as she planted her feet, put her hands on her hips, and hunkered down to take me on. I'd repeat my request in as kind a voice as I could muster, but I'd be met with, "Leave me alone. Can't you see I'm doing something else? Why does everything always have to be on *your* schedule?" or "God, I hate all the rules around here. You can be a real hard ass." My eyes would widen, and I could feel my blood pressure rising. My own children had never spoken to me this way. They didn't always like my limits, but they were always respectful. I'd watched kids act out like this in therapy with their parents in my office; I just never thought I'd be faced with a similar level of hostility in my own home. As she wore me down, I found myself becoming more reluctant to set the parenting and household limits I knew were good for all of us.

34
Melissa

Rules change everywhere, as I had quickly discovered, and, in foster homes, rules around food were always in the forefront. As a result, my eating habits would change with every placement. In some houses, I wasn't allowed to have candy. In other houses, I could eat candy, but only at a specific time of day.

Foster children often have food issues. They hoard food, they overeat, they undereat, they binge and purge. Fears that there's not enough to go around are standard, and you don't always know where your next meal is coming from. It's rare for foster kids to be allowed to help themselves in the kitchen, and lots of homes have locked cabinets. I remember sneaking into pantries, even in my mother's house.

Bob and Patrice ate what I came to know as "healthy food." I, on the other hand, loved McDonald's. I still do. That food may kill my stomach, but every now and then, I crave those delicious, chemical-infused French fries. It's what I grew up on.

"Can we go to McDonald's?" I asked Patrice one day.

"We don't eat there," she replied. "That food is not good for you." Her tone wasn't strict or condemning at all; she didn't say, "You can't have that." But all I heard was, "*We* don't eat there." I got that feeling where my chest caves in and I feel small.

"Oh, well *I* eat there," I thought, and I wanted to disappear. Patrice communicated with love, respect, and good intentions, but I interpreted her message in a completely different way. That happened frequently.

Luckily, Patrice's father, Richard, took me on McDonald's missions after school sometimes. He'd pull up after class got out and ask me what I wanted to do. "Let's go to McDonald's!" he'd say. Along with watching TV together, this was one of our bonding activities.

35
Patrice

Melissa frequently asked me if we could go to Kmart. It was probably a familiar place for her—or maybe even a special place to visit with her other families. While it was her cultural reference point for shopping, it wasn't one of my usual destinations. Still, about a year after Melissa had moved in with us, I asked her if she wanted to go to Kmart to get a Halloween costume.

My eyes popped open when we got there and I saw the number of carts filled to the brim with plastic bags of Starbursts, Mounds bars, and every other imaginable kind of sweet treat that would pacify little goblins and ghosts. "Oh, wow, can I have some of those bags?" Melissa was practically jumping up and down. "I love candy, you know, and we hardly ever have any around the house. Please, please, pretty please!"

"We'll be taking you out to fill your own bag in just a week. We're going to wait until then." I was thinking of how generous our neighbors were each year on Halloween and how wired Melissa got when she ate candy.

"Oh, whatever. You never let me get just what I want."

"Well, let's head over to the costume section and you can pick out the exact one you want."

When we arrived home, Melissa set her backpack and her new ninja costume on the edge of the bed and took out the tubes of makeup we'd bought to add to her disguise. As she did, the backpack tipped over and fell to the floor, spilling some of its contents. I reached down to help her and saw an unfamiliar wallet laying on the rug. It was made from red faux leather, and it had a gold star-shaped clasp. Melissa darted in front of me, grabbed both the wallet and the backpack, and turned away quickly. I narrowed my eyes and cocked my head. “Hey, Melissa, I've never seen that wallet before. Where did it come from?” She mumbled something about her aunt giving it to her as she moved toward her closet. She tossed the backpack inside and slid the door closed. "Really? Because I didn’t see you take it with us to the store. In fact, I’ve never seen it before. Do you mind telling me when you got it?"

“I’ve had it for a really long time. There’s nothing important in it.” I told her it didn’t look like something a kid would have and asked to take a closer look at it. She moved to stand guard in front of the closet and folded her arms across her chest as if daring me to say more. “Let’s just get back to putting my clothes away.” I told her that we had time for that, but that I wanted to take a look at the wallet. She walked empty-handed over to her desk, plunked herself in the soft office chair, and swiveled around a couple of times.

“Look, am I going to have to get it out myself?” I started walking toward the closet.

“Whatever. You’re nosy.”

I pulled the whole backpack out of the closet, took the wallet out, and opened it. I gasped as I saw a California driver's license with an unfamiliar woman's picture on it. The address listed was about five blocks from us. I quickly shuffled through the other personal items in the wallet: credit cards, photos, and the woman’s business card. I took a huge breath and asked her who the woman was. Just as the last word left my lips, I remembered that Melissa had taken our cart and wandered off on her own while I was in the housewares department.

She was silent for a few moments before she jumped up, pushed her chair back, and slammed her open fists down on the desk blotter. I held my breath as she arched her back and swung around. "Beats me." She stomped down the hall toward the kitchen.

Stealing was an issue that had come up in my therapy practice, but I'd never had to deal with it at home. I put my head in my hands and pulled on my hair. What would this woman think of our family? What if Melissa's stealing this wallet was the tip of the iceberg—a sign of some deeper pathology? What if we couldn't trust her when we took her to our friends' homes? I felt betrayed and really scared. I was embarrassed that I hadn't supervised her properly. All of my clinical expertise abandoned me at that moment. I stood up and yelled, "What the hell is going on? Get back here and talk to me!" I saw her disappear around the corner and heard the refrigerator door bang open against the wall. Clutching the wallet, I headed down the hall. She was sitting at the kitchen table, shoveling rocky road ice cream into her mouth from an overflowing bowl. "I just can't believe this. On top of taking this," I waved the wallet in front of her, "you lied to me."

"So, what's the big deal? I don't think it's any of your business. Anyway, everybody lies, that's just what they do."

I nearly had to grab the edge of the countertop. "You bet it's my business, and I'm going to take care of it right now. Just watch me." I scraped one of the stools away from the counter and sat down. I dialed the number on the business card I'd found in the wallet. The woman on the other end of the line confirmed that her name was the same as the one on the driver's license. I blurted out that I had her wallet, and before I could get any of the story out, she let out a yelp.

"Thank you so much!" She barraged me with gratitude for finding it and repeatedly told me how relieved she was. I couldn't get a word in. She asked if she could come get it right away and asked where we lived. I remember feeling guilty about my sense of relief; I just didn't want to tell the real story, and I didn't have to right then. My mouth was parched, so I got up and poured myself a glass of water. I stared out of the kitchen window at the sun coming through the redwoods and wished that I could be anywhere else but where I was. When the station wagon pulled into the driveway, I turned to Melissa. "Look, you're going out there with me to give this back to that poor woman and tell her what happened. You get me?"

"If you say so." She clanked her spoon on the table. Then she jumped up and grabbed the wallet from the counter. I followed her out the front door as the woman leapt from her car, dashed over, and threw her arms around Melissa. She immediately launched into a monologue about how distracted she'd been and how thankful she was that this darling little girl had found her wallet. She said things like, "You have no idea how much effort this saves me," and, "I didn't even know I'd lost it until I got to the checkout." Melissa and I stood like statues as she proceeded to open the wallet and take out a ten-dollar bill. My stomach lurched. "This is for you, sweetie," she said. "For saving my butt. I can't thank you enough."

Before I could decide what to do, she pressed the bill into Melissa's hand and told us breathlessly that she "had to run." I reached out, pried open Melissa's hand and grabbed the bill. "No, no, no!" I yelled. "You don't have to do that. Please no, no! Take it back."

She started to go another round of offering, but I interrupted her. I shoved the bill into her hand, took her elbow, and nudged her across the driveway toward her car. I looked back and saw Melissa sitting down on the front step with her arms crossed.

36
Melissa

Patrice got a migraine one evening after dinner. She was in her room, so I climbed the stairs and asked Bob what was wrong with her.

"She's not feeling well right now, but I'm taking care of her," he replied in a soft voice. I could see that she had vomited into a pot next to the bed. "Go wait downstairs, please." The shades on the windows were pulled, and Bob stroked her head slowly in the dimmed room. Anything could have caused the migraine, but I was sure that Patrice's headache was my fault, even though they'd said nothing to indicate that.

The honeymoon stage was over, and I was starting to harbor more and more resentments. Most of them developed over little things, but they added up to my feeling misunderstood. As much as I loved Bob and Patrice and wanted to stay with them, I was angry because they just didn't "get" me. I didn't have the skills to communicate that. "Things are getting bad," I thought, "and when things get bad like this, I get sent away." Although the Keets' home was the only one I had ever been in where I was treated the same as the biological children around me, I was still afraid of being sent away. After all, my aunt had said she loved me like I was her own daughter, and she'd put me on a plane and shipped me back to California. My kid reasoning said, "If they are going to send me away anyway, I might as well run away now. Then at least I'll have control over it." I was taking hold of the one thing I could.

Being understood was a big part of *The Brady Bunch* daydream. "If only I were with my real family, I would be understood," that internal voice said. Sure, most kids—especially pre-teen ones—feel misunderstood. But most kids, as children living with their biological parents, don't have the option of idealizing the homes they left behind. The ones they have are the only ones they know. I could feed my fantasy of the perfect family, and my mother and grandmother confirmed it every time I saw them. "No one can ever give you the home that we could give you. Melissa, come back. We're your real family, and you belong with us."

I really didn't stand a chance of finding a good home—not with all of these outside factors.

37
Patrice

We'd made it through the wallet fiasco. I'd taken an hour to cool off and then sat her down to talk about what happened. "I just don't get why this is such a big deal. Everybody I've ever known steals things," Melissa said. I tried to explain that there was no need for her to steal because we'd give her just about anything she asked for that she needed. Just as I did that, I realized that addressing her behavior with logic didn't make sense. She didn't steal the wallet because she needed money. There was something much deeper going on, something I could only address through continuing to provide the stability we were offering. So, I let the whole thing go.

A few days later, I got a call from Melissa's fifth-grade teacher. Apparently, she hadn't been handing in her homework and she'd been having "skirmishes" with classmates on the playground. I was surprised because, while homework was often a battleground for us, I knew she was doing it.

When Melissa walked home from school, I'd watch her from the kitchen window as she tossed her Hello Kitty backpack between her hands. I knew she was relieved that the school day was over, although she loved socializing in the classroom. Trouble would start when I asked her to take her books out and get her homework done before dinner. That day, after her snack, I told her about the call from her teacher.

"Yeah, so what's the big deal?" Melissa turned her head to face me and screwed up her mouth. "Those kids are stuck up.

And I know all the stuff they're teaching me already."

"Bob and I know you're smart. But one of the ways to show your teacher that is by handing in your homework."

"God, isn't it enough that I do it with you breathing down my neck?" She slammed her palms on the table so that her chocolate milk nearly toppled over. "You and the teacher aren't the boss of me! My mom would never make me do this crap."

I took a deep breath and reminded myself that this was new terrain for her, and that I had to keep being patient, no matter how many times this came up. Then, I thought of a new way to frame it. "Homework is your *job*. Just like Bob and I have jobs, you have one too. We expect you to do as well as you can at your job." I reminded her of the guidelines we'd set up for performance of that job—doing homework, paying attention, studying for tests.

"A job? I didn't sign up for a job. Are you crazy?" The pitch of her voice increased with its volume. "I'm going to talk to Bob about this." She stood up, shook her hands in front of her face, and stared down at me. Then, she turned and stormed off toward her room, muttering that I was crazy and mean.

That night, after everyone had gone to bed, I asked Bob to join me in the TV room. I told him that I was exasperated, exhausted, and stuck. I couldn't handle all of Melissa's lies. "Like, the other day, I asked her where her new sweater was, and guess what she told me: 'Oh, somebody at school stole it.' Am I supposed to believe that? That all her missing clothes have been stolen? You know how careless she can be with things." I stretched out on the couch and rubbed my eyes. "And the chore thing...is it too much to ask that she make her bed, hang up her wet towels, and put her dirty clothes in the basket? I'm going to make her start doing her own laundry."

"Oh, c'mon now," Bob chided. "That seems unreasonable. She's still learning what's expected of her. I think you need to slow down and lower your expectations." I should have known that Bob, the most patient man on Earth, would come back with this. "Remember, we have lots of years to help her change."

I huffed. "You're kidding, right? After nearly a year, I should lower my expectations? We're training her to be irresponsible." I was frustrated with her constant messes—in her room, in the kitchen, in the bathroom. But really, it was her attitude that had driven me to this point. She was rude to me a lot of the time, saying things under her breath, storming off in the middle of my talking with her. I described to Bob a few examples from the previous couple of days. "She's seething with anger, and it comes out at me." I knew he didn't see her this way often; she was typically on her best behavior when he was around. "I feel like I'm getting beaten up, Bob. It wasn't like this with Ellie and Colin." Bob stayed silent. "If we're going to proceed with the adoption idea, things are going to have to get a whole lot better."

"Honey, I think it will all be alright." Bob picked up his book from the coffee table and spread it on his lap. "I just think we need to give it more time. These things aren't that big a deal. And besides, she's kind of approaching the teenage years, right? Maybe this is all part of that. She's trying as hard as she can."

"Well, I am, too, and it's not working." I didn't say it then, but I'd resolved to get some outside help.

A few days later, I reached out to my friend Terry, who had recently adopted her foster daughter. We decided to meet over pastries and hot chocolate at Gayle's Bakery, our favorite local café. It was a foggy Monday morning, and the weather seemed to reflect my confusion and pessimism. Before venting to her, I asked how her things were going at her house.

"Actually, they've started to turn around." She described a

recent crisis in which her newly adopted daughter had threatened Terry's son with scissors. I was silently thankful that there was nothing like that happening in our house. "You know, I wasn't sure what to do until I found this amazing therapist over the hill in San Jose. We've gone to see her together a couple of times. I guess I'm hopeful she can make a difference for us." She went on to say that the therapist was helping her daughter get in touch with the feelings underneath her acting out, and that family life was gradually becoming more harmonious. Maybe this was what I was looking for.

Bob was skeptical about adding another therapist to Melissa's schedule, since she was already seeing one. "Well, that's all fine and good, but obviously that therapist is not helping Melissa behave better or get along with me." I had to hold back tears. "You and I have been together a really long time, honey, and we've never had any arguments about our kids before this." The ease of our dynamic while raising Ellie and Colin had added to my hubris around parenting. "We brought Melissa into our home to help her and to add meaning and joy to our lives, not to cause marital tension." I told him that I needed help and wanted to at least have a phone conversation with the therapist Terry had recommended.

He shook his head, took a deep breath, and said, "I guess that's what you need to do, then."

38
Melissa

I have one very bad memory of my time with the Keets, and it involves Olga, a child psychologist in San Jose.

I didn't understand why I had to go see another psychologist. I was still seeing my state-mandated counselor whom I'd met with weekly for years. We had a great relationship; I was attached to her and comfortable trusting her with the information I shared. I didn't ask Patrice why we were going to see someone else, however. I didn't know how to ask, or even how to put words to the uncomfortable feelings I was having.

I didn't like Olga from the moment I met her. She had a thick Russian accent which I had to strain to understand, and I remember thinking that there was something about her that made me uneasy. Unlike Patrice's eyes, which were always warm and smiling, Olga's were cold—empty, even. Her office felt the same way. The windows had thick shades over them, dimming the light and blocking the view of the busy street outside. Despite my distrust of her, I figured I had the meeting under control. Since I was used to being assessed by psychologists, psychiatrists, social workers, counselors, and teachers, I'd become kind of cocky about appointments with adults. "I do this all the time," I thought to myself, "I'm smarter than you think I am. Bring it on." The first meeting was fairly standard: paperwork and conversation. Patrice was there with me.

We started out the second session with me sitting on this little leather couch. Patrice was in a stiff-backed chair across from me, and Olga sat in another chair next to her. She started asking me questions. "So, Melissa, what made you decide to steal that woman's wallet?"

I shrugged and looked right at her. "I wanted to see if I could get away with it."

"And what were you feeling when you did that?" she asked with pursed lips.

"Nothing."

"Do you think you were trying to make Patrice angry with you?" I shrugged again. "Were you angry with Patrice?"

"No." I don't know if I was angry with Patrice or not, but I knew these questions were making me angry. I knew what Olga was doing. The feelings I didn't express were anger and resentment. She was deliberately trying to piss me off, and it was working. As I got more and more emotional, she came over to the couch and sat right next to me. I instantly shuddered. Her smell was what I remember best. It struck me as chemical and fake, like one of those perfumes that doesn't smell like anything real. She picked up my feet and drew them across her lap. Then, she wrapped her arms around mine, pinning them to the side of my body. My stepfather had held me down in just the same way, and I immediately flashed back to a time when he fastened a belt around my arms. There I was again, enveloped, unable to move, being held down onto a couch where I was being touched by a stranger. Suddenly, I was right back in the trailer, surrounded by my Raggedy Ann and Andy dolls, staring at the popcorn ceiling above my bunk bed. Olga's chemical odor morphed into Victor's sour and sweaty scent, and a wave of nausea ran through me. I had learned that when someone holds you down and touches you in a way that you don't like, you have a right to fight, and I did. I started screaming. "You fucking bitch!" I yelled.

My anger was so intense that I was able to wriggle out of her arms. Then, I bolted out the office door.

39
Patrice

I needed a life raft. I needed a boundary-keeper because I was exhausted from constantly setting and enforcing rules. I needed back-up—someone that didn't make me feel like the bad guy for wanting more peace in the house.

I called Terry's therapist. In our phone interview, she sounded sharp, experienced, and understanding. Most of all, she had strength in her conviction that she could help us. I made an appointment for the following Tuesday.

"I don't want to go to another therapist!" Melissa exclaimed when I told her the plan. "None of my other foster families made me go to two counselors." The strength of Melissa's reaction caught me off guard. I took a step away from her and sat down on one of the kitchen stools. I couldn't have known at the time that she'd accumulated piles of negative associations around going to counselors and being evaluated.

I want to say that we went to two sessions. My hazy remembrance of the first was of the therapist asking questions to get to know us and making some suggestions on how to improve our dynamic. I don't remember what those suggestions were, but I do know things did not improve the following week. I went into the second session thinking that Olga understood us a little better and that I had found an ally. We started that session talking about the events of the week that had passed, although I have no recollection of the details we discussed. At some point, Olga moved across the room to the couch where Melissa sat. The next thing I remember was seeing her with her arms around Melissa.

Immediately, Melissa started making a screechy, animal-like scream. The sound made me sick to my stomach. In a flash, Melissa broke free from Olga's hold and bolted toward the door, yelling, "I hate you!" on her way out. I sprang out of my seat, grabbed my purse and Melissa's jacket, and ran out the open door to find her. I could see her ahead of me as she disappeared around the corner at the bottom of the steps.

"Melissa! Melissa!" I yelled. But she didn't stop. I dashed down the stairs. When I got to the bottom, she was well ahead of me, weaving between live oak trees and flowering bushes, heading towards a grassy knoll at the edge of a manicured lawn. It faced El Camino, a busy three-lane thoroughfare with a constant stream of cars. She hesitated as she got to the curb. All I could see was the blur of traffic and Melissa's head swiveling to the right and left. She lifted up one foot as if to step out into the traffic. "Please, honey! Please, please, Melissa, come back! We won't ever go there again. I promise. I'm so sorry."

She jerked back, then she put her foot down and turned around to face me. I lowered my voice, stopped running, and walked slowly towards her saying, "Okay, okay," over and over. She stood like a statue, but her face was slick with tears. As I got closer, I could see that her chest was heaving. My whole body was shaking, and my legs felt weak. I was petrified that, at any moment, she was going to turn around and dash out in front of the passing cars. I didn't know if I should rush forward and try to grab her or whether that would frighten her more, since someone grabbing her was what started this whole series of events. In a split second, she stepped to the right of me and ran back to a tree. She collapsed with her back against the trunk and sank to the ground. I closed my eyes, dropped my head, and bent over, thinking I was going to vomit. I knew I needed to ensure that she wouldn't bolt again, so I slowly approached her and lowered myself onto a patch of grass about four feet away. We sat looking at each other, both breathing heavily. I kept telling her I was sorry and thanked her for stopping when I called out to her. Her arms were wrapped around her knees, and she rested her head on them. All I wanted was to erase the last hour and get her safely into the car with me.

She finally spoke. "Can we get out of here now?" I ran my hands over the grass and told her that I thought that was a super great idea. As much as I wanted to hold her and comfort her, I knew enough not to. I felt lightheaded as I stood up. It took me a minute of looking around to figure out where I'd parked. She stared at the ground as I unlocked the car and opened her door.

I grabbed the steering wheel, dropped my shoulders, and bit the inside of my cheek. I had no idea what to say to her. When I was sure I was composed enough to speak, I asked if she wanted any of the snacks we'd brought with us. She sat staring ahead and shook her head no. I wanted to find a safe place for us, so I just started driving home. The car echoed with our breathing, and the silence was only broken when I tuned into a music station.

Melissa didn't want to talk when we got home, and she went right to her room. I asked her twice through the door if I could do anything for her. Each time she quietly said no. About an hour later, she came out and sat on the trampoline until dinnertime.

As I was putting her to bed that night, I took a deep breath and again said I was sorry about what happened at Olga's. Again, I promised her we would never go back there. She hugged her stuffed orca and told me she didn't want to be read to.

40
Melissa

When I was a kid, I couldn't differentiate between the various adults in my life. Foster parents, counselors, social workers, and state employees were all "Child Protective Services" (CPS), as far as I was concerned. Adults were a unified force that kept me away from my family.

Somewhere along the line, one of these adults planted the idea that staying with the Keets meant never seeing Daniel again. I had thought that by living with the Keets, I was living in a foster home, as I had been for years, and I knew that foster children got to visit their birth families. Then, I found out that Bob and Patrice wanted to adopt me, and I was told that adopted children gave up these visitation rights. I could have accepted never seeing my mother again, but the idea of being cut off from all of my siblings—especially Daniel, who had always been my best friend and ally—broke my heart. I vividly remember Joe asking, "If we could place you somewhere with your brother, but it meant not living with Bob and Patrice, which would you choose?"

"I really like living with the Keets," I replied, "but I love my brother. I would always choose to be with him. I want to stay at the Keets, but I don't want to be adopted." I was upset that I was being asked to make this decision, and I was confused about why it had been brought up. Was this a real choice or a hypothetical one? How can you ask a child to choose never to see her family members again? It made me angry that no one had ever explained the details of adoption to me or even told me that I was being considered for adoption and not just for long-term foster care. "You can't just auction me off," I thought.

All of this came just after that horrible incident with Olga, which I blamed Patrice for. "How could she have done this to me?" I thought. "How could she not have known this would hurt me so badly?" *She* brought me there. *She's* the one who made me go.

My pile of resentments had gotten too big to manage. I wonder, too, if part of me wanted to hurt Bob and Patrice, to make them feel the way I felt. I started to plan an escape strategy. I knew running away was scary, and I hated doing it, but I had to get out.

41
Patrice

"Do you think you can come with me to that medical convention in Hawaii at the beginning of February?" Bob asked. We were sitting in the living room looking out at the rain, which had been constant for days. "We could use some time away." He laid out the logistics for me, and they tipped the scales of my indecision. Colin, who was almost fifteen by that point, would still be in South Africa with the private middle school he was attending. He and his fellow classmates were living with local families and going to school in their township for a month, so there was one less responsibility around the house. My dad could handle the daily routine with Melissa. Ellie, who was just a few miles away up on campus, would be his backup.

Hawaii. Time to ourselves. A break in the routine. What was not to like about that idea? The previous few months with Melissa had been rough, making me want to get away even more. During the holidays, she'd had extra visitation time with her mother, Paula. Two of those visits had included her three younger sisters and her grandmother. I wondered if these interactions were contributing to why she was so angry in her responses to me and why she had such a short fuse when approached about any issue that came up. On top of that, after meeting with her teacher, I was worried about her occasional aggressive behavior at school and her unwillingness to complete schoolwork. I thought that maybe having a break from each other for a week might do us both some good.

I made sure to give her extra attention before we left. We had a family dinner out, and I promised to bring her back something special from Hawaii. She assured me she'd be fine in a voice that sounded a little too chipper. She put on one of her fake smiles when she said, "Relax, Richard and I will have fun hanging out together." I saw my dad grinning and nodding his head in the way that he did to reassure me when I expressed worry. As an extra measure of caution, I called Ellie to reconfirm the dates we'd be gone.

The morning we left, I gave Melissa a big bear hug and told her how much I'd miss her. "Be a good girl, and don't get in any trouble, okay?" My smile widened when I added, "And please take good care of Richard for me."

When Bob and I got on the plane, I closed my eyes and felt a sense of freedom wash over me. Between swims and exotic meals under coconut palms, we called home daily and got nothing but positive reports. The last night of our trip, we took a moonlit walk along the beach. I said to Bob, "Honey, this has been great. And it looks like we'll be able to get away a little more now that we know everybody can manage without us for a few days."

We were folding up our bathing suits and stuffing flip-flops into our carry-ons for an early morning flight when Bob's phone rang. As I walked into the bathroom to pack up toiletries, I heard him shout. "Oh my God, are you serious?" I rushed back into the bedroom and saw his face go white. He held the phone away from his ear so that I could hear Ellie on the other end. I remember her saying a couple of times how much she hated to spoil our time away, but that she thought we should know what had happened before we got home. Bob and I sank onto the bed as Ellie filled in the details.

That morning, Melissa had insisted on riding her bike to school, and my father had let her do it. He didn't notice that she'd taken a small stuffed backpack in addition to her book bag. A few hours later, he got a phone call from the Scotts Valley Police Department—the one that had jurisdiction over the neighborhood where we lived. They told him that they had Melissa at the station and that she was okay, but that he needed to come and get her. "We'll tell you all about it when you get here," the police had said to Richard.

The story unfolded that a woman had seen Melissa riding her bike along the side of the highway a few blocks from her school and pulled over to find out why she was riding in such a dangerous place. When Melissa started crying, the woman called the police, who came right away. They questioned her about why she was alone on a bike on a major highway. She answered that a guy in a blue truck had tried to kidnap her, but she'd gotten away from him. "Of course, with that response," Ellie said, "they took her to the station and had to do a police report." When they questioned Melissa further, she broke down and told them that there hadn't really been an attempted kidnapping and that she'd been trying to get to her mother's house in Watsonville. Ellie explained that she had hurried home from campus when Richard called her. I took a huge breath and held Bob's hand as she went on to say, "I made some dinner for the three of us, and I'm spending the night. I'll handle things until you get home tomorrow."

Bob and I slept fitfully. Like zombies, we got on the plane the next day, each wondering what awaited us back home.

42
Melissa

I planned to run away during a week when Bob and Patrice were out of town. Richard was watching me while they were gone.

"So, do you want a ride to school today?" Richard had asked that morning.

"Nah, I feel like riding my bike today." I shouted from my room, as I emptied all the school stuff out of my backpack and shoved as much clothing into it as I could.

"Okay then, ride safe and have a good day at school," he said cheerfully. I remember feeling nervous, but I had a plan. I was going to ride my bike to my grandmother's house in Watsonville, about twenty-five miles away. I had driven there from the Keets' before, so I knew the way—on the freeway, at least. I took off on my bike towards school, making sure that I got past all the neighbors who knew me. Then, I turned and headed down the long rural road toward the highway.

I was doing pretty well for a while, feeling confident that I could pull this off—until I got to the freeway on-ramp. Cars were moving quickly, and the morning rush hour traffic was thick. But I was eleven years old and felt like I was wearing a superhero cape, so I took a deep breath and said to myself, "I got this!" I swerved into the shoulder and pedaled up the ramp, right next to the concrete barriers. I have no idea how I even got that far on a purple bike with a banana seat and streamers.

I knew I was in trouble when I saw a woman slow down and pull over. She was staring at me and rolling down her window. I felt myself starting to panic. "I am going to get into so much trouble," I thought. "What on Earth am I going to say?" But I tried to talk myself down, saying, "You can handle this, come on, think fast."

"Oh my God, are you okay?" she screamed. "What's going on?" At that, I instantly burst into tears; I didn't even answer her. Obviously, she called the police, since, in a few minutes, they were there too. I started freaking out because I was scared and worried about getting into trouble. So, instead of telling the police the truth, I told them I had been kidnapped. Of course, that made no sense whatsoever because, for starters, I was on my bike. I also happened to have a bag full of clothes with me. "Really?" one of the officers said. "How'd you get away?"

"He let me go!" Right, he let me and my bike go. They didn't buy it.

43
Patrice

"Oh my God, Bob. What are we going to do when we get home?" We sat poking at our in-flight chicken teriyaki. "How desperate was she that she'd go as far as running away and then lying to the police? I mean, she keeps saying that she wants to go back to her mother, but...risking her life by trying to get on the freeway?" I shook my head.

Bob pushed his tray away and stared out the window. I reminded him that things hadn't been easy for any of us during the previous few months. As I did so, I thought about our appointment with Olga and felt a wave of nausea. I didn't want to revisit that again, and yet, it kept popping into my mind. Bob took me by surprise when he turned to me and asked, "Is there any chance we're swimming upstream trying to adopt her at this point?" I grabbed his arm tightly and told him that I didn't even want to consider the possibility that adoption might not work. We knew how to be good parents. We had everything in the world to offer her. Failure had never been an option. I buried my head in my hands. "Maybe we're just not doing the right things with her," he added. "Although, for God's sake, I feel like I'm giving it my all." Bob, of course, was the one with the incredible patience, not me. How much more could he do? And, if he had nothing left, what did that say about me? "You know, she might just keep running away—in her heart, at least." He pressed his palms to his closed eyes. I had to lean in to hear him mumble, "How much of that could we take?"

On the way home from the airport, I reminded Bob that we had a complicated weekend ahead of us. We were going to pick Colin up at the airport the next day. On top of that, I was supposed to facilitate a day-long debriefing and family therapy session with the students who had gone to South Africa and their families. The meeting was scheduled for the day after the group's return. Bob looked at me with wide eyes and open mouth. "Are you still going to do that? Come on, we have our own crisis to manage." I told him that I couldn't see any way out of the commitment I'd made months ago and needed to follow through. Inside, though, I couldn't imagine how I was going to deal with this event and Melissa at the same time.

Then, I remembered that I'd also have to call Kristin to tell her about Melissa's running away. Bob suggested that we wait to do so until after we had talked with Melissa. He rubbed his brow as though trying to smooth out the situation in his own head. "Let's take our cues from Melissa. You know, see how big we want to make this incident based on how she treats it." He glanced over at me, then went on. "Let me pick her up from school today. We can take baby steps from there." I nodded and smiled at him, thankful that he had a plan, as always.

Later that afternoon, at home, Melissa came in the door just ahead of Bob. She was wearing her favorite t-shirt, the one with the cartoon kitten on it. I threw my arms around her, telling her how much I'd missed her and how glad I was that she was safe. She shrugged me off and didn't even stop to put her backpack down. "Thanks. Yeah, I'm fine." She turned around at the door to her room. "I just need to take a nap, okay?"

"Sure, whatever you need, we'll be here." I tried to put a little lightness in my voice, but I was unbearably sad. It looked like she wasn't happy to see us at all.

An hour later, when the doorbell rang, Melissa came out

of her room rubbing her eyes from sleep. "Goody, pizza!" She stumbled to a seat at the dining room table. My father was quiet at first, but then he got us talking about our trip. As soon as Melissa had eaten the last sausage and pepperoni slice, she stood up and asked if she could take her carrot cake to her room so she could finish the book she was reading. She seemed determined to be by herself. A part of me felt an internal sigh of relief that the conversation would be put off until the next day, even though I knew it ought to happen as soon as possible. Balancing her plate and a glass of milk, she walked away from the table. Then she turned back to us and said, "Oh yeah, Kristin's taking me to the movies and lunch tomorrow, okay?"

That timing seemed odd to me. "Uh, I guess so, but Colin's coming home tomorrow. I thought you'd come to the airport with us to meet him." He'd been gone for a month. While they didn't spend tons of time together, they had occasionally played board games or worked together on her math problems. I thought she'd miss him at least a little.

"No thanks, I feel like being with Kristin." She turned away and headed towards her room. "See you tomorrow, I'm going to bed."

I remember checking on her an hour later. I found her asleep with an open book and cake crumbs all over her comforter. As I turned out her light, I stood staring down at the girl I'd fallen in love with at Capitola Elementary. I looked around at the room—the room of her own that she'd dreamed of. Why would she run away from all of this?

The next morning, Kristin arrived to pick Melissa up. I had no idea what, if anything, Melissa had told her about what had happened. "Hey, gal, let's hit the road to get to that movie," Kristin shouted from the front doorstep. "What time shall I get her back to you?" She looked at her watch. I fumbled with my words as I told her and watched the two of them bustle off.

Early the following day, I stood in front of the families of the twenty-five students who had gone to Africa. Several months before, when I'd agreed to facilitate this debriefing, I knew it would take thought and energy. But, given what had happened, it now looked like it would take all the skill I had. While Colin had had a wonderful time, big issues had arisen with some of the other students. Three of them had been sent back home by the head teacher for breaking rules, and their parents—as well as other students—were furious about how the situation had been handled. Melissa hadn't wanted to come with us, but I explained to her that it was a requirement that all family members be there. I added a special emphasis on *family* as I put my arm around her. And there she was, part of our family, sitting alongside Bob and Colin in the front row. She was slumped in her chair and scowling. The headphones she'd insisted on bringing were clamped over her ears. I had to put her out of my mind for the next few hours in order to focus on the group of people in my care.

By the time we took a break for lunch, I was feeling a heady sense of accomplishment as I watched students and parents hug each other. My process had facilitated some difficult conversations. I felt emboldened to try to fix my own looming family problem before another minute got away from me. "Now's as good a time as any!" I thought, as Colin ran off to visit with his friends. Melissa, Bob, and I sat together at our own small table in the corner with our boxed lunches.

Before I had even gotten my bag of chips open, I said, "So Melissa, honey, can you tell us why you ran away?" Bob nearly choked on his turkey sandwich. Melissa looked down and sat with her hands clutched in front of her. She swallowed hard but didn't say a word. For what felt like a half-hour but was probably only a couple of minutes, the three of us sat there. I picked at my salad, and Bob stared across the table at me. "Um, because that's not how we act in our family," I added.

"We can't have you running away when there's a problem. We love you and want you to be in our family." Bob slammed his can of soda down on the table with a thump and intensified his glare. But I pressed on. "*Do* you want to be in our family?"

Melissa finally raised her head and leveled her eyes at me, "Actually, no, I don't." Her tone was steady. "What I want is to call Kristin and have her take me away from this stupid meeting." She turned to Bob. "Will you take me home?"

Just then, the head of the school rushed toward our table, leaned over, and whispered that he needed me because a family had started shouting at each other outside. I looked at Bob and Melissa, who now had her hands planted on her hips. "Melissa, Bob, I'm so sorry, but I've got to go. Melissa, honey, we'll talk about this later." Before I could gather my things from under the table, they were up and heading toward the door.

About five hours later, Colin and I dragged ourselves into the house. I was completely spent and flopped down on the couch in front of the fireplace. Bob walked in from the family room shaking his head. "Hi honey," I said, as I grabbed his hand without getting up from the couch. "Where's Melissa?"

"She was determined to call Kristin and go over there. I only heard the last of her conversation, but she got Kristin to come and get her." He said she'd offhandedly told him she might stay to watch a movie, so she took a sleeping bag and her backpack.

A few hours later, Kristin called and told Bob that she thought it was best for Melissa to have a little time away from us that night and maybe a few additional nights as well. Bob was so shocked that he didn't know what to say, and I sat in stunned silence when he relayed their conversation to me. As sad and confused as I was about Melissa's running away, a small wave of relief swept over me. I didn't have to tackle one more family problem that day.

44
Melissa

Immediately after running away, I knew I'd made a mistake. Still, I assumed that I would be sent back. I'd been returned to every other home I had run away from—including ones where I was living under the stairs and girls were being abused. I didn't get sent back to the Keets' though, so I figured that they didn't want me back, that I had messed up too badly for them. "I fucked that one up; time to move onto the next one," I reasoned. Not being returned to their home confirmed my suspicions that Bob and Patrice had been getting ready to send me away after all. In my mind, they'd done their community service. I was a nuisance that had been offloaded, and I was far too proud to ask to go back.

45
Patrice

What I thought would be a couple of days' break turned out to be four days of separation from Melissa. I had framed this time in my mind as a "cooling off" period, so I was shocked when Joe called to set up a time for Melissa to "come over and get her things." I was still in a fog and thought he meant that Melissa needed a few more essentials while she was at her temporary placement. We agreed he'd bring her over after school the next day.

I called Melissa every evening during those four days. She kept our conversations short and gave me brief answers like a polite stranger would. Before every call, I hoped that she would open up and tell me her feelings, but maybe that was too much to ask of an eleven-year-old. Bob talked with her on the phone a couple of times too, and he had tears in his eyes every time he hung up. We reviewed every incident we could think of from the previous few months—the increased visitations with her mother over the holidays, our talk about adopting her, my hard line on her schoolwork, my decision to take her to therapy—trying to figure out what we should have done differently. I kept beating myself up for my criticisms of her and made a promise to myself that I'd ease up when she came back.

As I waited for Joe and Melissa, I sat in my favorite armchair staring at the plate of oatmeal cookies I'd made to keep busy. Finally, there was a knock on the door. When I whipped it open, Melissa brushed past me and marched straight down the hall to her bedroom. Joe and I were already following her when I heard the door slam. We stopped in our tracks and faced each other. I shrugged and made a "what's a mother to do" face. Then, I said I wanted to go talk with her.

"No, I'll be joining you when you talk to her," Joe said quickly. Before he could say any more, I jumped in and explained that it would be good for Melissa and me to talk alone. I told him that I was sure things would get smoothed out once she and I were face-to-face.

He looked at me with a blank expression. "I'm taking her to a group home. You know that, right?"

"Sorry? I don't think I heard that right."

"She's going to a group home on the other side of town." He spoke slowly, enunciating every word.

"Really? A *group* home?" My voice was getting louder. "You'd rather put her in a house full of strangers for a while than keep her here and let us work things out?"

He shuffled nervously and nodded yes. I had so many questions for him, but first, I wanted to choke him right there in the hallway. Instead, I balled my hands into fists. Joe took a step back. "So, how long will she be in the group home before she comes back here?"

His eyes were cast down as he told me that the group home would be her official placement going forward.

"What? No!" I shrank back against the wall. Who was this guy who was about to take my daughter away from me without even letting me talk to her? I waved him away.

"I know this is hard."

"Hard? Yeah, it's hard, especially because I don't know where this is coming from. I thought you said, 'You're a great family, and she's lucky to have found you.'"

He glanced up at the ceiling.

"So, Joe," I spit out, "how exactly did this decision come

about?"

He cleared his throat. "Kristin and I both asked Melissa several times where she wanted to live, and, um...she was very clear when she told us she didn't want to be here. And, you know, our job is to listen to kids."

"Joe, please. You can see why I need to talk with her. She couldn't really mean that. You know all we've done for her and how much we care about her." I leaned in close to him. "Joe, you'll see that this isn't the right decision for her—or for you—to make."

I threw my hands up in the air and led him down the hall. Through Melissa's closed door, I asked if I could come in. "Sure," she replied in a breezy tone. She glanced up at my tear-stained face and quickened her pace as she shoved clothes, stuffed animals, books, and framed pictures into the suitcase and backpack we'd bought her. I flashed back to her unbridled excitement the day she had moved in with us nearly a year and a half earlier, carrying a different tiny suitcase, a threadbare backpack, and the rest of her few possessions in an overflowing garbage bag.

"Melissa, can we please sit down and talk?" She nodded, and we both flopped down on her queen-sized bed, as we'd done countless times before. I ran my hand over the African-print comforter and matching oversized pillows, thinking about the day she'd picked them out. She crossed her arms over her chest and sat stone still. "Melissa, honey, I don't want you to go." I couldn't hold back sobs, even though I was biting the inside of my cheek. I sputtered as I told her that I thought we could work things out. "You *know* that Bob and I really love you." I clutched one of the pillows, but my instinct was to grab Melissa and keep her from leaving me. She kept inching away, as if she could intuit my desire. Between gasps of air, I finally asked the big question. "Why are you doing this?"

Her words were steady and clear. "Because you want me

to be Ellie and Colin, and I can't."

I dropped the pillow, shook my head vigorously and waved my hands. "No, no, Melissa, that's not true!" I was nearly yelling as I reached out for her. She stared back at me as if I'd spoken a foreign language. Before I could get another word out, she scooted to the edge of the bed and hopped off. In swift movements, she slung the backpack over her shoulder and handed the shiny purple suitcase to Joe. After sweeping the room with her eyes, she dashed over to the desk and picked up a cardboard box labeled "dollhouse." Then she spun around, caught Joe's eye, and, with a flick of her head, motioned toward the door.

She didn't even say goodbye as she disappeared down the hallway. I ran to the open window and screamed out into the driveway, "Melissa, come back!"

PART II

46
Melissa

After I ran away from the Keets' in February of 1995, I was placed with the Larsons.

Jill Larson was a heavyset woman in her sixties, although the way she kept her hair in a close-cut perm made her look even older than she was. Her home had a good reputation, as far as foster homes went. There were a lot of girls in the house, though—ten when I moved in. Six slept in the master suite, in three sets of bunk beds, and another four girls slept in a downstairs bedroom. Like all foster children, I had lived in fear of being placed in a group home—an institution designed for kids just out of juvie. I'd heard horror stories of rotating attendants, dorm beds, and prison-style rules. Anytime I ran away, some adult threatened to put me in one. While the Larsons' wasn't technically a group home, it operated a lot like one. In retrospect, it's ironic that I ended up staying there for four and a half years—from just after I turned eleven to almost sixteen.

To make it in their house, you needed to outshine the girl on top. That was Kelly, their biological daughter, who we later learned was actually their granddaughter. Being pretty was also important there—the prettier you were, the better you were treated. We all knew Jill Larson only took in the pretty girls.

I tried to be a good kid there. I had a lot of chores: doing dishes, taking out the trash, watching the younger girls. During the week, I rarely watched TV because there was no time left after doing my chores and my homework. And my weekly cleaning tasks took up a whole weekend day. Most days, I also helped Peter, the foster dad, make dinner after he worked a full day as an electrician. I was like a sous chef, cutting, peeling, and putting things away while he cooked.

After spending time with the Keets, I had grown affectionate with Bob. I felt comfortable hugging him and snuggling with him on the couch. So, one night, after six or eight months at the Larsons', I wrapped my arms around Peter to thank him for cooking spaghetti and meatballs. I just went up and gave him a hug like any child would. The next day, I got reprimanded. "That made Peter very uncomfortable, when you went up and pressed your breasts up against him," Jill said, through her thin lips. My chest had started to develop, but I was still unaware of my changing body. I felt shamed. I was just looking for some connection, but, obviously, that was too much to ask.

There were benefits to being at the Larsons'. Once I climbed up the hierarchy, it wasn't so bad. Jill showed affection by buying people things, so I started to get more stuff. I was able to go shopping, and I got an allowance. I could pick out my own clothes. The food situation wasn't a free-for-all, but there was always something to eat. I connected with some of the other girls, especially towards the end of my time there, when there were only four of us left.

Most of all, the Larsons were dysfunctional in a lot of the same ways my biological family had been. That meant I knew the rules, and I knew how to play the game. The familiarity somehow made the defeat I felt easier to bear.

But I was not happy. I cried a lot when the other girls were out playing. I remember lying in my bottom bunk and staring up at the mobile I had made when I first moved in. I had taped twine to seven or eight of my favorite photos and strung them from parts of wire coat hangers. The whole thing dangled from the metal bed slats I looked up at, making them seem less like prison bars. There were a couple pictures of me and Daniel. He had been placed with a foster family he really liked, and I didn't get to see him nearly as much as I wanted to. There was also one of my half-sisters, and a few of my mom and my dad's family. Two of the photos were pictures of me at the Grand Canyon. In one, I was standing behind a fence, eyes wide. Patrice was on the other side of it, just at the edge of the frame. The other showed me sandwiched between Bob and Patrice, with an arm around each of them. It made me sad to look up at the mobile and think about what I had thrown away, what I had left behind. But the photos comforted me too. They reminded me that I had lived a different way for a while, at least.

"You should take those ratty things down," Jill Larson said, more than once. "That's your past. The past doesn't matter. You live here now." One by one, all of the photos disappeared. I have no idea who took them. When I asked around, no one would tell me. "Forget about it and move on," is the message I heard, again and again.

Despite Jill Larson's advice, I thought about life with the Keets all the time—especially when I had a bad day. "I wonder if I'd be feeling like this if I were at my old school," I'd think. Or "I wouldn't be fighting with this girl in the other bunk bed if I were in my own room at the Keets." But I never thought about calling them.

At first, I was too angry to consider it. "I didn't fit in with their family," I told myself. I could still see in my mind an image of Patrice crying as I left, but I didn't think she was sad. I thought she was crying because she was disappointed in me, because I had failed her. "What would be the point in calling?" I thought. "They don't care."

Then, the anger shifted to remorse, sadness, and shame.

I'd always thought that my problems stemmed from not having enough food or clothes or money for basic needs. I thought that, once I had those taken care of, I'd be a better kid, a loveable kid. But at Patrice and Bob's I didn't want for anything, and I had still messed up. "I must be unlovable," I concluded. "They must be relieved to be rid of me."

I remember lying to social workers and counselors about my time at the Larsons because I just didn't know where I would end up next. I thought about running away all the time, but I knew how the system worked. I wouldn't be allowed to go back to my birth family until I was considered an adult and had aged out of the foster care system. So, I waited. "If I'm going to run away, I need to make sure I'm going to get all the way home," I reasoned.

Nevertheless, I did run away from the Larsons'. Because I was fifteen and a half and they were exhausted from dealing with me, CPS treated me a little differently this time. They were more willing to place me with family members. The only suitable ones were my maternal grandmother and my uncle, who I had seen off and on over the previous handful of years. I hated my uncle's wife, and I knew she didn't want me, so I went with my grandmother, Vera.

The way I see it, Vera was the source of all of the dysfunction in my birth family. She's not a bad person; she's just twisted. That's the word I like to use. She reminds me of one of those matriarchs in a movie on the Lifetime channel—the kind that portrays a very rich family who has to keep all family matters sealed up from the outside world. Those ladies do whatever it takes to keep their families together, even if it means they have to cover up rape or incest. That's my grandmother in a nutshell.

She and her first husband, Buddy, had five children. Within the family, Buddy was always described as a hard worker, someone who brought home the bacon and did what he had to in order to support his kids. He also physically and sexually abused both my mother and my aunt. From what I understand, my mother experienced frighteningly violent abuse. I hate to categorize the severity of abuse, since it's all bad. But what I went through doesn't compare to what she had to endure. It started at a very young age and never really let up. She told me that her father would throw her up against a wall while he was raping her because she wasn't being quiet enough. And he raped her and her sister repeatedly for years.

My grandfather abused his sons as well, and it's quite possible he abused his wife. None of this would be surprising, because it's rare for men like this to have abusive interactions with some family members and normal, healthy ones with others. I know that at some point, legal action was taken against Buddy for having abused my aunt. The charges were dropped, although I don't think it was my aunt's choice to do so. I'm almost certain my grandmother convinced her to "leave it alone."

Even though Buddy had done horrible things to his family, he was never excluded from their lives, even after my grandparents divorced. He's even in some home videos. That seems sick to me, that a man who raped and abused his daughters was welcome to celebrate birthdays with the whole gang.

It's no surprise that the reality of living with my grandmother and her second husband, Bill, was nothing like the fantasy I had dreamed up over the years. The honeymoon period at her house ended after only two weeks, when my uncle came down to visit for a night. He had been accused of molesting several girls, and Vera knew all about that. Still, she put him in my room.

The next morning, I woke up to him fondling my breasts as he masturbated. Instantly, a hundred thoughts ran through my head. What if I scream? What if I don't scream? Should I slap his hand? What should I do? Even though I was sixteen, I felt like a little girl again—like the seven-year-old who had to deal with Victor. Somehow, I reasoned that my uncle thought I was asleep and wanted me to be asleep. So, I decided to pretend I was just waking up. I stretched my arms and made a yawning noise. He froze. But then, after a few seconds, he started again. So I stretched my arms out further, flipped his hand away, and ran to the bathroom. I locked the door behind me and lay down on the floor. Sometime later, the sound of my grandmother banging on the door woke me up. I let her in, but I wouldn't let her touch me.

"You better not tell anybody about this because they just let you come back home, Missy," she said. "It's been nine years, and we just got you back." So much for my fantasy that my grandmother never knew what was going on with Victor, that she had never done anything wrong. She must have known all along.

That was my first time being abused as a teenager. In this one encounter, I felt like all the progress I had made flew right out the door. Maybe it was my fault, I started thinking. Maybe I shouldn't have hugged my uncle when he first showed up; maybe that made him think I wanted his attention. Not only did I slip right back into a victim mentality, but I also lost any hope I had for feeling at home at my grandmother's.

But I didn't have anywhere else to go. I knew that at my age, I wasn't going to be placed in a great home. "Shit happens in the world, but I'm not the only girl it happens to," I told myself. "Suck it up." I stayed with my grandmother for six more months, until I turned sixteen.

47
Patrice

From the start, Kristin and Joe had been brimming with optimism that we were the "right" family for Melissa. They both knew we planned to adopt her. Since I had no idea that Melissa's departure was going to be permanent, it didn't occur to me to say to either of them, "Hey, how about arranging for Melissa, Bob, and me to go to family therapy together?"—nor was it suggested to me. Not only had Bob and I not been consulted about what might be the best thing for Melissa, we weren't even told what was going on with her until she was in our house packing her bags. Maybe to Kristin and Joe—and even Melissa—we hadn't been that special after all. Maybe, in their minds, we'd just been one more home along the string of foster placements that had failed.

The days after Melissa left felt like a foggy June in Santa Cruz—long, gray, and chilly. They all looked alike, and they all ran together. I don't remember going to the social services offices to fill out paperwork, nor do I remember getting any documents in the mail, although there must have been some necessary bureaucratic procedures. I do remember that we got a letter from Melissa a couple of weeks after she left. Its tone was similar to one a child would use when writing an obligatory message to a grandparent from summer camp—breezy and newsy. It contained a request for us to bring her some things she had forgotten. I felt so conflicted and hurt because it was another sign of the permanence of her being gone. I reasoned that if she loved us and missed us or had any wish to come back, she could have asked to come get them herself. Since I didn't think I could experience the intensity of her rejection again, Bob dropped the items off at her new foster home. She wasn't there to receive them.

While he was out delivering her things, I thought about the year Bob and I spent apart when we were seventeen. I came back to the house crying one evening after working at the store. I burst in while my mother was watching TV. "Mom, this is so hard," I said. "How can I do this 'being apart' thing? It hurts so much."

She pursed her lips and said, "Well, Patrice, life isn't all a bowl of cherries." I decided then and there that I would make sure my life *was* a bowl of cherries. Why shouldn't it be? If life didn't give me cherries, I'd pick my own.

I'd succeeded at that, for the most part. Until this, anyway. Maybe my mother was right. Maybe I was too selfish—always wanting people around, always wanting new experiences, always wanting to have my life be as full as possible.

Over the course of the previous year, I had often turned to Kristin for help with Melissa. At that point, however, it felt like we weren't on the same team. As I look back, I can see that my feelings of shock and abandonment may have clouded my thinking. Kristin might have been able to be a confidant for me, but I didn't give her a chance. When I called her hoping she might say that Melissa and Social Services wanted to return her to us, she began telling me that Melissa was adjusting well to her new place. I felt cold all over. Of course, I wanted Melissa to be happy, but the selfish part of me wanted her to be happy in our family. Kristen, who I thought knew Melissa so well after spending time each week with her, spoke so definitively, with a finality that I could feel in my bones. "Kristen," I asked in the most mature voice I could muster. "Has Melissa asked about us or said she wants to come back here?"

"No, she hasn't." Kristen said in a steady voice. I politely thanked her and got off the phone.

I had many of the same feelings about Joe, but my anger with him was more on the surface. With him, I didn't expect that there would or could be any negotiating about bringing Melissa back into our family. So, I decided to cut my losses. After he escorted her out of our house, I never spoke with him again.

48
Melissa

I fell in love with Greg when I was sixteen years old. He was seventeen and a half. Our relationship was a whirlwind, and we dove into it head-first.

He was incredibly handsome. On more than one occasion, we were stopped by strangers in grocery stores who said, "You're Justin Timberlake!" and asked him for his autograph. He had curly blonde hair which he wore in long ringlets when we first met. He always shaved his facial hair into a goatee or a soul patch. Although he had a small frame, he was very muscular and compact, with broad shoulders and a thin waist. More than anything else, it was his big, bright smile that drew me in. It curled up playfully at the edges, like the Joker's. Greg's smile reminded me of my father's, and it warmed my heart in the same way.

I met him when my mother, Paula, was down visiting us from Mt. Shasta, the town in far northern California where she was living with my three stepsisters. Whenever she was in the Watsonville area, she basically toured me around, bringing me to all her friends' and extended family members' houses to show off the fact that we were together again. My mother knew Stephanie, Greg's mother, because Paula had dated guys who were part of Stephanie's extended family. That made Stephanie's house on Ohlone Parkway in Watsonville one of our stops. I stayed in the car doing the anti-social teenager thing while she went in—until I noticed this blonde guy walking around. He was definitely checking me out, and I was checking him out too, though I pretended to be napping. Eventually, I got out of the car and talked to him, and, by the time my mom had emerged from Stephanie's, I had a huge crush on him.

After my mom left town, I was the one that initiated contact between us. Greg was very shy at first, but then, he wooed me. When we started dating, he'd leave presents on the stoop. I'd walk out the door to go to school and find a little gift sitting there on the mat waiting for me. Sure, the presents were from the Dollar Tree, but they were wrapped in newspaper and had little hearts or flowers on top. They made me feel special.

We discovered we had very similar life stories. We'd both grown up in broken homes, and we'd both been in foster care. His father had left the family at a young age, and mine was absent from my life for long periods of time. Because we had so much in common, we shared our deepest secrets. I told him things that I had never told anyone else—things that made me feel broken and scarred. He heard them and accepted them. He loved me despite the darkness I carried. I didn't think anyone would ever do that.

Before long, Greg and I were spending all of our time together. You could not have separated us with the Jaws of Life. My grandmother and mother sure tried to, though, because neither one of them liked him. Since we were a year-and-a-half apart, they said he was too old. They even argued that he was committing statutory rape by being with me. Although they knew Greg's family well—and Paula would later end up marrying into that family—they considered them "bad seed." Vera and Paula thought of themselves as different, like Greg's family's dirty laundry was somehow worse than ours.

I was already fed up with Vera for protecting my creepy uncle after his visit, and we were fighting all the time because she wouldn't let me see Greg. Then, Vera's second husband, Bill, started to show me extra attention. I knew where this was going, and I decided it was time to get out of there. I figured I'd go live with my mom. "There's no way they're gonna let you do that," my grandmother said, since my mother had been deemed unfit to care for me.

"So, how 'bout this. You give me the money for the bus ticket up to Mt. Shasta. Then you tell CPS I stole the money and ran away." She agreed. And I guess social services was okay with it, because no one ever came after me at my mother's house.

Sadly, the fantasy I had created around returning to live with Paula lasted about as long as the one with my grandmother had. My mom was using—methamphetamines, primarily, and lots of them. There was never any food in the house, and she wouldn't even buy me the simple things a sixteen-year-old needed, like toothbrushes and notebooks and new pairs of socks. I hated my school; I couldn't make friends and felt completely alienated. I pleaded with my mother to let me switch, but she refused. So, I stopped going to school altogether. I had been a very successful student back in Watsonville, when I was living with my grandmother. I was set up to graduate six months early there, which was no small feat for someone who grew up with instability. I threw all of that success away. I couldn't help but think about Patrice then. School was so important to the Keets. If she knew I might not graduate from high school, she would be crushed. I had to shake off the shame when an image of her disappointed face popped into my head.

When my mother was faced with truancy charges, she finally said I could transfer to another school. But by then, it was too late. I had gotten too far behind in my credits and had to attend an alternative school where I was bored out of my mind. I'd go through assignments in an hour that took the other kids three, so, for the rest of the day, I'd leave to hang out with friends. When I realized how easy it would be to get the credits I needed to graduate, I decided to get a job. Since there was never any food in the house, and I had started stealing clothes and shampoo, I figured I'd better begin to provide for myself. I went to work at McDonald's.

In the meantime, Greg and I maintained a long-distance relationship for the eight months that I was up there. We talked for hours at a time. I read him my poetry and complained to him about school. He listened so carefully, and he, in turn, told me about all the drama in his family. We always seemed to be on the same page.

The first time he came up to visit, it was a total surprise. He called to tell me he had already bought his bus ticket and was on his way. I had to beg my mother to pick him up at the bus station, and she made us sleep in the living room rather than in my bedroom—not that it made any difference. We'd been having sex since shortly after we met, and we did that night too. He brought me a promise ring. It was a ruby red heart on a gold band. "I want you to know that I am here to stay," he told me. When he had to go back to Watsonville, I was overwhelmed by sadness. I wanted to go with him. I had spent all this time trying to get back to my mother, and then, there I was, completely willing to leave her to go to the ends of the Earth with Greg. That said a lot to me.

He visited again in December. Just before he arrived, I came down with a cold. I was planning to call in sick to work when my mother, who, up until that point, had been completely uninvolved in my life, decided to intervene. "You need to be responsible and go to work," she said. "You are not calling in sick."

"Who the fuck are you to tell me to go to work?" I replied. "You sit on your ass and collect welfare and buy drugs with it while I'm putting food on the table. I don't have to go to work if I'm sick. I haven't called in sick once in two months!"

Not only did I not go to work that day, I ran away with Greg. We hitchhiked three hundred miles—half the length of California. We slept on the streets under a camper shell for a night before we found a truck driver to take us south from Shasta County to Watsonville. We got to Greg's mother's house on Christmas Day and settled into living there. I was just weeks away from my seventeenth birthday.

Two months later, I was pregnant.

49
Patrice

"Hey, honey, Sam asked me again about that big dinner party he's hosting this Friday night. Do you want to go?" Bob asked me, about a month after Melissa left.

"No," I said. I returned to washing the breakfast dishes.

"Yeah, I guess I don't really feel like it either. But you're the social one. I was hoping you could get me to rally." He was staring into the overstuffed refrigerator as he said this. I still couldn't admit to myself that Melissa wouldn't be eating with us anymore.

My shame at failing had no boundaries. I worried that my friends—many of whom would be at that party—thought less of me now that Melissa had run away and been moved to a different home. It was hard to think that the ones who had cautioned us back when we were first thinking about fostering her had been wiser than I'd been. Bob and I had gone from zero to a hundred miles an hour in the process of incorporating Melissa into our lives. We'd told everybody that we had a new daughter. Our enthusiasm and optimism had burst forth at every opportunity. This made our conspicuous public failure all the harder. "I'd really rather not have to explain once again to people that Melissa's gone," I said.

Bob shut the refrigerator door without taking anything out of it, then looked at the counter, pulled an English muffin out of a bag, and dropped it into the toaster. "What's on your plate today?"

"The usual. I'm at Bay View this morning. I think, anyway. It's Tuesday, right? I don't even know anymore."

I moved through many of my days on autopilot, swept into a vortex of grief and confusion. I'd sit in front of my computer typing case notes and realize I'd been staring off in space for a half-hour, thinking about Melissa. I wondered how people could believe that I was a good family therapist when I couldn't even be an adequate foster mom. My confidence at work unraveled like a poorly crocheted shawl. Having two successful kids must have been a matter of luck, not skill. I was an imposter who had been unmasked by an eleven-year-old foster child.

At night, Bob and I would find ourselves trying to comfort each other. "I think maybe this is the best thing for her," Bob kept saying. "She has her own ideas and opinions. Maybe we weren't the right fit."

I'd often push back. "The best thing? Are you kidding? Bouncing to another foster home?" Or I'd shift the blame onto her family. "It must be what her mother and grandmother were saying to her. It's all their fault that she couldn't bond with us." These angry outbursts would alternate with painful self-recriminations. And then there were the justifications I came up with for not going after her: "Maybe she was lonely here and being around more kids will be better for her," and, "Maybe we tried to move too fast." Most often, though, I'd berate myself for being so critical and demanding. I'd think about how relieved Melissa must have been to not have someone riding her about homework.

"We have to respect Melissa's feelings and choices," Bob said more than once. "She knows herself better than we do."

Melissa hadn't brought much stuff with her, yet her absence filled the house. She'd touched every aspect of our lives—from daily logistical issues to big decisions about the future. We had planned vacations and college savings around her. I found myself walking into her now-tidy room and sitting at her desk thinking about the times Bob and I talked about how smart she was. We both pictured her in college and going on to a career where she excelled. We pictured her happy, having moved past much of her childhood trauma.

My father, too, felt responsible for Melissa's leaving. "I'm so sorry that I didn't watch her more carefully the day she ran away," he said to Bob and me at dinner the first night she was gone. "I should have noticed the bag she packed and talked her out of that crazy behavior. She's made a big mistake by leaving this house."

I got up from the table and pulled him against me, rubbing his nearly bald head and telling him he'd done nothing wrong. "You were always wonderful with Melissa. You drove her to school, took her out for ice cream, laughed with her at movies, and listened to her chatter. You made her feel loved just the way she is."

Apparently, I hadn't done that. I heard her voice ringing in my head: "You want me to be Ellie and Colin, and I can't."

50
Melissa

I didn't know I was pregnant until I wasn't anymore. I had been having horrible stomach pains and was unable to get out of bed for a few days. Then, I passed a mass into the toilet and went to the hospital. The doctor told me he thought the fetus had been dead for a while, which is why I'd become so sick. Two weeks after I'd started sleeping with Greg, I'd gotten a Depo-Provera shot, so I must have gotten pregnant during one of the first couple times we had sex.

Even after I recovered physically, I still struggled emotionally. I wondered if I would ever be able to have kids, and I felt like I'd been robbed. I'd never really thought much about being a mother, but, once it was a possibility, and that possibility was taken away from me, then I really wanted it. While I didn't put any effort into getting pregnant again, neither Greg nor I tried to stop it. Six months after the miscarriage, I was pregnant with my daughter, Trinity. At that point, I was seventeen years old.

I was really excited about having a baby, and so was Greg. My family wasn't too pleased though—not just because they didn't like Greg, but also because I was so young. I was essentially following in my mother's footsteps. She had given birth to my brother Daniel a week before her eighteenth birthday. My due date was three weeks before my eighteenth birthday. Paula eventually accepted it, though. She'd have her first grandchild, and she was happy about that. Daniel wasn't. He didn't like Greg, and he didn't like the choices I was making, so I assume that's why I didn't hear from him much then.

My pregnancy was miserable. I had morning sickness the whole way through, couldn't keep food down, and still managed to gain a ton of weight. Some of this was probably due to my own physiology, but I think my living situation made it worse. We were sharing a house with Stephanie—Greg's mother—and several of his siblings. The initial honeymoon stage was over, and Stephanie wasn't treating me that well. At the same time, the minute we found out I was pregnant, Greg's possessive and controlling side came out. I had never seen even a hint of it before. He wouldn't let me go anywhere by myself, and he didn't want me to see my family. He started making rules about what I ate and what I did with my time. I'd already noticed a trend with Greg's family: The women who'd had children with Greg's brothers all took off with their kids. Apparently, they wanted to get as far away from the family as possible. Both Greg and Stephanie knew this, so all of their efforts were dedicated to making sure that my baby stayed with them. I felt smothered and didn't see how I could raise a child there.

Six months into my pregnancy, I convinced Greg to move to Stroud, Oklahoma. My mother had a new boyfriend, Scott, and they, along with my three stepsisters, had driven there in an RV in search of a cheaper place to live. They'd rented a two-bedroom house in this dumpy town with one traffic light and a couple of stop signs, halfway between Tulsa and Oklahoma City. My grandmother bought me a plane ticket, and Stephanie bought one for Greg so he could follow me. We flew there on October 6, 2001, just three weeks after the 9/11 attacks. There was a motor home behind the house my mother had rented, so when it was warm, Greg and I stayed in it. On colder nights, though, we had to sleep in their two-bedroom house with the five of them.

I thought it might be a good place for us to build a life—mostly because it would be away from Greg's controlling family and friends. I also thought that somewhere cheaper would be good for us, and that my mother and stepsisters would offer me support. But I didn't know anything about the place, really. I was just looking for a way to escape from Stephanie.

As I got closer to my due date, I decided that being married meant something to me. Next to Paula's rental was a triple-wide trailer that had been converted into a church. We'd had some interactions with the pastor—not because we went to church, but because we saw him around from time to time. We decided to get married there.

Paula had to sign off on the license because I was a minor. My grandmother sent me $70, which covered the fees but nothing else. So, I wore a pink flowery summer dress of my mothers to a December wedding. I also wore her size 9 high heels, because my feet had swelled so much that I couldn't fit into my size 7 shoes. Scott, my mother's boyfriend, walked me down the aisle. My heels made a hollow clicking sound on the trailer floor. Besides Scott, my mom, and my stepsisters, the only other people there were the pastor, who had agreed to do the service for free, and a man who worked for the church. He and his wife brought us a cake.

Trinity was born five days later.

I thought about Bob and Patrice a lot while I was in the hospital—in part because medical facilities always reminded me of Bob and the tidbits of doctor talk I'd heard over dinner when I was a kid. But I also thought about what the Keets would say if they knew I had a baby at seventeen. It was a good thing they'd never find out, I remember thinking.

From the outset, Greg wasn't the father I thought he would be. He had been so nurturing and attentive with me in the time we'd known each other. When I'd had cramps, he'd sit by me all day. He'd bring me warm compresses for my abdomen and do whatever he could to cheer me up. I thought this would translate into caring for a child. It didn't; but in the early days, I still thought he could learn.

I'd gotten him a job working at a restaurant, but the base pay was only $2.14 an hour. There just weren't any other options in Stroud. All I wanted for us was to live in a studio apartment somewhere as a family. I knew that, as young people, we were going to have to work hard to get what we wanted. I didn't even want another child. I just wanted a simple life—the three of us together, on our own. Greg said he wanted this too, but I don't believe he really did. Regardless, this dream was clearly not going to work out in a town with so few work options.

Nothing about life in Stroud was working. I'd gone to Oklahoma to run away from my problems, but, of course, I just took them with me. Greg was half of that problem, and my willingness to do anything for him was the other half. I even looked the other way when I suspected he was smoking meth with my mother. They both denied it at the time, making me doubt myself and my judgment. Years later, though, they admitted to it.

Four days before my eighteenth birthday, we moved back to Watsonville, back to Stephanie's house. I tried to hold out some hope that it would be different now that Trinity was in the picture, but I was skeptical.

51
Patrice

I was putting on my favorite gold teardrop earrings and running a brush through my hair one more time when the thought hit me: Melissa was about to turn eighteen. It was January 12, 2002, and Bob and I were heading out to meet friends for my birthday—which meant Melissa's was the next day. She and I had been surprised to find out that our birthdays were only a day apart, and I remembered the two years of joint celebrations we'd had. The first birthday together, we went all out and took her to Tahoe where she tried skiing for the first time. The party there had involved a firepit, s'mores, and way more hot chocolate than it should have. We spent the other birthday in Santa Cruz. Melissa wanted a bowling party, since she'd been recently introduced to the activity by Colin and his friend, Jared. The afternoon had been fun until she came in last in the second game, and then there'd been a bit of a scene. In hindsight, I think the day was too long. We'd packed it in, as usual, going out to lunch first, then stopping by the Boardwalk arcade on the way to the bowling alley. She was really cranky when we finally got home. I now think her mood was a reflection of deeper feelings. I imagine that on each memorable day of the year—her birthday, Christmas, Mother's Day—Melissa was reminded that she wasn't with her biological family. She never articulated her loss on those days, but a notable disturbance would always occur, and I would end my day feeling inadequate. The way I saw it, I kept failing to help her be happy. I wish I had sat down with her and asked her about her feelings rather than pushing forward with my agenda of fun.

Eighteen was an important age in the life of a child in foster care. She'd be aging out of the system if she hadn't been adopted. She'd be thrust into adulthood and responsibility for everything from decisions about where she lived and who she lived with to how to support herself and whether to pursue higher education. I felt dizzy thinking about how ill-equipped the girl who lived with us would be for these huge challenges. I wished again that we had been the family who shepherded her to adulthood, no matter how challenging that would have been. But that girl had had seven years to grow up. Maybe she'd lived in a house where they were able to prepare her for adult life. That's what I hoped for.

I tried to picture what she might be doing to celebrate, but I didn't even know if she'd finished high school or if she'd opted to live with her mother and grandmother. If she'd stayed with us, we probably would have hosted a huge party and invited everyone we knew to celebrate and honor this milestone. Of course, that would have been my idea of the perfect birthday, though—not necessarily hers.

52
Melissa

I was eighteen when Greg introduced me to drugs.

Later in life, Child Protective Services told me that my stepfather had been a cocaine user. As for my mother, I remember her sleeping a lot when I was a kid. It's quite possible that drugs played a part in that, although she said she didn't start using until I got taken away. In Shasta County, it had been clear that drugs were ruling her life. She'd get her welfare payment and take off to a hotel for a few days.

Regardless, I don't think my family history contributed to my drug use. Greg was really the catalyst. He smoked pot constantly—from pipes he made out of foil, or from soda cans, or apples, or anything else he could convert into a bong. When he didn't have any weed around, he'd take off on what he'd call a "boonie." He'd drive all over looking for pot, leaving me at home for hours or dragging our infant daughter and me along with him. If he couldn't find anything, he'd get really agitated. There were times he pulled the seats out of the car checking to see if he'd dropped a nugget somewhere. It never occurred to me that he had a problem. I just thought marijuana was really important to him. I didn't understand drug addiction. And I was addicted to Greg, so I went along with anything he did.

Greg was out on a boonie when one of his dealers said, "I don't have any; nobody does. But I have some of this." It was a baggie of cocaine, about sixty dollars' worth, and the dealer offered it to him for twenty. I remember asking him what it was. I'd seen it in movies, but I had a newborn baby; high-end drugs weren't a part of my life.

"I want you to do it with me just this once," Greg said. "I don't do this stuff all the time. This is special." It was like that phrase you always hear, "What happens in Vegas stays in Vegas." It would only happen once. No one would ever know.

"Let's get Trinity to bed first," I said, because that was always a process when she was six months old. I remember him being antsy and excited. I've seen that kind of energy in a lot of addicts since then.

We snorted the cocaine. It made my skin feel like it was covered with insects, like their little legs were crawling across my body, heading straight for my face. I was totally nauseated the whole time, and I passed out and woke up vomiting. It was then that he told me that not only had he done cocaine before, but he'd also done a lot of other drugs—just about everything out there, in fact. "Happy Birthday, son, here you go!" his dad had said to him when he turned nine, right before they did methamphetamine together.

Meth is what Greg and I did next. I figured it would be different from cocaine, so maybe I'd like it. But really, I didn't do it out of a desire to get high. I did it because he did it. I wanted to be with Greg. I wanted us to be a happy family, a family that stuck together. I was so committed to that fantasy that I was willing to do meth to keep it alive. In retrospect, I can hear how crazy that sounds. But at the time, I was desperate. Besides, if I didn't go along with him, he'd be gone for hours without me. I'd be stuck in that horrible house with Stephanie. I wouldn't be able to leave because he'd take off with the car. In my weird co-dependent logic, this all made sense.

About a week after the cocaine incident, Greg asked his sisters to watch Trinity so we could go out with one of his friends. At first, I felt uncomfortable because there were other guys there. Greg had always been a very jealous person, and I knew that if someone was attracted to me, I'd better not talk to him. So, when we got to his friend's garage, I sat quietly while these guys played dominoes. Then the stuff appeared. It looked just like the cocaine, but Greg said, "Don't worry, you're gonna like this one, it's different. It's really fun. It gives you lots of energy." I argued with him, saying that I didn't know what it would do to me. I hadn't realized we were going to be out this late, and I was worried about Trinity.

I was sitting there watching these guys pass around a glass pipe made from a vial—the kind single roses are sold in. There was a bulb in the end and a little hole on top. I watched one of them pour the stuff from the baggie into the little hole while another held the lighter very carefully. If it gets too close, the meth burns, but if it's too far away, the stuff doesn't liquefy, they told me, as they repeated this delicate technique of making sure the flame was in just the right spot while spinning the pipe slowly.

"10 o'clock and 2 o'clock," Greg was saying. "You've got to move it between 10 and 2. As you're moving it, you inhale."

The bulb at the end filled with thick white smoke. Apparently, when the smoke started escaping from the hole, I was supposed to start inhaling. Since I was new at this, Greg was holding the pipe to my mouth and doing the turning for me. "I don't know what to do. Do I go now?"

"Yes. Breathe in now. A little faster." He was watching me like a hawk. "No, that's too fast; slower."

As soon as I began inhaling, I wanted to cough—not because of the smoke, but because it tasted horrible. It tasted the way burnt plastic smells. But Greg was telling me I needed to push past that coughing reflex and hold my breath. I did that, then watched the smoke come out of me with the same white thickness it went in. My initial reaction was nausea. But then, the taste went away, and, instantaneously, I felt energized. It was like an adrenaline rush, like going down the steep drop on the Giant Dipper, the big roller coaster at the Santa Cruz Boardwalk. Only, instead of ending after a few seconds, it just kept going and going. For hours.

All I could think was, "God, I could get so much accomplished on this!" That first time, I did one hit at 10pm and was up until 7pm the next day. I didn't crave doing it again, though, because the comedown was so awful. It felt like having the flu. I couldn't eat, so my stomach felt gross, like it was eating itself.

Still, I kept doing meth for a few months. It turned into a habit for me because it was a habit for him. My addiction was Greg, not drugs. I didn't know the effects of what I was doing, but I knew what I was doing was wrong. I lost a ton of weight, and I was so tired so much of the time. After coming down, I just slept and slept and slept. I remember not being able to get up and take care of Trinity when I was coming down, so she was often with Stephanie or Greg's sisters. That ate at me. As young a mother as I was, I tried to be caring and diligent. Most of the time, Trinity had been fed at normal hours and she'd had a regular bath time. I tried to keep her on a consistent schedule, but it was hard, given Greg's erratic behavior. So, there were times when I just said, "Okay, we'll put Trinity in the back seat, and she'll fall asleep. Let's go."

Other times, we left Trinity with Greg's sisters, who, I came to find out, treated her horribly. They'd fed her spicy Cheetos, Oreo cookies, and all sorts of other foods that were totally inappropriate for a six-month-old. I returned more than once to find Trinity with a horrible diaper rash, or with a diaper overflowing with urine. When I told Greg I wouldn't leave my daughter with his sisters anymore, he said he'd get his mother to watch her instead. I don't remember where we went, but we came back to the house in the early morning hours. When Trinity woke up, I noticed a blistered burn on her leg. It was in the shape of a cigarette. I confronted Stephanie about it, but she wouldn't give me a straight answer. I didn't think she'd hurt Trinity deliberately, but Stephanie always had a cigarette in her mouth.

I couldn't trust any of them to watch Trinity, so I quit doing drugs with Greg. I used for three or four months, and then I quit cold turkey. Physically, it wasn't hard on me; I had never really liked it all that much. What made it hard was knowing that Greg was going to be gone all the time without me. Meth is a sensory drug, and it increases your libido. I knew he'd be out with a lot of other women around, and I knew he liked to have sex when he was high.

People always ask me why I didn't leave then. For starters, I was madly in love with him. Looking back, I think I was more in love with his potential than with him, but the feeling was all-consuming. I still believed in him and in the life I thought we could build. Maybe this was just a phase he was in, I thought, since I didn't know at the time how serious a problem his drug use was. We could move past it. He could get a job.

And what else was I going to do? Where else was I going to go? My mother was a mess. My grandmother was still around and offering me a place to stay, but I didn't like her and, after the incident with my uncle, I definitely didn't trust her. I still talked to Daniel occasionally, but not only did he not like Greg, he resented the fact that I was associating with the maternal side of our family. He was still living with his foster mother, who, understandably, thought my mother and grandmother were trouble. Since I had gone to live with both of them at various points, I don't think she was a big fan of mine back then either. I suspect she thought that I was a threat to Daniel's stability, and that the farther she could keep him from my dysfunctionality, the better chance he'd have of getting through the college work he was trying to do. Getting some kind of help from my brother clearly wasn't an option. I thought briefly about checking into a women's shelter, but that was like going back into foster care. I'd just gotten out of the system; I sure didn't want to throw myself back into it voluntarily. And, if I told them how I was living, they'd take Trinity away for sure. I just didn't see any other solutions.

With no support system, no job, and a baby girl I was responsible for, I kept turning to Greg. I knew he loved me, no matter how bad things got. That was more than I had anywhere else.

53

Patrice

A few months after Melissa's eighteenth birthday, Bob and I were diving into our salmon dinner when our host, Dale, asked if we'd heard about Melissa. Dale had known Melissa's brother, Daniel, well. He'd been the boy's CASA Advocate—like Kristin was for Melissa— for eleven years. Bob and I shook our heads no. In fact, we hadn't heard anything about her during the seven years that had passed since she left our house. Of course, we hadn't inquired either. That didn't mean that we didn't think about her, though.

We met Dale a couple of years after Melissa left, when Bob and I became involved with CASA. I hoped that I could make a difference in the system and help other foster parents do better than I had done. Among many other wonderful and dedicated people I encountered there, Bob and I had gotten to be close friends with Dale and his wife. Until I joined the CASA board and met Dale in person, I had only known him as the pesky voice on the phone who had wanted to get Melissa and Daniel together when she lived with us. That had been when I was doing everything I could to prevent that from happening. As Dale and I worked together on the CASA board, he learned how heartbreaking Melissa's departure had been for us. It must have seemed natural to him to give us news of her.

"Uh, no, we haven't heard anything," I said, trying to avoid Dale's eyes. Leaning back in his chair, Dale told us that Melissa had given birth to a baby girl who was now nearly a year old.

She was married to the baby's father, and they lived with her in-laws in Watsonville. I looked across the table at Bob. His eyes darted back and forth between me and Dale. I could feel my face flushing as I tried to steady my breath, but I felt like the seas were rising around me, and I had to get to higher ground. I said something about hoping she was happy and then scurried away from the table.

In the bathroom, I put my face up close to the mirror and leaned heavily on the wash basin. I felt lightheaded and slightly sick to my stomach. Hadn't I come far enough not to be thrown into an emotional tailspin after hearing a tiny snippet about Melissa's life?

I wish I could have let this information be just that—information. On the face of it, it was good news. Melissa was in a relationship, had family support, and was a mom—albeit an eighteen-year-old one. Our fondest dream for her was that she would escape the cycles of abuse and poverty she had experienced as a child and find stability and happiness. So, I should have been able to quash the niggling feelings of guilt and shame that were crowding the borders of my consciousness.

I pushed even harder on the bathroom sink, trying to grind my discomfort into the porcelain. Outside the bathroom window, I saw a lemon tree dripping with ripened fruit, and I walked over to the window to inhale its sweet fragrance. I closed my eyes and forced myself to picture Melissa hugging her new baby while surrounded by a loving, supportive family. Then, I pulled the door open and headed back to the dining room.

54
Melissa

I felt like a prisoner at Greg's mom's house. Stephanie and Greg wouldn't let me go to school., and they wouldn't let me apply for welfare to access the services that would allow me to get a job. "If you get on welfare, they're going to make you pay all of that money back," Stephanie said. We all knew of people that ended up having to pay back some of the benefits they'd received. Usually, this was the result of some reporting or accounting error. I don't think Stephanie was really concerned about that happening, though. She was just trying to control me, yet again. "Don't let her do that, Gregory! Don't you dare let her do that!"

Stephanie was a powerful woman. Although she was only five-foot-one, she was built like a tank. She had a masculine frame, with short stocky legs, broad shoulders, and a huge belly. Her hair was dark and long, and, in it, you could see her family's Cherokee heritage. She had a distinct way of wearing her hair, too; she always pulled it back into a high and tight ponytail, braided the hair that was hanging down, and then wrapped the braids into a bun.

Stephanie's house was always full. Greg had two sisters and three brothers, and there were often a lot of other people hanging around and sleeping there as well.

Greg rarely worked. In the time I knew him, he never held down a job for more than a couple of months. Stephanie did work, and she was committed to her job at a senior housing complex. For the most part, she supplied Greg with money.

I had always assumed that living with Stephanie would be a temporary situation, something we'd do to get on our feet before finding our own apartment and creating our own family life. At some point, however, I realized that Greg thought of his mom's house as a permanent arrangement. Before I got pregnant, I had kept a job and was going to adult school, and I knew I would return to doing both of those things. What I didn't know is how long it would take to do so.

When Trinity was about eight months old, I noticed Greg's interest in other women. I was spending all my time caring for my newborn child, and I was already feeling sensitive about my looks. I shouldn't have been. I wasn't heavy at all; actually, I had an hourglass shape that attracted a lot of attention. But I had stretch marks, I suffered from a host of body image issues that my history of abuse had created, and my husband was checking out other women. Greg was gone from the house much of the time, using. I heard him on the phone with a woman trying to figure out how and when they could meet up. She was a convenience store clerk who worked at the gas station where he bought his cigarettes. "How did you get her number?" I asked. "And why are you talking to her?"

"You're making a big deal out of nothing." He looked away and laughed. He may have been high, but I wasn't used to him being so cold and distant.

"What the hell are you laughing about?" I shouted. "Why is this funny to you? Do you understand that if you want to see other women, I'm going to leave you?" When I said that, his demeanor completely shifted. He raised his voice and tried to turn the tables on me.

"Well, Tom is always staring at you. His eyes were all over you the other night, and you know it. And those guys at the supermarket yesterday, they were totally checking you out."

"I can't help what someone else does. But you don't see me

on the phone with them trying to make plans to get a date."

He got up close to me and pushed me on the shoulder. "Whatever, you're the slut."

"I'm going to go. Zoe, bring Trinity to me," I told his sister. "We're leaving." I had just gotten out of the shower and was in my nursing pajamas—a pair of shorts and a top that had slits down the front that allowed access to my nipples. I had no underwear or shoes on, and my hair was still wet. But, as soon as I had Trinity in my arms, I planned to run.

"No, you're not going to get her. Get down on the bed," Greg yelled. Then he grabbed my arm and threw me down onto the futon couch that we folded out every night to sleep on.

"Don't fucking touch me like that!" I tried to stand up from the bed, but he grabbed my shoulders and threw me back down. I jumped up again, but he pushed me harder, and my head flung back against the wall behind me. I was pissed, but more than that, I was panicked, because I could see no way out of a situation that was escalating rapidly. So, I kicked him away from the bed, and when he came back towards me to throw me down again, I hit him across the face with my open hand.

In the meantime, Stephanie was standing in the door, blocking my way out. There were other people gathering too, listening but doing nothing. "Get the fuck out of my way!" I yelled, as I ran to grab Trinity from Zoe.

"Block that door," Stephanie said to Lynette, Greg's other sister. Lynette locked the front door and positioned herself between me and it. The only way out was through the sliding glass door in the back of the house. I threw it open, ran out, and climbed over the rickety wooden fence behind the house—in my nursing pajamas, with Trinity on my hip.

Once I was over the fence, I walked swiftly through the complex's entrance gate and out onto the main street. It was foggy that morning, and I could feel the moisture saturating the flannel next to my skin. Greg and Lynette followed me, with Greg shouting, "Please don't leave. Just please don't leave me!" I kept moving. I continued past the railroad tracks, with the idea of heading towards my grandmother's house. "Get the baby! She won't leave without the baby!" Greg yelled, as he rushed up from behind me and yanked Trinity out of my hands. I didn't want to release her, but if I had held on, she would have gotten hurt. So, I let her go. Greg passed Trinity off to his sister as though they were running a football play. I was still planning to go to my grandmother's house to call the police, figuring they could help me get Trinity back. So, I kept walking away, thinking Greg would eventually leave me alone. He didn't; he just kept following me down the street. "Missy, don't leave! Come back, just please come back already. I'm sorry, I'm sorry!"

I stayed silent and quickened my pace. He grabbed me and wrapped his arms around me—at first in a hug, but, since I was jerking and fighting, it felt more like a wrestling hold. "Get off of me! I don't want you to touch me, you bastard!"

With that, neighbors noticed us. "Take your hands off of her!" they shouted from their balconies. "Let her go, we're calling the police!"

The police showed up—and I ended up going to jail.

Even though I was the one being attacked, he was the only one with marks—"physical evidence," as they called it—on his body. "Did you hit him?" the cops asked me.

"Yes. He was holding me hostage, and he wouldn't let me leave. So, I hit him. I have a right to my own body!" I guess that was the wrong thing to say. This was my first lesson in what would happen if I tried to escape from my abusive situation. *Don't trust the police. Don't tell them the truth. They are not there to help you.*

I spent the night in jail and cried the whole time. I was afraid for myself, but more than anything else, I was afraid for

Trinity. I had no idea where she was or what was happening to her. I thought about the Keets while I was in there. This was so much worse than not doing my homework or stealing a wallet. Of course, I probably wouldn't have ended up in jail if I had kept living with them. But that meant I wouldn't have Trinity either. She was the best thing in my life, and I wouldn't change anything that would take her out of it.

I was given the option of a trial. I knew that if I had the opportunity to explain my story to a jury, they would sympathize with me. I could have fought the charges and they would have been dropped. But where would Trinity have been the whole time I sat in jail awaiting the trial? No one was going to post my bail. After the incident with the burn on Trinity's thigh, I couldn't trust Greg's family to take care of her. And, while my own mother wouldn't have harmed Trinity, she would have neglected her. If I told the authorities I was afraid for my child's safety, I would run the risk of Child Protective Services showing up and taking her away. I had lived through that myself; I sure didn't want my own daughter in the system. I might as well have been a rat in a cage at that point. There was no way out.

So, I sucked it up and pleaded "no contest." They got me for child endangerment because Trinity was present at the scene, even though Greg was the one ripping her out of my arms. I had to pay piles of fines, spend three years on probation, and attend domestic violence counseling at my own expense. On top of that, I earned the title of "violent offender." And who got the protective order for Trinity? Greg.

"She can't leave now," Stephanie said. I had ordered a birth certificate for Trinity, and Stephanie stole it, as though it was proof of ownership. "Trinity doesn't know that Melissa's her mom," Stephanie would say around the house. "She thinks *I'm* her mom."

We didn't leave. And, before long, I was pregnant again.

55
Patrice

Sitting on the dock at Lake Colby in my new neon blue bathing suit, I felt a deep sadness come over me. The lake was one large reflecting pool, glowing with the early light of dawn. The humid air was so close to saturation that it became an entity of its own—the familiar weighty stillness before a thunderstorm. The canoe was tied up to the ladder, and I found myself thinking about an early morning paddle Melissa and I had taken years before. Even though she usually hated getting up before noon, she'd been a different person in this environment. She'd scamper down the pine needle path, leap onto the dock, and bounce on her toes. She'd want to take a swim or pull one of the kayaks out of the rack to look for minnows scurrying beneath the boat.

After swimming out to the floating raft, I climbed the ladder, lay down on the splintering wood planks, and stared up at the building bank of clouds. We gave her everything a child could possibly want—from food, clothing, and her own room to travel, books, and classes. We showered her with love and attention. We sent her to a good school and supported her learning. And still, she rejected us. Or me. The breeze kicked up a notch, and I felt goosebumps emerging all over my body. After so much success with Ellie and Colin, I had failed at the most important job in my life, the one I thought I was born for: mothering. And, to top it off, I was still upset about it. How could I still be so rocked by this, so many years later? I was a therapist; how come I couldn't talk myself out of this corner?

My goosebumps turned into actual shivering, and I curled myself into a ball, clutching my legs to my chest and rocking back and forth, not caring about the tiny wooden daggers digging into my back.

As I dove back into the lake, I thought about the two of us cuddled up under a striped wool blanket on the screened-in porch, waiting for a flash of lightning and its accompanying not-so-distant crash of thunder. I wondered, like I often did, what she was doing at that moment. I wondered too, if she ever thought about the lake and me.

56
Melissa

I was twenty when Heaven was born. I was ecstatic—both to have another child and to have another girl. Just a few days after I got out of the hospital, we moved into an apartment in the Vista Montaña complex, on the east side of Watsonville. We were living with Stephanie and Greg's sisters again, but this time, everyone was on the lease. I hoped that the combination of a new home and a new baby would shift the dynamics at least a little bit, even though there were still three families living in a four-bedroom apartment together, and I knew I'd end up being the cook and housekeeper again.

I had a little extra hope, too, because both my probation period and Greg's protective order were about to expire. I had taken GED classes and the GED exam through Watsonville Adult Ed, and just after I gave birth to Heaven, I received my certificate in the mail. I'd also applied for and gotten a spot in a one-year, fully subsidized dental assistant training program through Welfare to Work. I finally got on welfare, which gave me a little more room to breathe. I had to apply without Stephanie knowing, and it took me a long time to talk Greg into it. But I made it happen. I went to the office to sign up and found out I needed every kind of financial documentation imaginable. The hardest part was providing a birth certificate for Trinity, since Stephanie had stolen the one I'd ordered. Stephanie's mother, Janet, was really into genealogy, and I discovered that she had birth certificates for everyone in Greg's extended family. I got her to give me a copy. As far as I know, Stephanie never found out.

Within the welfare system, the woman is named as the head of the household. That always irked Greg, because it meant that the money went to me, and he couldn't take it and spend it on drugs. I got $730 a month for the three of us, and it was put on a debit card in my name. It enabled me to pay for the rest of my domestic violence classes and buy more of the basics we needed, like food and diapers. Stephanie eventually found out that I was receiving assistance, but, since it meant she didn't have to pay for as many household expenses, she didn't make a fuss about it. With all of this support, I was starting to feel like I might be gaining some ground.

But, at the same time, Greg started disappearing regularly again. I don't think he'd ever stopped using, but at least he had been around the house more while I was pregnant. I wanted to work, and I was getting ready to start the training program, so I needed childcare. Greg was unable to provide it. If I left the girls with him, he'd dump them on his family and go out looking for drugs. I was still scared to tell the authorities about our living environment, knowing that, once they found out about it, they'd say I was neglecting my kids and take them away. So, I had to manipulate the system to get what I needed. Somehow, I convinced them that Greg was out job searching every day, when, in fact, he was out getting high. CalWORKS gave me the money I could use to pay a local woman for childcare, and I got a job at Carl's Jr. right away.

I was good at my job. Knowing how to please people had been part of my skill set growing up in foster care, so adapting to customer service was easy. I started off as a closer, so I cooked, but I also did a lot of dishes and mopped. I cleaned out the fryers and filtered the oil. Then, I got moved to the opening shift and did a lot of prep work—slicing onions, filling the lettuce containers, making pico de gallo, putting away the food that was delivered every day. Fast food work is all about anticipation—knowing what you are about to need and preparing for that during what little down time you have. I did that well. I worked hard and got along with the other people there, so my boss took me under her wing.

I liked working, and I really liked how being there provided a break from Stephanie's. But my schedule was running me ragged. I'd work eight or nine-hour shifts, pick up the kids, come home, clean up the mess left by nine people, cook for nine people, clean up all of *that* mess, bathe my kids, get them to sleep, and then maybe catch three or four hours of sleep myself. I'd get up a couple hours before work—not just to get myself ready to go, but also to feed and dress an infant and a fussy toddler.

Greg and I argued constantly then, and we argued about the same damn thing every single day: the fact that he was gone all the time. He routinely left with the car, knowing full well I needed it to get to work. We lived out in a rural area where one bus passed by every two hours, and my work was in town. There were times when I called Leticia, my day care lady, to pick me up. There were times when I had to ask Stephanie to drop me off. There were times when he took the car from my workplace and left me stranded there. I'd have to walk a mile and a half to Leticia's to pick up the kids, and I'd almost always be late. You can't live with someone like this and function normally.

One of the many times I confronted Greg about disappearing, he told me this wild story about some guy pulling a gun on him in downtown Watsonville. Knowing his drug habit and the kinds of gangs there are in Watsonville, it wasn't hard to believe his tale. The following week, he disappeared for three whole days. I wondered if he'd been shot, and I decided to file a missing person's report with the police. "I wasn't getting shot," he said when he got home. "I was just ignoring your calls."

When he said that, I felt like something had shifted in him. It was like he just didn't care anymore. I saw that same disconnection then that I had seen when he was holding me hostage in that room years before. He turned cold, and his eyes said, "I don't give a shit about you." It was like a fist to my gut.

57
Patrice

In the early years after Melissa left, walking on Pacific Avenue in Santa Cruz became extra stressful for me.

Our downtown's main street had been a common spot for homeless people to congregate off and on over the course of the time Bob and I had lived in the area. Some days, there were people camped out on the sidewalks with their dogs and possessions. I had come up with a strategy to walk these blocks—one that involved donating to the local homeless services nonprofit and paying more attention to housing advocacy issues. That enabled me to walk past the older women, men, and boys without too much distress. But young women could push me over the edge.

There was one girl with long brown dreads that I always tried to smile at. She often sat with her chihuahua in the tiled alcove by El Palomar, the Mexican restaurant next to the movie theater. She always had a chariot with her—one of those fancy baby strollers with the extra durable tires—but she used it for her dog and her possessions, not for a child.

When I did see girls with babies, I had to look away. Girls with long blonde hair made my heart beat faster, too. I wanted so badly to believe that Melissa had ended up just fine, but I could never quite convince myself of that. Every time I thought about trying to find Melissa, the pain I felt when she left at eleven would overtake me. "Why would things be any different now?" I'd wonder. So, I never did anything.

58
Melissa

I was running myself ragged attempting to maintain appearances and keep Greg's lifestyle—and, by association, my lifestyle—a secret. I was working my butt off to climb out of the quicksand, but much of the money I made went to paying Greg's fines and court fees. He'd gotten a DUI which racked up $2000 in fines and required that we pay for a $2000 drug counseling course. He'd been busted for driving without insurance, driving without a license, and driving an unregistered vehicle, and he'd received more speeding tickets than I could keep track of. One of the car accidents he was involved in cost us $1500 in damages. One month, he had a $230 phone bill. He sold my brand-new cell phone to a drug dealer in exchange for meth, and he tried to steal my wedding ring to pawn it off. He kept disappearing without a trace for days at a time, and he always came back strung out and exhausted.

I snapped. I called my friend Daryl, a counselor I had met at Camp Opportunity, a program that enables kids in foster care to spend a week at summer camp in the Santa Cruz Mountains. I remember crying and telling her that I thought that something was wrong with me. "I just don't really want to live anymore," I said. I was distraught, exhausted, and done.

A week prior to this conversation, I had bought a bottle of Tylenol PM. I never took pills. I just wanted to sleep and couldn't seem to manage it. Daryl said, "Just don't do anything, Missy, I'm coming, I'm coming right now!" But, as soon as I hung up the phone, I took the whole bottle. Then I just lay down.

Somewhere in there, I had also called Daniel. He understood how trapped I was, but he had no way to help me get out of my situation. By that point, he had moved out of his foster mother's place and was couch surfing everywhere from friends' places to our place—which he could only do for a couple of nights before Stephanie would get upset about having another person in the house. Daniel couldn't stand being there anyway; he would get upset watching how I was being treated there. While I was on the phone with him, I told him that I thought I was in danger and that I was probably going to die. I said this because I was afraid for Trinity and Heaven. I knew that if something happened to me, their lives would be a living hell from that point forward. There would be no way for them to have any kind of success living with Greg's family or with my family. They'd have no future at all.

Daniel got to the house before Daryl did. He called 911. I remember just lying in bed, telling him, "I'm going to go to sleep now."

I was released from the emergency room that same night; for some reason, I wasn't held for the customary seventy-two hours they generally require for suicide watches. Greg had been gone for this whole episode. He showed up at the ER while I was in recovery.

I needed help. I needed a counselor, I needed support, and I needed to clear up my record to make sure I could keep the kids in my care where I knew they would be safe. So, I did what I had to do: I went to my CalWORKS case manager—the woman who facilitated my welfare payments—and told her about Greg's drug use. I knew full well she'd tell CPS, since they were in an office upstairs, in the same building downtown. I had no choice. To them, I'd looked like the bad guy; I was the violent offender with the record of jail time and assault, and I was the one who had tried to kill herself. I knew that if I redirected the spotlight onto him and his drug addiction, then it would be off of me. Greg had accumulated enough of a police record that all the local cops knew who he was. What I told my counselor didn't surprise anyone, and it relieved me of the burden of concealing his lifestyle and maintaining his fabricated job search log.

I wondered what, at age twenty-one, I would have been doing if I had kept living with the Keets. I probably would have been in college. I definitely wouldn't have been running around to every social services agency in the county to get assistance for me, my two kids, and their deadbeat dad. The future would have probably looked a heck of a lot brighter. But I couldn't think those kinds of thoughts for too long; they'd make me desperately sad.

All I could do was stay afloat. All I could do was keep breathing.

Meanwhile, in October of 2005, Stephanie and the other three family members on our lease gave the landlord a thirty-day notice without consulting me. At the same time, Stephanie had decided that I hadn't been doing enough work in the household. She and I had made a verbal agreement when we moved in that, in exchange for keeping the house clean, providing all the food, and cooking all the meals, Greg and I wouldn't have to pay rent. She changed her mind when it came time to move out. She sued me for back rent and a portion of the deposit—a total of $6800. This left me living in an empty house, unsure of where to move next. I was working full-time and taking care of my two kids. My husband was still doing drugs, and I was being sued.

To add insult to injury, my dad died while all of this was

happening. While we'd had very limited contact between the time I was taken away from my birth family and the time when Trinity was born, I had made an effort to find him shortly before Heaven was born. We'd been rebuilding our relationship slowly since then. After his mother had a stroke, he was permanently placed in a halfway house for homeless men with mental health and substance abuse issues. A few times, he'd shown up unannounced at Stephanie's when he wasn't stable, so things with him still weren't easy. But that didn't change the fact that I unconditionally loved my warm and wonderful dad with his Santa Claus smile, rosy cheeks, and big belly laugh. I'd visited him at his house just two weeks prior to his death. Then, just like that, he was gone from the world.

Family members that I hadn't seen since the age of seven—like my aunt Jenny—came in for the funeral. I had to face the woman who shipped me away after telling me that she loved me like she loved her own daughter. So much was falling down around me that I became numb.

I know exactly when I hit my breaking point: when Greg stole my debit card in the middle of the night. I had just gotten paid, and I had two days to get out of the house Stephanie had left me to clean. He emptied my account for drug money.

I figured out how to get Medi-Cal to pay for me to see a counselor. My counselor knew I wasn't an alcoholic, and she knew I didn't do drugs. However, she repeatedly told me that a lot of services existed for people with these issues. "Have you ever had *these issues*?" she would ask. "Have you *ever* used drugs before? Or had problems with alcohol? You know, there are a lot of services for people out there who have had *these issues*. Are you sure you haven't ever had *these issues*?" Finally, I caught on. I said, "Well yeah, I have, actually." I didn't want to say I had drug problems since drugs are illegal. So, I said I was an alcoholic. It seemed like the safest option.

"Really? Well, that's amazing, because it turns out there's this place for people in recovery that provides housing."

If it hadn't been for that counselor, I would never have thought to manipulate the system in that way. But I did, and I got an apartment out of it. It was tiny; I called it my "walk-in closet." But it was mine.

There was a catch, however. Because I was in a housing development for alcoholics in recovery, I had to sit through AA meetings every week. Every week, the leader would call on me to speak, and, every week, I would pass, claiming that I just wanted to listen. Since I didn't drink much, I couldn't come up with anything to say. I sat in those meetings feeling like a fraud. People were baring their souls, and I was just trying to keep a roof over my head. After each meeting, we lined up to collect the leaders' signatures on our attendance sheets. Eventually, I figured out that people forged these signoffs, and I stopped going. Faking signatures made me feel bad, but not as bad as going to the meetings did.

The housing complex was for women and children only, so Greg wasn't supposed to be around. It wasn't too hard to keep him away for the first three or four months I was living there, since he was so deep in his addiction that he had no time for us. But in the spring, he showed back up, and, after a while, I started sneaking him in. When he was coming down from a high, he'd get really emotional and plead with me to let him stay. "I know I have a problem," he'd say. "I'm going to get clean, I am. But I can't do it without your help." I wasn't going to turn down the father of my children. And it was hard on me to be separated from him. I still loved him and just couldn't let go. So, I let him stay sometimes, and I ended up getting kicked out of the complex. I tried fighting it. There was one girl in the building who snuck multiple men into her house, and I was only hiding my husband. Besides, I was the only one there with a job. I was the only one not receiving Section 8 housing assistance and paying any portion of the rent on my own. But that's what happens in the system. Anyone who's doing what they're supposed to gets ripped off. When you're on welfare and you get a job, you get penalized. You lose stuff. When you have nothing, you get all the services.

An organization called Families in Transition helped me to get my own apartment out in Lakeview, east of Watsonville. When I think about my year there, I have mixed emotions. Independence has always been important to me, and I had it there. But Lakeview is where my marriage really fell apart.

Greg didn't move in with us right away. I set out a game plan and established expectations. "If you want to stay here, this is what I need to see,"—that kind of thing, because I knew by this point that he routinely said things and didn't really mean them. I didn't want him around when he was coming down from a high. And, when he was around, he needed to keep a low profile because I didn't want to lose my childcare. If welfare found out he was living with me, they'd say that he could take care of the kids, even though he'd proven that he couldn't. So, once again, I had to manage a juggling act. Luckily, my landlord didn't really care who was there. I paid my rent on time, so she was happy. I wasn't, though. I wasn't sleeping.

I'd started working at a dental office on the west side of Santa Cruz. I put in ten-hour days and commuted for over an hour in heavy traffic. One morning, shortly after Greg had moved in with us, I was so tired I could barely move from my bed. I thought he was clean, and I assumed he was doing everything I had asked him to do in order to stay with us. "Greg, can you watch the girls today?" I asked. "If I don't have to bring them to day care, I can get just another hour of sleep, which would be so amazing."

"Sure thing," he said, and I fell back asleep. An hour later, my alarm went off. I fed the girls breakfast and drove to Santa Cruz for work. Sometime during my lunch break, I started feeling panicky and didn't know why. My mind started racing with possible scenarios. I was the only one in the family with a phone, so I couldn't call Greg to check in. I had an hour-long lunch break, and I had to do something.

"I have an important errand to run," I quickly told my boss. "I may be back a little late." Saying any more would have made me sound like a crazy person, or it would have required that I divulge my secret life, my secret dysfunction.

I raced to Watsonville, thinking the whole time that I was being paranoid, that there was almost certainly nothing wrong, and that I was wasting time and gas money. But, as soon as I pulled into my parking space, my landlord approached me and said, "I saw your little daughter walking around outside by herself. I knocked on the door and no one answered, so I opened it to put her back inside. Your husband was just lying there, sleeping." Sure enough, as she was telling me this, two-year-old Heaven wandered up to us. "Mommy," she said, "I was looking for you."

How did I know this? I was freaked out not only by what was happening, but also by the fact that I had known in my gut that something was wrong. How did that work?

Greg was crashed out in the bedroom when I walked in. He had to have been high and coming down. It was one o'clock in the afternoon, and he was dead asleep. Apparently, Trinity had tried to make herself more breakfast, because I saw an empty bottle of maple syrup on the counter and a gigantic dark brown spot on the beige carpet near the kitchen. Meanwhile, Heaven's shoes were over in the corner. She'd been wandering around outside without them and without anyone to keep her from walking into the street.

That was the last time I ever left the kids with him. I knew I could never lose my childcare benefit, no matter what.

"You've got to go," I told Greg. "You have to go stay with your mom." It wasn't that easy to say it, and it was even less easy to make it happen. He battled me day after day.

"Please, let me come home, please," he'd say. "Why are you doing this? It's not fair. I never see the kids," and, "I just want to be with you." It wore me down.

The chaos at home started to show in my performance at work, although I think I was able to hide it most of the time. I had all sorts of other problems at that job, though. When I had started working there, I had accepted a lower wage because they were willing to work around my training program schedule. But, after I graduated, I took on additional hours and responsibilities, and I was routinely coming in on my days off. It was time for my raise, and I asked to be bumped to normal entry-level pay for a dental assistant—about fifteen dollars per hour. They offered me thirteen-fifty. I said, "Thank you, but no thank you," and then things unraveled.

They didn't fire me. They would have needed a reason to do that, and they didn't have one, other than that I had come in late three times in that one week of craziness with Greg. If they had fired me, I would have been able to receive unemployment, which would have been great. Instead, they just refused to let me come into work. They took away my income under the pretense that I had "medical issues." I had a hand tremor, which I had told them about when I was hired, and I had been gaining a lot of weight. They were convinced that I had Parkinson's disease and wanted me to provide a doctor's note saying otherwise. I brought them one, but it wasn't good enough. They wanted a second one. I spent a month in limbo waiting to be seen by doctors, with no money coming in the door.

I couldn't make rent, so I put in a thirty-day notice at Lakeview. I had to come up with a living situation that would keep me out of Stephanie's house. My sister lived up north in Redding, so I thought I'd try that. The house was too small, there were rodents everywhere, and I didn't get along with her boyfriend. I spent eight months there unsuccessfully looking for work. I'm pretty sure the dental office in Santa Cruz had blackballed me.

With no other ideas, I went back to Watsonville, back on welfare, and back to Stephanie's, again. At least I knew how life worked there.

59
Patrice

On a chilly fall day in 2008, Bob walked in the front door from work and blurted out, "You'll never guess who I met at my office today!" He was out of breath as he unzipped his bright yellow bicycle jacket and laid his backpack on a kitchen stool. I looked at him with an expression that said I wasn't going to bother guessing. "Melissa," he said.

"What? Are you serious?" I leaned back against the kitchen counter to steady myself.

"There she was, standing right next to me at my office door."

"Oh my God, Bob! Tell me everything! Why was she there?" I made my way over to the couch, and he followed me. He told me that she'd been in the office to see one of his partners, and they nearly bumped into each other as she was walking to the reception desk. He hadn't recognized her at first, but then she asked him if he was "Dr. Robert Keet." When she told Bob who she was, he motioned her into his office. At first, she hung back at the doorway, but eventually, she went in.

"She didn't seem well. She had a sort of pale and pasty look." He went on to say that she was overweight and looked like a very large version of herself as a child. The two of them stood there in disbelief until she said that she wouldn't have recognized him without his beard. "I think I said something like, 'And you're all grown up,' and watched as she shuffled back and forth and clenched her hands like she wanted to get out of there." Bob explained that Melissa brightened up when she told him that she had two little girls named Heaven and Trinity, four and seven years old. "She said they all live in Watsonville, at least for now." Bob explained that she started talking very quickly after that. He couldn't remember everything she said, but she had told him that she'd worked as a dental assistant at an office on Mission Street but had lost that job. She did say that she wanted to go back to school "when things settled down." Bob took a deep breath. "I didn't get to find out what needed settling down because she reached over and grabbed my arm. She got a pained look on her face and asked me how you were. I told her we thought about her and always hoped she was doing well." Then he described how, when he said that, she stepped close, gave him a quick hug, and mumbled that she had to go. Bob said he could feel her crying.

"Before I could say anything, she disappeared around the corner, and then I saw her sitting in the waiting room. I didn't know what to do. She kept her head down, and there were other patients sitting there." Bob told me a big part of him wanted to go find her and get her whole story but that another part of him felt like he needed to respect her privacy. It seemed to him that she'd gotten as close as she could handle.

"Bob, maybe she's seriously ill." I felt my body tense up. "Maybe she's in trouble. Maybe she can't take care of her kids." After the hundreds of times that I'd wondered and worried about her, I finally had some pieces of the puzzle—and they weren't good. I felt a pull to learn more about her, but that feeling was eclipsed by panic. Getting reconnected with Melissa could draw me into something I wasn't ready for. My gut was telling me that whatever her situation was, she might need too much. I knew that Bob and I never did things partway; if we were going to dive back into this ocean, it would be all or nothing. An image of Melissa with in-laws, young kids, health issues, job problems, and who knew what else rose up like a sneaker wave. Bob moved closer to me on the couch, took me in his arms, and held me tightly.

Finally, he said that he wasn't allowed to find out about her medical condition. "I'm just hoping I saw her at her low point." He leaned back and ran his fingers through his hair. Then he gave me one of his cautious looks, and I thought, "Oh, no, what's next?"

"I'm just thinking out loud here, but do you think we should make contact with her, maybe meet her kids?"

I turned my gaze toward him and moved a foot or so down the couch. "Of course, that crossed my mind." How could I explain the rush of conflicting feelings I was having, especially when he seemed so open to the idea of reconnecting with Melissa? I started massaging my temples and reminded him what an emotional year it had been for me. He knew that I was barely coming out of my grief at having lost my father earlier in the year. We'd also just had two grandchildren born in the space of four months. I'd been on a roller coaster of joy and sadness. Adding anything more to that felt overwhelming. I shored myself up and told him that I just didn't think I had the capacity to get involved in anyone else's life, especially one that could be a minefield of emotions and needs. "Remember, honey, we never just stick a toe in the water. We always jump in all the way." I didn't think I was ready to do that—not at that moment anyway, anyway.

Bob held my hands and told me he understood. "Is there something small we could do for Melissa and her girls, maybe?"

Something small? Like what? Like being part-time friends? I couldn't imagine what he had in mind. I felt selfish thinking about the privileged life we led. But I also knew that it had taken me years of therapy to come to terms with Melissa leaving us, and I sometimes still felt like I hadn't fully recovered. I didn't feel like I could start up a new relationship with her, and I couldn't imagine having a superficial relationship with someone I had loved and wanted to adopt.

As hard as it was to say, I finally told Bob that I wasn't up to reconnecting with her. The relief I felt at voicing that confirmed that it was the right answer for me, but it didn't stop the waves of worry and guilt from invading my consciousness and taking shape in my dreams.

60
Melissa

When I stopped starving myself to try to lose weight, I ballooned up to 247 pounds. I had been seeing doctors off and on to get the clearances the dental office wanted. While I certainly didn't have Parkinson's disease at the age of twenty-three, it was clear that I had something. Nothing moves quickly for Medi-Cal recipients, so it took two years to figure out that I had a tumor on my thyroid gland that had to be removed. I scheduled the surgery for April of 2008 and quit looking for work shortly after my twenty-fourth birthday.

Shortly before the surgery, I needed to see the endocrinologist in person. His office was in a medical complex in Santa Cruz, and, as I got ready to leave, I randomly thought to myself, "Wouldn't it be funny if he were in the same building as Bob?" I quickly dismissed the thought as I climbed into our old green Ford Taurus, which we had nicknamed the "patty wagon."

Once I got to Santa Cruz, I followed the directions the receptionist had dictated to me over the phone. I realized that I was, in fact, going to the same medical building where I had once spent time with Bob. I wasn't nervous until I walked up to the building and saw his name on one of those classic medical office signs—the ones where the doctors' names are printed in white capital letters on plastic sliding strips. "He *does* still work here," I thought, as I walked up the stairs to my appointment. When I arrived at the door to the office, I saw two names on it: my endocrinologist's and Bob's. They shared an office, their spaces separated only by a reception desk. I felt an instant flood of anxiety. Should I say something? Should I not say something? What if I don't say anything, and he finds out that I was here? My last name was different, so maybe he wouldn't know, I rationalized. I felt this pull to talk to him, but I didn't know what I would say. I didn't want to be disrespectful, but, at the same time, I was feeling awful about myself. I weighed almost 250 pounds, and I didn't want Bob to see me like that. And I sure didn't want to tell him about the state of my marriage or my living situation.

My mind was rushing around with all these thoughts when the receptionist called me up to the desk. I stood up and walked towards her. When I looked over at the door, Bob was right there. He looked very different, but somehow, I still recognized him. "Are you Dr. Robert Keet?" I asked. He said yes, so I blurted out, "I'm Melissa. I used to live with you. Do you remember me?" It was so awkward; I was so awkward. I'm certain that I offended him with my words and the way I just spat them out and ran away. It seemed to me that Bob could see right through my tough exterior and down to my shame, my sadness, and my turmoil. By the time I got down the hall and into the specialist's office, I was shaking. I couldn't focus on what the doctor said to me because I felt so bad about the interaction with Bob. I distinctly remember thinking that I never wanted to have an encounter like that again. I didn't want to see Bob again. I couldn't deal with that level of shame.

Late 2008 and early 2009 were very hard for me—harder by far than all the other years that came before. I felt like my whole life had been a fight. Being in foster care had felt like a fight. Going home was a fight. Leaving home was a fight. Being with my husband was a fight. Getting out of his mom's house was a fight. Trying to climb out of poverty was a fight. Bettering my life was a fight. I was tired—really, really tired.

On New Year's Eve, we had someone to watch the kids for a change, so we went out with my brother and his girlfriend as well as our friends Bo and Julie. The plan was to get a bottle of wine and go somewhere together to drink it, but Greg kept trying to convince us to go over to this woman's house. Supposedly she was someone he had met at Watsonville Adult Ed. "She's really cool, and her parents are out of town," he said.

"Her parents are out of town? How old is this woman?" I asked.

"She's like, nineteen."

"Why the hell are you hanging out with a nineteen-year-old girl? The only reason a nineteen-year-old girl is going to hang out with a married twenty-seven-year-old man with two kids is because she wants to sleep with him. No. Stay away from her."

Soon after that, I noticed Greg being secretive with his phone. He was disappearing more and more frequently, but he kept denying that he was seeing her. "There's nothing going on. You're totally paranoid, just like your father," he said. And, although I didn't like being told I was crazy, I also didn't want to be right. But, of course, about a month later, I saw the text messages from this same nineteen-year-old, Candace.

Learning about Greg's affair was a sharp blow straight to my gut. "Fuck you! Fuck you, you ungrateful shit!" I yelled at him. "I have literally supported you financially, emotionally, physically—in every way—for seven years. Do you think I've sacrificed everything for you, just so you can run around and get high and sleep with a nineteen-year-old? I've paid hundreds of dollars per month towards your fucking fines, I've kept you out of jail, I've cooked meals for your whole family, I've cleaned your mother's entire house from top to bottom so many times I can't even count, I'm raising our kids by myself, and now this?"

I was waiting around to have surgery and taking care of my kids, and I wasn't doing a very good job with that. I could handle their basic needs; I bathed and fed them. But I couldn't bring myself to do much more, which made me feel even shittier and contributed to the ugly running dialogue I heard in my head all day. "My husband doesn't want me, I feel rejected as a human being, I can't save my marriage, and now, I'm a horrible mother too." It got me down and kept me down.

I asked Greg for one thing. "If you're going to cheat on me, that's fine; but let me get through this surgery, please. I've been a good wife to you for seven years. I'm asking you to be there for me for this one time."

He did it. For eight months, he didn't see Candace. I didn't trust him, and I felt insecure every time he left the house. But we didn't argue. And he stayed.

During my surgery, we lived with Greg's mom and sisters, who had unsuccessfully sued me. So, as soon as I was feeling better, I moved in with Daniel. He had recently gotten a two-bedroom place with his son. They shared a bedroom and let us sleep in the other one.

At his house, I wasn't sleeping at all. The physician I saw through Medi-Cal had me on a whole cocktail of medications—psychotropic meds, anti-depressants like Trazedone and Wellbutrin—even a booster to make the anti-depressants more effective. None of them helped. Most nights, I watched my mind dart all over. I could never stay with any idea long enough to work it out, but I couldn't stop the flood of words and images from coming at me either.

"Please don't leave, I want to be with you, you know that," I heard Greg say. I was missing him so badly that I had taken his calls. "I'm not seeing her anymore. I want to come home.

Please don't go." This is the voice that rang in my head—the sweet talk, which I wanted so badly to believe. I couldn't get a grip on the facts; I couldn't figure out if I should listen to what he was saying and try to trust him, or if I should ask him for a divorce. From minute to minute—second to second, even—I was changing my mind.

I had to know if he was telling me the truth about Candace. He was working the graveyard shift at a gas station about a mile away from Daniel's. My brother was asleep, so I couldn't leave the girls at home. I put them in the car, drove across town, and parked across from the station. I sat there looking at the tall neon sign and the glowing gas prices and debated whether or not to go in and say hello. "You're acting like a psycho," I thought while I was sitting there, watching and questioning. "Why are you doing this? There's no point in bothering; you know he's not being faithful." And then: "But what if he means what he's saying, and he really wants to stay? There have been plenty of good times too; he does love me. He stood by me through the surgery. I could give him another chance."

As I was sitting there under the ugly yellow light of the sodium streetlamp listening to my internal voices go head-to-head, I watched Candace walk in the door. I watched them make out passionately as he pressed her against the front wall. I never went across the street.

I went home and bawled my eyes out.

"Why are you crying, Mommy?" Heaven asked.

"Because I'm sad." I didn't know what to say. Heaven was only four years old. Trinity was seven. What do you tell them? How can you possibly begin to explain?

We all got into bed together. Our room had a bunk bed with a double futon on the bottom and a twin mattress up top, but most of the time, all three of us piled into the bigger bed. Heaven was on the wall side of the bed, and Trinity was in the center. I was on the edge, sobbing quietly, trying not to keep them awake.

Trinity rolled her little body my way and said, "Mom, can I tell you something?"

"Yes, baby."

"It's something about Daddy."

"What is it, do you miss him?"

"He told me not to tell."

At that moment, I already knew. I already knew what she was going to say. I stopped crying instantly, and my heart started racing. I was trying not to show emotion because I didn't want her to feel uncomfortable, so I took a deep breath and said, calmly, "That's okay, you can tell me."

Her breathing was choppy and gasping. I could tell her heart was pounding. In a shaky voice, she said, "Daddy crawled on top of me and rubbed up and down."

I knew it. I totally knew it. And, in that moment, I knew it had to be true. There was no way for her to come up with this on her own. There was no way she could have gotten it from TV. There was no way she knew about my history, since I hadn't yet shared any of my experiences with her. There could only be one way she could know about this kind of abuse: by having been a victim of it.

I took a few more deep breaths, tried to steady my voice, and kept going. I'd had enough experience with suggestive questioning that I knew to be careful about what words I used. "Did you have clothes on when he was rubbing on you? And what about Daddy, did he have clothes on?" I couldn't believe I was asking these questions. Here they were again, back in my life, like familiar old ghosts that seemed to always linger around my world.

With the information I got from her that night, I was able to establish that Greg had sexually abused her at least six times over a period of three years. The first incident that she remembered was in Vista Montaña, the apartment we lived in when Heaven was born. Trinity was three when we lived there. The most recent event had happened only a few weeks prior, in my brother's home.

"It's okay, you did good." I wrapped my arms around her and gave her the strongest hug I could without hurting her. Then I left the room and dissolved. Where my body had been, there was now emptiness. I couldn't feel my own skin, and I didn't know where I stopped, and the room began. I don't even think I cried; there was no person left to do the crying. There was just hollow, vacant breathing. I called my grandmother and told her what I had just heard. Then, I hung up the phone and called the police. Nobody came. Not right then, not even that night. I was crushed.

No one showed up until the next day, and, when they did show up, everything they said was dripping with insinuation. "Are you sure you're not just angry with him? Are you sure your daughter has no reason to make this up? Does she have any reason to be angry with her father?" they asked.

I could imagine a kid making this up if she were eleven or twelve—old enough to understand what sexual abuse is. Old enough to have had sex ed in school. But Trinity was seven. I could not imagine her thinking, "I'm going to accuse my daddy of molesting me because I'm mad at him for hurting my mommy's feelings." Not a chance.

The investigation went on for weeks. The police put me on the phone with Greg a number of times in an effort to get him to confess. He never did. At the same time, once I started talking to him again, I got confused. He got under my skin and started planting ideas. "I'm not saying that nothing happened to her, Missy; I'm just saying it wasn't me. What about Gary? God only knows what he's capable of these days, and we look alike, especially in the dark." Gary, his younger brother, had been starting to show more and more signs of mental illness and had developed a serious drug addiction.

That got me. Children get confused. And, as I knew all too well, once you're victimized, you're marked with a target. Abusers can spot you a mile away. When I was little, it wasn't just Victor coming after me. I remember being handcuffed to a fence at my schoolyard by a gang of boys who lifted my skirt. I was held at knifepoint by a pre-teen boy in his trailer who forced me to strip down and show him my vagina. I was chased by older boys in Salinas all the time. For victims of abuse, it often feels so constant that you can't keep the events straight. As a result, there are many documented cases of kids being convinced they've been sexually abused when they haven't. So, I had my gut instinct on one side, and doubt and Greg's defense on the other. I was totally overwhelmed by feeling like this whole thing was a nightmare I just wanted to wake up from. I believed my daughter; I just didn't want to. I didn't want this to be true.

"Has anybody else ever done anything to you that you don't like?" I asked Trinity. It turns out Gary did molest her. "Holy shit," I thought. "What if it was Gary all along?" Later, I became convinced that both of them did it. But then, I was just confused—confused, sad, upset, and frustrated. The police weren't doing anything. I couldn't get services to help my daughter. And, to make matters worse, I couldn't leave town because we were involved in an investigation. I just wanted to get Trinity as far away as possible from both Greg and Gary, but my hands were tied.

I told Daniel about what had happened, and it really rattled him. He had sustained a lot of abuse when we were little, most of which I had been forced to watch. I remember Victor taking a long phone cord and wrapping it first around Daniel's waist and then between his legs. He tied my brother to the wall in such a way that, if he moved in any direction at all, circulation to his penis was completely cut off. We always tried to have each other's backs, Daniel and I, because we were in that mess together. But, in reality, we were totally helpless. Victor tortured Daniel to sustain the hierarchy in the home and he had me watch in order to make sure I took on some of the blame for my brother's suffering. I wanted to make it stop, but if Victor laughed, I knew I had to laugh too—or else. Daniel couldn't protect me from my stepfather, no matter how much he wanted to, and I he'd always felt guilty about that. When I told him about Trinity, it was like a quadruple whammy for him: One, his niece was being abused. Two, she was being abused in his home. Three, he failed in his role as protector with me, and, here he was, failing at the same role again. And finally, he was being forced to remember and relive his own abuse. Looking back, I can see how this made him crack.

At the time, however, I didn't understand that. I knew things weren't right between us, and I was sure that he was angry with me, but I didn't know why. We got into a huge argument—I don't even remember what it was about—and he lost his temper. I could tell he didn't want me around anymore, and I had to leave. Once again, I didn't have anywhere to go. So, once again, we went back to Stephanie's. Greg was living there. He was away from the house with Candace most of the time, but I was terrified that I might fall asleep and leave Trinity unprotected from him. So, I did what I needed to do to stay awake, which was meth. I knew Greg would have it around. Ironically, I used his stash to protect our daughter from him.

I couldn't protect myself from Greg, however. He knew exactly how to work his way into my brain. "It wasn't me, Missy, it was Gary. Trinity said so herself. She's just confused; she's a child, after all. We need to leave town. We'll get away from here, we'll get away from my brother. I want to leave with you guys, you know that. Please, please, don't leave without me."

During the six weeks that Trinity's case was open, the police were unable to gather any information. Trinity could never say whether or not there had been any penetration; she didn't understand the anatomy of a vagina. A physical exam, which I thought was protocol since I'd undergone one, could have cleared that up. But they never gave her one. Based on what she had told me, whoever abused her slid himself in and out of her labia. I knew that Greg and his cousin and sister had performed this exact act on each other as kids, because Greg and I had talked about it. It wasn't abuse then, of course; he was just a kid. But kids don't do that kind of thing to each other unless someone has done it to them.

It turned out that Greg never had any intention of leaving with us. All that begging and pleading was a ploy to get me to drop the case.

And it worked. I walked into the police station and told them that I had made everything up. "I was angry at my husband for having an affair," I said, "and I created this story to get back at him." They had never taken me seriously when I was trying to prosecute him. They doubted me when I told them my daughter's safety was compromised. They ignored me when I asked for some kind of protection from Greg. But no one questioned me when I told them I had lied. Twenty minutes after I walked in, there was no longer a case against Greg. Instead, there was a case against me: perjury. It's still on my record. Someone sees it every time I apply for a job that requires a background check. As if it's not bad enough that I have to live with the guilt I feel for putting my husband before my child, the guilt I feel for believing him, and the guilt I feel for going back to him after knowing what he did—on top of that, the general public has access to a record that says I'm a liar.

I don't know how he manipulated me to that point, I really don't. I'm sure my mental and emotional instability had a lot to do with it. I wasn't sleeping, and, of course, I was doing meth to stay awake. I'm glad I was, too, because one night, when I accidentally fell asleep, I woke up to find Greg alone with Trinity. The look on her face told me exactly what he was going to do. That moment convinced me that Gary was not the only abuser. I knew that look. I knew he had done it. And I knew he would do it again.

I left town the next day. I packed the car, putting the girls in first and then fitting as much of our clothing and possessions as I could around them. I went to my grandmother's and borrowed $100 from her. Then, we drove north to Redding, as fast as we could—as though we could outrun all the demons that were chasing us. I had no hopes, no dreams, no ideas about what we might do. I was just holding onto the steering wheel.

61
Patrice

"After that meeting in his medical office, I could tell Bob wanted to reach out to her. I mean, I think he'd do it, if I weren't stopping him." I blurted this out as I walked into my therapist's office, before I even sat down.

"You sound angry about that," Virginia said as she got up to close the door, her stylish asymmetrically cut gray hair swinging as she did so. I'd seen her on and off for years as I'd worked through career changes and the deaths of my parents, so we'd long since done away with the standard formalities.

I wasn't angry about it exactly—more like confused and frustrated by how, while Bob and I saw eye to eye about so many things, we were often not on the same page when it came to Melissa.

Back when Melissa lived with us, she and Bob had a special relationship—one that was much cleaner and less fraught with tension than her relationship with me. It didn't take long for Bob to get attached to her. He was never short with her or critical of her actions, and his generosity towards her was limitless. On an intellectual level, I appreciated his unconditional love, but sometimes it pissed me off. He could watch her explode at me and still rationalize her behavior. In the midst of a conflict, he would see my distress but take her side. Sometimes his justifications of her defiance felt like betrayals. This feeling would be complicated by a sense of relief. I'd think, "At least one parent can keep cool and not overreact." Was he ever hurt by her? Did he ever feel angry?

"I just don't understand how he could think we have the emotional resources to try to connect with her now, given what she's going through. I don't. I can't bear the idea of being rejected by her again, and yet, here he is, willing to just put himself out there. I don't get it." I threw my head back against Virginia's comfortable wing chair.

She folded her hands in her lap. "Well, you and Bob are different people, for starters."

"Yeah." I thought about why I loved this man: He knew something about everything and a lot about many things. He read voraciously about topics ranging from particle physics to history. He taught our kids to fix the plumbing and build a chess table. But, most of all, he gave. He gave 100% to his patients, and then he came home to help in any way he could—pitching in to fix dinner, repairing whatever might be broken around the house. His open heartedness set the stage for bringing Melissa into our family all those years ago.

"We're really similar in a lot of ways. But we're different in one distinct way." Virginia tilted her head, encouraging me to go on. "I have high expectations of most everyone in my world, and I'm not always quiet about those expectations."

"How does that show up?"

"I give a lot to the people I care about, but I hope for some kind of reciprocity. I remember nearly all my friends' birthdays and expect them to remember mine. I cook elaborate meals for people, but I want to be thanked for them."

"And with Melissa? How did that show up with her?"

I pressed my fingers down into the arms of the chair. "I guess I wanted to be thanked. Maybe not verbally so much, but through basic actions, like following my rules. Some of those I never made explicit, like 'no stealing wallets' or 'no lying.' Others, though, like 'do your best in school,' I mean...I repeated those nearly daily. I couldn't have been clearer."

"You think Bob didn't need to be thanked so much?"

I threw my hands up. "I guess not. And his expectations were so much lower. When she did something wrong, he'd always say things like, 'She's had a rough go; she'll get it eventually,' or 'You just need to be patient with her.' But kids need structure. They need rules and expectations to thrive. You and I both know this, right? I mean, it's my mantra: 'Nurturing, limits, and love are the cornerstones of parenting.' I was just trying to give her what I thought she needed, and..." My speech was accelerating as I felt myself get ramped up. Why did it seem like these basic principles had backfired with Melissa? I dropped my head into my hands.

Virginia paused before speaking. "It sounds like, in some ways, you and Melissa weren't a great fit."

I looked up. "What do you mean by that?"

"Well, you're someone that has high expectations and wants to be appreciated. Melissa came from a background where there were no expectations, and I'm guessing there wasn't much of an emphasis on appreciation and thanks in her homes. She may not have had the tools to give you what you needed. So...she pushed back. And I'm guessing pushing back was a kind of survival strategy for her. Why wouldn't she keep up what had worked in the past?"

Not a good fit. These words echoed in my head then and for weeks to come. I had been such a good parent to Ellie and Colin and such a good counselor to many children in schools and in my private practice. I had hoped these successes would translate into helping Melissa start over. Was it possible that Virginia was right? "Not a good fit" made it sound like Melissa's running away hadn't all been my fault.

Virginia let me sit with that for a while. "I know you well enough to know that you apply those high expectations of other people to yourself too. I wonder if that's what's going on here."

I nodded, but, in my head, I still fought back. I should have been able to change her life.

Virginia asked one more question before I left that day: "Is it possible that there are issues that nurturing, limits, and love can't fix?" I didn't have an answer.

62
Melissa

When I first got to my mother's apartment in Redding, all I did was sleep. I wasn't using; once I didn't need to stay awake to guard Trinity, I immediately stopped. I was just exhausted and sad. I had so much ammunition to use against myself, so many examples of what an awful person I'd become. I stopped taking all my meds. I lost sixty pounds, and I was suddenly single. This led to my getting a lot of attention, so I started going out a lot, partying most nights with people in the building. I just wanted to stop feeling so awful.

I left the girls with my mom when I went out, since I knew she would be up all night, anyway. She and her boyfriend did a lot of meth then, so while I wasn't leaving them alone, I wasn't exactly leaving them in good care. I had gotten to a place where I couldn't take care of myself, let alone them. Trinity missed a lot of days of school because I couldn't get her there. I couldn't get out of bed.

After a couple months, my mother told me I needed to leave because I wasn't on her lease. With only $300 a month coming in from welfare and no work to be found, I couldn't contribute to the bills. I did convince her to let the girls keep sleeping inside while I slept outside in the car. Three-year-old Heaven started walking out alone into the street each morning to come and wake me up, and that worried me. I couldn't keep an eye on my kids from the car, and my mother was obviously not watching them. It was clear that I had to keep them by my side no matter what.

In desperation, I started knocking on the doors of complete strangers who I had heard might have extra rooms. One man let us stay with him for a little while. He was young, and he fit the definition of the classic "nice guy," so I didn't feel threatened by him in any way. "I don't have any cash to give you," I said. "I get $300 a month for the three of us, and we eat off of food stamps. But I know how to cook. If you let me stay with you, I will cook you dinner and clean your house until I can get a job and my own place." After a month, his ex-girlfriend found out I was staying there. She decided she wanted to get back together with him, so he kicked me out.

Once we were homeless again, I started spending a lot of time with my cousin. She was doing a lot of drugs, but I hadn't touched meth for eight months. "I know this guy," she said. "He's kind of a 'trick.'"

"What's a 'trick'?"

"You know, an older guy who has money and drugs. He sees a pretty girl and gives her drugs because he wants to have sex with her." I didn't know. This is the kind of thing I learned up in Redding, where there's drugs and poverty everywhere you turn. The ring of people I was running with sold their bodies and stole in order to survive, and they did meth to numb themselves to it all. I didn't blame them.

I went to meet this guy, and, as soon as he opened his windowless wooden door, I started crying. "I just got kicked out of a place. I have nowhere to go. I'll clean your house, I'll cook your food, I'll do the dishes, and, if I find a job, I'll pay you rent. Please help me." He was retired, and he owned his house. In the backyard was a travel trailer, and he let us stay in that. But it was November in the northern California mountains, and, after a week or two, it started to snow.

I asked him if I could stay in the house. "Yeah, you can stay in the house. Wanna come do this stuff with me?" It wasn't really a question; it was more like an arrangement. If you want to sleep inside, you'll do this with me; that's the deal on the table. So, I did it. It was meth, of course.

I never asked for drugs, not once in my life. I never paid for them, I never carried them, and I never did a single deal. They were just always around. Drugs were the social currency of the scene I ran in, and, as a young, attractive woman, I could use whatever I wanted, whenever I wanted by just showing up at the right place at the right time. I knew how to do that.

I thought that doing meth with this guy wasn't that big of a deal. By then, I'd used and quit a handful of times. Trinity and Heaven had a warm place to sleep, and there was food around, always. He wasn't a bad guy, really. But he had his vices, and he had his agenda. On top of having to do drugs with him, I had to deal with sexual advances that grew stronger and stronger until I just couldn't handle any of it anymore. I didn't want to use. I couldn't get the kids to school on time. I was failing.

Right about when I was at my lowest point in Redding, Greg started calling me. I don't know how he got my number. He said he had some questions about our taxes, and I tried to keep the conversation to that. I still had a lot of feelings for him though, and I struggled with them. How could I still care so much about the man who abused my daughter? How could I have feelings for someone who had locked me in a room, lied to me, and cheated on me? I didn't understand this crazy mix of emotions then, and I still don't now. I just know that I could never quite let go of the dream I'd built around him when we met—the one where two kids from totally dysfunctional families find love and a way forward together. My inability to give up on that fantasy kept me from cutting the cord, even though, by that point, I knew it had to happen.

When I told Greg about our living situation, I broke down and said, "We really need help. We can't stay here but don't have anywhere else to go." He called back a few days later to suggest that we move in with his older brother's family in Modesto. I knew that this would probably be a bad idea, since he was still in this other relationship, and he was still using constantly. Plus, Greg almost certainly had an ulterior motive. But it felt like life or death to me. I had been thinking about killing myself every day. I couldn't get the kids to school. I was doing drugs with this man for a warm place to sleep. I felt volatile and fragile, and, most of all, I felt like a complete stranger to myself. I just wanted to get back to the me that I knew I could be.

So, we went to Modesto, to Greg's older brother's house. We only lasted a month at Steve's before he threw us out. The ulterior motive then became clear: Greg was trying to make me look as crazy and unstable as possible. The worse I looked, the better his chances would be to get custody of the kids, and the less likely anyone would believe my story about Trinity's abuse. If Greg had really done what I said he'd done, why would we come back to live near him? We had no other choice, that's why. But our return to Watsonville and Stephanie's house made me look more like the perjurer the police believed me to be. Greg knew all along that there would be no other place for us to go.

I asked Greg not to be there when we were in Stephanie's house. I just couldn't handle the idea of doing meth yet again to stay awake, and, at the time, he was mostly living at Candace's anyway. But, one night, I woke up, and the kids weren't there next to me. I ran out into the yard and found them with Greg in the motorhome behind the house. I looked at Trinity and again saw that expression on her face—the one that said she didn't want to be alone with him. The fear in her eyes triggered all the anger I'd felt when I first found out he was abusing her, not to mention all the confused and painful feelings I still had about my own experiences.

I completely lost it. I started screaming at him and calling him a disgusting pervert and a sick, sick man. "If you ever touch me or touch the kids, I'll kill you! I'll find someone to kill you. I hope you die!" It came out, it just all came out.

He headed right at me and started pushing me against the wall of the trailer. I was whipped up into a frenzy, so I fought back. I scrambled toward the door and stood in it, with Heaven behind me. I couldn't leave the trailer yet because Trinity was trapped in the far corner, behind Greg. Greg started pushing me again, as if he were trying to throw me down the trailer's stairs. I clawed at him to try and hold my position. Finally, he shoved me back so forcefully that I fell backwards out the door, shifting my weight to avoid falling on Heaven. I hit the metal stairs hard, but the tumbling distracted Greg, so Trinity was able to bolt towards us and out the door. I grabbed both of the girls and ran into the house to get my car keys. Greg moved faster than I did and snatched the keys off the bed. He locked all the doors to the house and barricaded us inside. Then, he went after Trinity, yelling at her for "all the things she said about him." I put myself between them, in front of the ratty couch where my daughter had curled up into a ball, crying. I had never seen Greg like this before. I was so terrified that I wet myself.

Meanwhile, the neighbors overheard the commotion and called the police. They arrived and forced Greg to unlock the door. He instantly transformed. In a totally calm voice he said, "It's alright, Officers, this is a misunderstanding. This woman is crazy." But the three of us were crying and trembling on the couch, and they had the neighbor's story, so it was clear that they'd walked into a domestic violence scene.

The cops took the girls and me out of the house and set us up with Families in Transition, the domestic violence service organization that had helped me before. They assigned me a home health care nurse because I'd told them I was suicidal.

"I'm not just thinking about it occasionally," I told them, "I'm actually planning it. I just need to find someone to take care of the kids after I'm gone." That was all the help I got.

I moved back in with Daniel. I hadn't spoken to him for about a year, but, when he saw me, he saw that I had become a ghost of my former self. It showed all over me—in the hollowness of my face, my eyes, and my physique. I had gone from the 250 pounds he last saw me at to the 147 pounds I weighed then. The only word I can use to describe how I was feeling then is "vacant." Emotionally, I couldn't pull it together. It was like the circuits weren't firing, and the power cord had been severed. I knew something was wrong with me, but I didn't know what it was. I knew I needed help; I just didn't know what kind. Daniel saw that and opened his home back up to me.

Still, I felt judged by him. By him, by the girls, by the school—by myself, even. I could not get out of bed to do what I needed to do. The girls were missing school because I couldn't get them there. Daniel took them when he was able to, but he was going through his own struggles with his son's behavioral problems and his dead-end job. I wasn't helping him any by being a marginally functional body in his living space.

I remember thinking about Patrice one night, as I was sitting on Daniel's couch and found a book stashed between the cushions. A book—I hadn't seen or touched one of those in a long time. Patrice would be so sad, I thought. She got so excited when I read on my own—and even more excited when we read together, and I asked questions about the characters or got anxious about what might happen next. I learned to love reading at the Keets' house. Once upon a time, it had been important to me, but it had gotten lost somewhere in my chaotic life. I had always envisioned myself cuddled up in a big armchair, reading to my daughters, but the thought of that was a joke now. I didn't have the time, the space, or the motivation. It felt like just another way in which I had failed.

Greg started coming around again, which further muddled my already messed-up emotions. Just seeing him sparked feelings of powerlessness and feelings of worthlessness, shame, and guilt. I knew we were never going to get back together, but I couldn't turn off the attraction I still had for him and the sense of connection that a decade together had built. "I should be strong enough," I kept telling myself. "I should be able to retract those feelings," but I couldn't, even though I knew being around him was unhealthy. I wasn't telling anyone I was seeing him, although my brother clearly had his suspicions.

Using became a logical decision. I self-medicated during the week so I could get the laundry done and the house cleaned, and, when I got through everything, I would sleep.

I attempted suicide for the second time with a combination of methamphetamine, alcohol, and a bottle of Wellbutrin. I didn't feel any effects at first, but a couple of hours in, I started to hallucinate. Just then, I realized that I was going to die, and I hadn't made a plan for my kids. I panicked and pumped my own stomach by vomiting, drinking tons of water, and then vomiting again until I couldn't taste the pills. Then, I put the girls in the car and drove out to Stephanie's to talk to her about taking the kids. Greg was there. He said, "No, I don't want them. Not by myself. I don't want them if I can't have you." I was exhausted and too scared to return to my brother's, so I spent the night out there. The girls slept in one of the bedrooms, and I stayed up all night with Greg and his girlfriend, figuring that if I was with him, he couldn't get his hands on Trinity. With meth in my system, it was easy to do.

The next morning, I drove the kids to school and then returned to Stephanie's to sleep. The home health care nurse went to Daniel's to check up on me, since I had told her I was planning to kill myself. When she didn't find me there, she drove out to Stephanie's looking for me. She found me there, and I was high.

My kids were taken away from me, and I was taken to jail.

"How could you?" I thought, hating the system and everyone who worked in it. I went to them for help, but instead of helping me, they waited until I did something criminal to act. I had to strip in front of the officers. I had to have my orifices searched and undergo the humiliation of being hauled off to jail. All of this could have been avoided when I told them I was making a concrete plan to kill myself. I should have been evaluated by a mental health professional. Someone should have looked at my cocktail of medications. If I only could have gotten childcare, all of this could have gone very differently. I just needed someone to take care of my kids for a little while so that I could take care of myself. But I could never get that, no matter how hard I tried. You just can't get help until you've done permanent damage to your life.

63
Patrice

The scene at Dale's played itself out one more time, four years later, in 2012. We were, once again, seated around his dinner table, talking about CASA happenings and venting about the politics of the day. During a lull between salad and dessert, Dale asked if we'd heard the latest about Melissa. Bob and I looked blankly at each other and turned to listen to what was coming. She wasn't doing well, Dale said. She'd had another baby girl, but her marriage was over, and she'd been living with her brother. However, the always-tolerant Daniel had finally kicked her out of his house, Dale said. Apparently, Melissa's erratic behavior had become disruptive to him and his newborn son. Dale thought that her behavior was the result of her using drugs. I gasped and made some horrible noise that expressed a combination of shock and sadness. I could feel my pulse quickening as he went on to say that she'd found housing with a friend. My feelings were crowding out logical questions, so I quietly sat there, willing her new living arrangement to be just what she needed.

Dale suggested that we get comfortable in the living room as he got up to clear the table. I remember telling Bob how overwhelmed I felt. I know I mumbled that I couldn't imagine getting involved in Melissa's situation, and I hated hearing myself say that. He put his arm around me, and we both put on smiles as our friends walked in with tea and coffee. I didn't have the stomach to ask more about Melissa.

64
Melissa

I didn't stop using right away. I knew I could stop because I had done so many times in the past; I just didn't want to. When my kids were around, I was doing meth to get the energy I needed to take care of them. Once they were gone, I was using because I just didn't care anymore. I did it because it was there. There was no reward—but there were no consequences either.

I was just waiting to come to a decision. Should I kill myself or try to get my kids back? Can I guarantee that my kids will be safe? If so, then I can kill myself. Maybe they'd be better off in foster care. Besides, no one ever gets their kids back once they've been taken away. My family had assured me that they did everything they were supposed to do and failed. "We fought for you tooth and nail, Missy!" they said. What made me think I could succeed where they hadn't?

I may not have known whether I wanted to live or die, but I knew that, in the meantime, I needed a job. I went back to Carl's Jr., and my old boss hired me right away. I was staying at Stephanie's, of course, and Greg's whole family was pushing me to try to get the kids back. Stephanie was living in an in-law unit behind her mother's house, and her mother made my staying on the property contingent upon going to church on Sundays. I did it, although I was high as a kite every time and had no problem saying that. I was also telling anyone who would listen that I was planning to commit suicide. I just didn't care anymore.

Greg's grandmother signed me up for a Christian women's retreat being held at a facility in the Santa Cruz Mountains. She was paying for it, and I didn't want to be rude, so I went. When her friend came to pick me up for the weekend, I hadn't used in a day or so, but there was definitely meth in my system.

The facility was nestled into a grove of giant redwoods. Barely any light came through their branches, except in the grassy field in front of the assembly hall where the trees had been cleared. The air was saturated with moisture, even though it never rained while I was there. It was like the forest created its own rain, and walking through it felt more like swimming. After the friend dropped me off, I was shown to my cabin. It was a little dark brown building with lichen growing on the sides and a screened door that slapped closed. All I wanted to do was lie down and sleep for a long, long time. But we were required to see the opening speaker, so I made my way over to the assembly hall, which was basically a modern-style church that had a stage, a PA system, and ugly brown wall-to-wall carpeting. I deliberately sat alone and a little apart from everyone else, feeling disconnected and numb.

The opening address was being given by a woman who spoke about her childhood in North Korea. She described how, as a four-year-old, she had been abandoned by her mother at a train station. For the next two or three years, she lived on the streets and was raped by several men. She avoided being murdered three times, and her young life was filled with physical abuse. Her story was truly horrific.

I was listening to her, but, at the same time, I was thinking about my own life experiences. "I know how that feels," I thought. "I know how it feels to be sexually assaulted, I know how it feels to be betrayed by people, and I know how it feels to be shunned by the society that's supposed to be helping you." I was just sitting there on this hard wooden church pew, looking at these built-in shelves with books and little pencils stuck in them, running down a list of all of the shit that I'd been through, tallying it up in my mind. "I'm so young—just twenty-seven. I already have a seven-year-old and a four-year-old. I've been married. I'm probably going to be divorced soon. I've been homeless. I've been raped. I've been abused. I've been kidnapped. And now, I'm broken. Really, really broken."

It was the first time in my life I ever felt the unbelievably heavy weight of everything I'd been through, the overwhelming amount of crap that I'd endured. "After all of that, now—*just now*—am I broken!" I said to myself. So many people would have given in so much sooner. It took that incredible list of horrors to get me to break.

It suddenly dawned on me that I wasn't weak at all—that, in fact, I was strong. *Really* strong. "Maybe I don't want to be strong anymore, but I am," I told myself. "This is who I am. Not everybody gets to have the strength that I have."

And then, I just sat there and cried. I cried a river of totally effortless tears. I could not control the flow; it just poured out of me without any strain on my face, without anxiety in my mind, and without any fear in my heart. It was a complete and total release. I didn't question what was happening; I just sat in that moment and let it happen. And, when I was finally done, I left. I walked back across the sunny clearing to the woods that surrounded my cabin. I stood there with my hand on the doorknob for a minute, encircled by huge, shaggy redwood trunks on all sides. I followed the path of one particularly thick one up and up and up, into the canopy where its branches intertwined with all the others. Then I took a deep breath, drawing in the musty air of the forest. My blouse stunk from my own smell, and it was soaked with sweat and tears. I peeled it off right there on the doorstep. Then I walked into the cabin, crawled up into the top bunk, and went to sleep before anyone could talk to me.

I woke up the next morning and tried to analyze what had happened. I was at a Christian women's retreat after all, so I knew everyone was going to say I was "touched by Jesus." I didn't—and don't—believe that, so part of me didn't want to talk about it. Do I believe I was touched by something? Possibly. But was it Jesus? Was it God? I don't know. What I do know is that whatever happened in there was profound enough to rewire my psyche. Whatever it was completely reframed my entire way of thinking. I realized that I was so strong and so capable, and, in doing so, I forgave myself—for everything. Then, I experienced a vivid and undeniable sense of not being alone. I was surrounded by a very warm aura, a very comforting resonance. I could sense support all around me, and I rested in it.

I did end up describing the experience I'd had to some of the people at the retreat. I was honest with them. I said I wasn't really sure what happened or what I should call it. I let them perceive it however they wanted to; after all, I was along for the ride. And, of course, Greg's grandmother was thrilled to hear that I'd had this profound experience.

In the end, what mattered is that something shifted for good.

One week later, I appeared in court. The judge outlined all the steps I'd have to take to get my kids back. There's a reason why many people never go through with it—the list of tasks is daunting. If I hadn't just had a life-changing experience, I probably would have lost all hope right then and there. But I was determined.

I tried meth one more time, a few months later, to see if I wanted the feeling again. No way. It was completely revolting. Any desire I had to use flipped itself off like a light switch and

I stopped using drugs altogether. Meanwhile, I was in mandatory drug counseling, labeled as an addict; only, I was not going through any of the experiences that other people were describing. I needed their signatures on my attendance sheets, so I played the role, just like I had done in those AA meetings. And, just like in those AA meetings, I felt like a fraud.

In addition to the drug counseling, I also had to go to personal counseling and family counseling. I had weekly parenting classes, drug classes, and periodic visitations with the girls in their foster home. I was working thirty-five hours a week at Carl's Jr. and taking the bus everywhere. More than a few times, I just broke down at work. I'd show up there and cry and cry—because I missed my kids and had made such bad choices, but also because I was exhausted to the core. My boss and I were good friends by then, and she'd just say, "Missy, take as long as you need. Get it all out, and then, when you're ready, you can go take some orders."

Somehow, I was managing all of it—except for my living situation. I was beginning to feel like living with Stephanie and her mom might cause everything to crumble. Greg and I had concocted a plan that we thought would move the reunification process along faster: presenting a united front. He had seen children in his family taken away from their parents permanently, and, of course, I had *been* one of those children. We were convinced we needed all the ammunition we could find to have a chance at getting the kids back. I didn't want to work with him, but, in the eyes of the law, Greg was still a viable custodian for the girls. I was the one with the multiple criminal charges, and I was the one the authorities believed to be a liar. I thought that if we stuck it out together, eventually he'd show his true colors. Everyone would see that I was the responsible one, and their opinions of me would shift. So, I went along with the "functional couple" facade.

I couldn't make that illusion last for more than a month.

The family counseling sessions that included all four of us were painful. Greg was doing his best to win an Academy Award, acting like the perfect father that none of us had ever seen. Then, as expected, he stopped showing up. Because we were on the case together, I was being held accountable for his lack of attendance. I didn't want him taking me down again.

I broke down and confessed everything to CPS. I told them that Greg and I had been performing for them. I explained why I was so afraid of his getting custody of the kids. I told them about the abuse, and I explained that the perjury I had committed was not in telling the police about the abuse, but in telling the police that the abuse was a fabrication. I said I was living at Stephanie's with Greg because I literally had nowhere else to go.

Finally, the system started to support me. CPS separated my case from Greg's and got me into a sober housing project in Capitola for people with drug charges who are working to kick their addictions. If you're homeless and this "significant life stressor" puts you at risk of sliding back into drug or alcohol abuse, CPS can put you in a rent-free sober living situation. As I'd learned, when you're at rock bottom, you can get services—but not until then. The house was near the mall and had a little patio and a succulent garden out back. I shared a room with an older woman. Living there came with a bunch of additional required meetings, like regular AA or NA gatherings, again, as well as curfews and scheduled chores to fit into my already crammed schedule. I had to get signoffs on everything I did and show my signatures to the woman who ran the house. But I wasn't at Stephanie's, and that's what counted. I stayed there for eight months.

65
Patrice

"I can't believe I'm still dealing with this, but here we are again," I told Virginia a few weeks after Dale had shared his news about Melissa. I explained what had happened and how paralyzed I'd felt listening to his story. "All the progress I've made, and here I am, fifteen years later, slipping back into beating myself up about my failure with Melissa."

Virginia took a deep breath and exhaled loudly. "Okay. I'm thinking we should try something different today," she said in her always-soothing deep voice. "Something I know you do all the time when you work with families." She stood up and walked over to her supply closet. She pulled out a small bag of magic markers and an oversized sketch pad. "I haven't used these in a while, so this will be fun for me, too." She put the art supplies down on the coffee table in front of me. "I want you to draw your relationship with Melissa. You can take that to mean whatever you want. Just put the pens on the paper and go for it. I'm going to go out to the lobby to get some tea. Take your time."

I pulled a cap off the red marker, inhaling that familiar acrid scent. I felt a little silly holding it and was glad Virginia wasn't there to watch me. How could I draw this relationship? I bit my lip, laid back in the chair, and closed my eyes. This was ridiculous. I opened my eyes and looked around this office where I felt so comfortable. There was the photo of Big Sur on one wall, another of Yosemite, and another of the Grand Canyon. The Grand Canyon—that place where the differences between Melissa and me became so obvious, so difficult to cross, like the canyon itself.

That was it. I'd draw us with a chasm between us. I made a line to indicate land, then a big ditch, then another line on the other side. On the right side of the canyon, I drew myself, poised at the lip, stretching my hand out as far as I could into the empty space. I tried to show that the figure was as close to falling in as she could be, even though my stick figure drawing skills didn't make that obvious. I put Melissa on the other side, standing with both feet firmly planted, as she always seemed to do. I added crossed arms and a frown. It looked like something halfway between a standoff and Michelangelo's "The Creation of Adam." Virginia came back with tea for both of us, and I showed her what I had.

"Okay, yeah. So, I'm seeing a gap between you two, one that looks hard to cross. That makes sense, given all the differences we've talked about—cultural differences, differences in values, differences in habits." I nodded. "Do you need to add anyone else to this picture, or is the relationship really just about you two?

Right, of course there should be more people in the drawing. I put Bob next to me, in a more solid position where he could hold onto on to me but still be close to the edge. Then I drew Ellie and Colin back behind him. I added my father, Richard, back a little further. He'd passed away in the intervening years, but he still belonged in this family portrait. I showed Virginia the picture again.

She nodded silently. "What else belongs on your side besides people? How about the things you're offering her? Why don't you go ahead and add those in."

That was easy. I grabbed a different color and drew a big house. While I was at it, I drew a school next to it, as well as a bike and a pile of toys. I added a dollar sign to the air around the house and a shopping cart to represent groceries. “I mean, I could go crazy here,” I said after a few minutes. “I could add clothes and a diploma and a college account and an airplane to symbolize all the trips we would have taken—and a big set of arms for the endless support.” I could feel my throat tightening.

“Okay, then maybe add a couple of those—just to show there’s a lot of stuff there behind you.” When I was done, I pushed the sketch book back over to her. “That’s a lot. There’s a lot being offered over there.”

“That’s just it,” I said. “As I’ve asked myself a million times, how could she have rejected all of that?”

She nodded and shrugged but didn’t say anything for a while. Then she pointed to all the white space behind Melissa. “So, do you think anyone belongs on that side, behind Melissa?”

“You mean supporting her? No. There’s no one over there; there never was. Why wouldn’t she just make the leap?”

“Are you sure no one belongs on her side? What about her birth family?”

“They were telling her she should run away and go back to them! They were holding her back.”

Virginia tilted her head. “That sounds like ‘negative support,’ right? Seems like that could go in there.” I put Paula and Vera, her mother and grandmother, behind her. And Daniel, of course. Then, I drew a couple of squares and streets to represent Watsonville as an area—a concept, almost. “So, these people—and forces, I guess, since you’ve got a whole city in there—you said they were holding her back, yes? Can you indicate that somehow?”

“Yeah, sure.” I drew some arms from her birth family, to show them tugging on her and keeping her from getting over the gap.

“And how about Joe and Kristin? Where do they go?”

"Huh, yeah. Good question." I stopped just short of rolling my eyes. "I mean, they should be in the middle, with one leg on each side, helping me grab Melissa's hand. But they didn't really end up there." I reached for another color. "Maybe I'll just put them in the air over the chasm, like they could see and hear more than I could." I started putting stick figures up there, but they looked too much like angels, so I drew exaggerated elephant-like ears on them. They extended close enough to Melissa as to both smother her and make it impossible for Bob or me to get a word in.

Virginia watched me further clutter the piece of paper. "It's looking pretty messy in there. And I don't think that's just a result of your drawing skills."

"Yeah, I suppose there are a lot of players. And this doesn't even count the parts at war inside of her. Or any of us, for that matter."

She turned the drawing around and looked at it more carefully. "So, Melissa can't make it across this ditch even if she does jump because she's got all these folks clutching at her. And you're on the other side trying to hand her all these gifts." I nodded as she kept studying my scrawl as though it were a museum piece. Finally, she placed the pad back on the coffee table and looked up at me. "What's interesting to me is that she's got her arms folded. What do you think about that—the way you drew her arms?"

She was in that position so often. Defensive, protective, ornery. "She took that stance all the time. Against me, against the world." And it pissed me off, even though I was able to recognize where it came from. "I know it was her way of blocking all the shit that came her way. You know, given what she grew up with, she had to protect herself."

"Yeah. It still hurt you though, it sounds like." I nodded. "So, in order to protect herself from the shit, she has to bury her hands in her arms. Kind of hard to accept gifts in that position, isn't it?"

I felt a twisting sensation in my gut. Of course. *Of course.* You can't fold your arms in defense and open them to accept love at the same time.

I looked at the drawing again, thinking about the stick figures clinging to Melissa as well as all of the other ones I didn't draw but could have—her stepfather, her Aunt Jenny, some of her previous foster parents, other girls she lived with—and I saw the complex, knotted mess, to which I could have also added Child Protective Services, the foster care system, issues of income inequality and education inequality, and so much more.

I closed my eyes and felt the burn behind their lids. The tears leaked out, and I sensed that they might be flowing for a while.

66
Melissa

Of all the things I had to do, visiting the girls at their foster home was the hardest. They'd been placed in the same house together, which was fortunate. It was a lot like the Larsons', the home I had lived in after leaving the Keets', only it was in Watsonville, off Freedom Boulevard. There was a special needs girl living there, so there were always a lot of grunting and yelping noises in the background. The first few visits were supervised by CPS employees to make sure that the girls weren't at risk. I had to go into them numb. Those disassociation skills I had developed from my own childhood trauma served me well, since you can't be too emotional when the supervisors are scrutinizing you. If you're too emotional, then the kids are emotional, and that looks bad. If you're not emotional enough, then they think you don't care. It's a lot like being on trial.

Trinity and Heaven almost always cried. They wanted to be with me and just didn't understand that I had no control over that. My heart ached to see them so sad and so confused, and, at the same time, I kept flashing back to being in their exact position. It became hard for me to separate their experiences from mine, which made the emotional charge even more powerful. I decided to focus only on what would help the girls get through this. "What was it I needed to hear when I was in their shoes?" I asked myself. I needed reassurance. I needed to know that I wasn't being abandoned. I needed to know that I was going to be okay. So, that's what I told them during our visits. "Even though you feel lonely, and it's scary, and you don't know what's going on, know that everything is going to be okay," I said, "And you know that I love you, right? Well, that's all you need to know." I also remembered that, when I was in their shoes, I had felt guilty for what had happened. I was certain that I was the cause of all the trouble. If I had been a better kid, or if I hadn't caused my mother so much stress, things might have turned out differently. I couldn't bear the thought of Trinity and Heaven coming to those conclusions, so I kept saying, "There's nothing that you did wrong. There's nothing you can do to change the way things are right now. That's my job. Trust me to do that." Over and over, I said, "This is not your fault. It was my responsibility to take care of you and keep you safe, and I lost that privilege. Now, I am going to get it back."

At the same time, the girls told me horrible things about the home they were living in. Heaven had become the "whipping boy" of the household. The mother blamed her for everything that happened. She mocked her and isolated her. Not only did this make me angry at their foster mother, it brought up my own painful memories of eating behind the stairs and being told I was too ugly to sit with the other kids.

The girls had both been assigned CASA advocates, and, when I told their advocates about the environment in the house, they offered to stand behind me in whatever course of action I wanted to take. If I complained and had them removed from the house, there was no guarantee that they'd be placed together again—nor was there any guarantee that the next house would be any better than this one. Of course, I had rolled the dice again and again by running away when I was a foster kid. I had been willing to take that risk for myself, but I was not willing to take it with my children. "We just need to wait it out," I told the CASA volunteers. And, to Heaven, I said, "Remember, it's not you. It's her. Do the best that you can. She doesn't need to like you because you have me, and I love you."

June 24, 2011, was a big day—one of those days I will always remember. I was awarded custody of my children after only ten months.

I knew things had been going well; I had been doing everything they asked me to do. I had attended every class, meeting, and court date assigned to me and collected every signature I needed. I had formulated a "reunification plan" that included setting up a support network, finding childcare, and renting a place where children were allowed.

I had to leave the sober housing project because kids weren't permitted to live there. My nine dollar-per-hour job at Carl's Jr. didn't allow me to get my own place, so I moved into a shelter for women in recovery run by the Salvation Army. There were eight women and their children living together in one building. Each family had its own bedroom, but we all shared a kitchen. I had to pay rent on a sliding scale because I had a job. Only one other woman in the house was working; the rest were not, and they didn't need to pay for their housing. On top of that, my food stamp benefit was reduced because of my "supplemental" nine dollar-per-hour income. I couldn't collect welfare at that time because I had already been on it for five years. In addition, I could never collect welfare for Heaven because I got pregnant with her while I was already receiving assistance.

I stayed in the women's shelter for about a year until I felt held back by that environment. I had outgrown it, and yet, I didn't have anywhere else to go. I moved back in with Daniel.

As if working to get my kids back hadn't been enough, I decided to take on the process of closing my criminal cases at the same time. I had the perjury charge out there, which I had been appearing in court for periodically. There was also the drug case that was connected to both the perjury case and the child neglect case; by attending drug classes and rehab sessions, I was working towards getting that one removed from my record. The third case concerned my drivers' license, which had been revoked back when I was in Redding. I had accumulated tickets because I had to keep appearing in Watsonville for court dates associated with the perjury charge, and driving was my only way to get there. In Redding, I had driven folks around in an unregistered vehicle on a suspended license in exchange for cash—cash which I used to buy groceries—and I had gotten more tickets that way. Every ticket I'd received had fines and "failures to appear" tacked onto it, and, during the six-month period when I got these tickets, I had no job and no money to pay those fines.

In December of 2011, I had an appointment at the county courthouse to close my last case. I put on a dress suit and walked into a drab courtroom in downtown Santa Cruz. I had just gotten promoted at work, and I'd gone to the salon and had my hair dyed for the first time in years—red with plum undertones and platinum highlights. That made me the brightest thing in the place. I walked up to the bailiff with a thick file of paperwork, including records of every AA meeting I'd attended, a certificate of completion for family preservation court, a certificate of completion for an outpatient drug counseling program, a certificate of completion for my time in the sober housing program, and a certificate of completion for parenting class. The woman with all those charges no longer existed. She had been replaced with someone new.

Judge Gallagher looked over the file, handed it to the bailiff to hand back to me, and said, "I just want to take a moment to acknowledge all of your accomplishments, Melissa. When you first came in here, you were at a low point. I look at you today with all of these successes and all these accomplishments and I see them in your face. Your changes show."

I broke the cycle.

PART III

67
Melissa

When CASA approached me about giving the speech, I couldn't say no. Never mind that I had never spoken in public before; I just knew I had a story to tell, and I knew I was the perfect person to tell it.

The idea was to provide the audience with the parental perspective on the CASA experience. Trinity's and Heaven's CASA advocates were instrumental in helping all three of us get through those ten months of time apart. Since I'd had my own CASA advocate as a kid—Kristin—I had this unique 360-degree view of what the organization did. Back then, I had no idea what Kristin's role was. I didn't realize how much continuity she provided, how steady and regular a presence she was in my life. I just didn't get it until I got it, and that happened when my girls were taken away from me. Only then was I able to appreciate everything CASA had done for me growing up.

The way I saw it, this speech could be my way of expressing my gratitude. I sure hadn't thanked anyone when I was little, and it seemed about time to do so.

I knew I'd need some backup for my first-ever speaking engagement, so I called my best friend, Julie. Julie knew my whole story, and she agreed to come along for the ride.

I can get pretty excited about dressing up for important occasions, so it didn't take much to convince me that giving this speech required a new dress and pair of heels. I even did my hair up really nicely, and I was feeling pretty good when I left Daniel's place in Watsonville. The girls and I were sharing a one-bedroom apartment with him and his son at that time, and I was working nights at Burger King. I couldn't get that night off, but I was on the late shift. I knew I had enough time to make the speech and grab a bite to eat before I needed to show up.

The fundraiser was an afternoon banquet at Chaminade, a luxury hotel in the mountains above Santa Cruz. "I think I ate there one time, with the Keets," I said to Julie. As we drove up the winding roads in my yellow Chevy Cobalt, I said, "This is so weird, but I know that this is exactly where I am supposed to be at this moment. Something important is going to happen, I just know it." It was so certain, as if I had proven it with a scientific formula, beyond a reasonable doubt. We both got all emotional, so I had to pull over to the side of the road. We sat there for a few minutes, crying our eyes out and laughing at ourselves at the same time. I had to be careful not to make a mess of my mascara, so I took some deep breaths. Then, I pulled back out into the road and proceeded to make a bunch of wrong turns.

When we arrived at the parking lot, I got nervous. I realized that I wouldn't know anyone there. "It's a good thing I made Julie come with me," I thought. We walked inside together. I grabbed a glass of wine, but I couldn't sip it because my hand was shaking so powerfully. Julie was eating hors d'oeuvres off every passing tray, and she tried to lighten the mood by saying, "Oh, *this* is what rich people do with their afternoons. I could get used to this!" We spotted Anne, Heaven's CASA advocate, across the room and found seats at her table. It was then that I looked around at the sea of faces in the banquet hall. There were over two hundred of them. My stomach seized up with fear. I noticed the tiny square podium—the one I would have to climb up to in my stiletto heels and cocktail dress. The little steps leading to it had no railing.

"Julie, what if I fall?" I said, in a panic. "Now I know what Miss America worries about!"

I scanned the room again and noticed two familiar faces: Judge Gallagher and Judge Guy. They were seated together at the next table over. Judge Gallagher was the county's family court judge at the time, but he'd previously been the criminal judge. Judge Guy was the current criminal judge, but she'd previously been the family court judge. I had been seen in both of their courts—and it hadn't been for pretty stuff. I took another deep breath. Then, as I looked over towards Judge Gallagher again, I remembered what he'd said to me after he closed out my criminal case.

Judge Gallagher went up to the podium and recited a beautiful poem about CASA, so I was already crying when it was my turn to take the stage. Apparently, I didn't fall on my way up there, but I know the first thing I said when I got to the stage was, "I'm so nervous!" After that, I don't remember any of it. I have a copy of the speech I gave but no memory of saying any of the words. I do remember feeling like everything was happening in slow motion, and I know that, at the end, everyone was standing and clapping and crying. At that point, I was relieved, mostly because I was no longer crying alone. Thankfully, someone helped me down off the stage and escorted me back to my table because I'm not sure if I would have found my way alone. Along the way, I shook a lot of hands and was thanked by a lot of people. "That was really brave," one said. "People really need to hear what you have to say," another commented. "Thank you for your courage."

Back at the table, I chugged a glass of water and then got up to leave. I knew we needed to get moving if I was going to make it to Burger King on time.

68
Patrice

It *was* our Melissa. There she was—a real person—an adult, even, looking healthy and vibrant and telling her story. I hadn't recognized her until the end of her talk, but when she mentioned that her CASA advocate was named Kristin, a picture of her as a ten-year-old child came together in my mind like an old Polaroid slowly developing. A part of me wanted to run up and envelop her in a giant hug, but the bigger part of me wanted to run like hell.

"So that's the story of me and my girls. Thank you to CASA and to all of you here," Melissa said to wrap up. The room went silent. She hunched her shoulders, pursed her lips, and tucked her chin to her chest. I'd seen this gesture before when she'd felt self-conscious as a child. The sound of chairs being scraped back along the shiny wooden floor replaced the silence, and, in one fluid movement, everyone in my line of vision stood up and started clapping. Melissa's head jerked up, and a huge smile spread across her face as she looked from one side of the room to the other.

After Bob and I had recognized Melissa and collapsed into one another, we'd continued to clutch at each other's arms until the applause erupted. Then, I felt Bob's firm grip under my armpits as he helped me to my feet. My hands shook as I reached for my water glass. After my fingers brushed the rim, I watched the full glass topple over, soaking the cluttered tablecloth, and finally pulled away from him. "I'm so sorry, honey, but I've gotta get out of here. I...I... need air." When I reached down for my purse, I had to steady myself by grabbing the back of my seat. I stuffed my bag under my arm, turned, and fled through the nearby door.

Out in the corridor, I pulled out my phone to call Ellie, who, by that time, was thirty-seven and living in Baltimore. I trembled as I muttered, "Oh, Ellie, please be there. I need you; I need you." I wanted her to tell me I was okay. I needed to hear that I had been a good mother. My call went to voicemail.

The metal railing along the wall supported me as I made my way, hand-over-hand, down the hall ramp to the bathroom. Jimmy from the CASA office hurried toward me carrying a large bouquet of flowers that I figured were for Melissa. I fussed with my hair and gave him a cursory nod. When I got to the ladies' room, I pushed the door open with my whole body. Then, I walked a few feet inside, leaned against the wall, and sank to the floor. I brought my knees up to my chest, curled into a ball, and let the tears that had been pressing against my eyelids flow. Through my sobs, I heard a familiar voice. I lifted my head slightly and saw my old friend Cindy standing at one of the marble sinks in front of me.

"Oh my God, are you okay?" Cindy asked, watching me in the mirror. She turned, lowered herself to the floor next to me, and encircled me with her arms. "What's the matter?"

I took in a gulp of air. "I feel like I might throw up." My sobs got louder and tumbled out on top of each other. "That was Melissa up there speaking. I just can't believe it. Right there, in front of us." Cindy and I met when we first moved to Santa Cruz, and she knew all about our time with Melissa.

I curled up tighter on the tiled floor and dug my fingernails into my shins. I felt Cindy's arms around me as she patted my hair. "Bob and I didn't even recognize her until near the end of her speech. Twenty years later, and with a different last name." I closed my eyes. "What if we had just kept her—or if we didn't let her get away?" I let my chin hit my chest and covered my face with my bent arm. "I only heard part of her horrible story. Her life could have been so different if, if...."

"Do you think you'll talk to her?"

"God, I don't know. What could I ever say to her?" Cindy walked over to get a paper towel and wet it under the faucet. As I watched her, I could see in the wall-sized mirror that my mascara had made black drizzles down my face. My eyes were puffy, and my skin was covered with red blotches.

There was a knock on the bathroom door. I watched it open slightly and heard Bob's voice come through, asking the same question I'd been asked twenty years earlier, in my office at Capitola Elementary: "Do you want to come and meet Melissa?"

Did I? Yes. No. Maybe? I really didn't know. "I'll be there in a minute," I shouted through the door. Then, I shook out my hands and pushed myself up. With Cindy's help, I got to the sink and threw cold water on my face, making my mascara run even more. My carefully arranged hair now stood up in clumps. Fixing myself up was hopeless.

What would Melissa think of me? I was a pathetic mess—an older version of the distraught, pleading woman she had last seen when she packed her bags. "Cindy, I'm such a sight. Can I really go out there looking like this?" I fussed with my scarf.

"You're okay. Just go out and be yourself." She hugged me and opened the door. Bob was leaning against the wall with his eyes closed.

"Honey, I'm a wreck. Do you think this is a good idea right now?" I grabbed the collar of his shirt. "Have you already talked with her? Where is she?"

"It's okay. You'll be fine. *We'll* be fine." He ran his fingers through my hair. "I just went up to her after she came down off the stage and told her who I was. I thought she was going to collapse into the arms of the woman next to her." He told me that when Melissa got her bearings, she reached out and took his hand, looked around, and asked where I was. "I asked her if she had time to meet you, and she grabbed me tighter. She nodded, and I saw tears come to her eyes. I told her I'd go get you."

Together, we made our way back to the ballroom. We'd only taken about a dozen steps when I saw a group of three or four people coming at us, led by Melissa. She seemed to be galloping toward me, tall and sturdy, with her hand undoing her braid so that her long hair swung loosely as she moved. I froze, pulled my shoulders and head back, and squeezed Bob's hand in a death grip. Melissa loomed before me, larger than life. Meanwhile, I felt like I was actually shrinking. I took a deep breath and let go of Bob's hands. Melissa and I collided in the middle of the hall. She wrapped me in her bare arms and pulled me tight to her. When our cheeks pressed together, I was flooded by the odors of floral perfume and sweat.

"I'm so sorry I hurt you," she whispered. "I love you so much. I never should have left."

My full weight collapsed into her. "Oh, Melissa, honey." I closed my eyes and breathed her in. I buried my head beneath her chin and kneaded my fingers into her back. She, too, was sobbing, shaking, and gulping air. We stayed in our tight embrace until I felt Bob's hand on my arm. He stepped closer, encircled both of us, and dropped his face into the mass of our wet hair. I could feel his chest heaving. I don't know how long we stood there.

69
Melissa

Julie and I were collecting our things from the table when a man stopped me and said, "There's someone here you should meet." I paused and spun around, and there was Bob. I wrapped my arms around him and gave him a long, long hug. There was no awkwardness at all, just intense feeling. Of course, I asked where Patrice was, and he said he'd go find her. Someone ushered me out of the banquet room and around the corner. And there she was, in the middle of the hall, just looking at me with the same open, generous face I remembered.

"I love you," I said.

After that, everything became a whirlwind of emotion and activity. There was hugging and sobbing and gasping and talking, and, to top it off, somewhere in there, Judge Gallagher came by to ask me if I'd be willing to do more public speaking for the court.

In the parking lot, Julie said, "Missy, what you said in the car—you were right! You're exactly where you need to be!"

70
Patrice

Bob shepherded Melissa and me through the closest open doorway and into a long conference room. I don't remember who started talking first, since we couldn't seem to get our words out fast enough. I asked Melissa about her girls. She told us that Trinity was twelve and Heaven was nine. But, before I could find out more, Melissa waved her hand and barraged us with questions about our family, starting with my father. I explained that he had passed away seven years prior but had been able to live with us for most of that time. "Richard was a really wonderful man," she said. "I'm so sorry." She reminisced about how good he had been to her—the many meals he'd cooked for her, the rides he'd given her to and from school, the time they spent together watching TV. "We were buddies. I remember when he used to take me to McDonald's after school, and it would feel like we were kids breaking your 'no fast food' rule." As she said that, I realized that Melissa was talking to me like a grown-up—a sympathetic and caring grown-up. She was meeting me as an equal in my loss. We had both experienced the loving, fun-spirited man who indulged her wants, as he had mine when I was a child. That bond had never occurred to me before.

When she asked about Ellie and Colin, I tried to keep my responses general, feeling self-conscious about my embarrassment of riches. Where my own children were in their lives seemed too perfect, and the last thing I wanted to do was draw too much of a contrast between their situations and hers. "They're both doing fine," I answered.

"I want to know about Colin," Melissa insisted. "I remember him so well. We were only what, three or four years apart? But he always seemed a lot older than me." Blushing, she added, "And, I remember his friend Jared, who I always had a crush on." She wasn't going to let her questions be brushed off. She'd wanted to fill in the blanks of the twenty years that had passed and make my kids real people again.

"Colin married his high school sweetheart. They met at sixteen, so you wouldn't have known her." I told her they lived in Santa Cruz and had two adorable daughters, four and six years old.

"Does he work here? What does he do?" Her blue eyes seemed extra wide. I explained that he'd become an internal medicine doctor, like Bob. When Melissa heard that Ellie was a pediatrician specializing in allergy research at Johns Hopkins Hospital, she turned to the small audience of onlookers that had joined us and took a couple of steps back. She waved her hand towards Bob and me and said, between sobs, "See, that could have been me." She hung her head. I felt like I'd been kicked in the belly.

While I was trying to figure out how to respond to that, a man who I remembered seeing on the podium walked up to Melissa. He introduced himself as the juvenile court judge and thanked her for sharing her story. "That's a hard thing to do," he said. "You were wonderful up there." He went on to ask Melissa if she knew about the court's speakers' program. When Melissa nodded her head no, the judge explained it and asked her if she would be willing to be one of their featured speakers. "Your story could help other people who are struggling."

Not missing a beat, Melissa stood up straighter, locked eyes with him, and said, "Thank you. I would be very happy to do that." As she went on to talk with the judge about how they could connect, I noticed that Melissa was speaking with him as if he were a peer. And, in turn, she was being respected and honored for having made it against great odds. We had just heard that she'd worked her way through sexual abuse, poverty, neglect, abandonment, drug abuse, and the loss of her own two daughters to foster care. Now, she was going to be a positive force in the judicial system.

Melissa was owning her own success—the success that she had experienced without us. In that moment, I realized that, as horrible as parts of her story were, they were hers. They were *her* failures and *her* successes. Her journey had been her own.

71
Melissa

Even now, I still sometimes think about how things might have been if I hadn't run away from the Keets'. I would have graduated from college long before I did. I'd probably still be single. I wouldn't have kids. I might be a doctor, like Ellie and Colin, or a lawyer, which is what I wanted to be when I was little. At this point in my life, it's clear that I'm not going to be either of those, which in some ways is sad and in others is just fine. But, if I had stayed with the Keets, I wouldn't have my kids. They're the only good things that came out of all my crappy mistakes, and I wouldn't trade them in for anything.

And yet, if I had to do it over, I wouldn't. I say that not only because I wouldn't want to experience the pain again, but also because I could never ask my children and the many other people who were pulled into my story to be harmed in seeing me harm myself. I can live with the consequences that my choices have had on me; I have a lot more trouble living with the consequences my choices have had on my loved ones—Trinity, in particular.

72
Patrice

"Well, Miss Superstar, it's time to get you out of here and off to work," Anne said, as she put an arm around Melissa. "The real world calls."

"Yeah, *that*. Back to the grease and a stinky kitchen!" She wondered out loud what might be waiting for her this evening: what equipment might have broken down, who might have called in sick, what deliveries might be late. A smile crossed her face as she stood taller and ran her hands down the sides of her shiny dress. "But, thank God, at least I have a job."

While Julie and Melissa collected their things, Anne twisted toward me and caught me in a tight embrace. We'd known each other casually for years from CASA work, but I had no idea she had a connection to Melissa. She grabbed my hand, pressed a piece of paper into my palm, and said, "Call me!"

Bob and I stood in stunned silence watching them disappear. I leaned into him. "Take me home, please."

What I had expected to be a relaxing social evening had instead been an emotional rollercoaster of shock, fear, relief, and joy. When I finally went up to our bedroom to change out of my party clothes, I sat on the bed and gazed up at the bank of family photos on the sage green wall. There was a sepia print of Bob's father, Ernest, an internal medicine physician who had handed down the art and love of healing to Bob, Ellie, and Colin. Alongside his picture was one of my own parents, Richard and Eleanor, on their wedding day. Richard was handsome in his Navy uniform, and my mother looked healthy and gorgeous even after a crowded cross-country train ride from Upstate New York to California. The fresh faces of our own four grandchildren tickling each other on a trampoline brought a smile to my face. Then I blinked as my eyes came to rest on the only professional family portrait we ever had taken. "Christmas 1993" was written in a script-style font at the bottom of the photo.

I got up to look at it more closely. Melissa sat front and center surrounded by Ellie and Colin. Bob stood like a carved Greek statue behind me with his hands holding the elbows of my formal black jacket. My hair was short and curly, and I stared straight ahead while clutching Melissa's shoulder possessively. My father looked dignified and serious. Really, Melissa was the only one in the photo who looked comfortable. She looked like a child model showing off her lace-collared, flowered dress. Her blonde hair was pulled back and tied with a bow, and, in her self-confident pose, I could see the resemblance to the thirty-one-year-old woman I had just watched on stage.

I remember thinking at the time of the photo shoot, "This is our new family, and we've succeeded in making Melissa a part of it." I could still conjure up the joy and awe I'd felt at the idea of having three children. I guess I'd thought that memorializing the moment in a photo would ensure the permanence of those feelings and the situation that created them.

I took the picture off its hook and held it tight against my t-shirt. As my tears made dark blotches on the paper backing, the longing for what I had hoped for back then returned. And even though I'd stopped assuming full responsibility for what I used to call my "failure" with Melissa, the disappointment I continued to feel pushed against the walls of my chest. I could sense a migraine coming on. Still clutching the picture, I made my way downstairs to the sunroom where Bob was drinking tea. I grabbed an ice pack from the freezer and lay down on the cushioned bench, tucking an oversized chenille pillow under my head. Then I slid the photo across the table to him.

He leaned forward to look at it, then he grimaced and closed his eyes. When he opened them, he said, "I texted Melissa to set up lunch for the three of us. Are you free on Tuesday at noon if she can make it?" His voice had the weight of both excitement and weariness.

"Yes."

73
Melissa

I talked a mile a minute the whole way down the hill. Julie drove, since I was shaking all over. "Julie, I just knew there would be something special about this night. I can't believe it—the Keets, the speech, the judges—everything! I mean, I just feel like my intuition is so right on lately. I'm on the right path, and everything is telling me that." I was blown away by re-meeting Patrice and Bob and floored by the crowd's reception of my speech. But I was just as amazed by the fact that I had known in my gut that something special was going to happen at that event. "Julie, pull over!" I shouted, as we approached the scenic vista on Highway 1.

Julie swerved into the big parking lot about five miles north of Watsonville. The sun was hovering just above the horizon. "I know we're tight on time, but I just need to sit here and soak this in for a moment." This lot was the only spot along the freeway with a view of the Monterey Bay, and we were just in time for sunset. I sat and took deep breaths, watching the sun get bigger as it descended, watching the light splash on the water in different patterns. I just needed to stop moving, to let everything catch up with me—at least until the sun vanished. "Okay, let's go," I finally said.

Julie drove us to her house, then I hopped in the driver's seat and headed to Burger King. I was a little late, so I slid in the back door and went straight to the bathroom. I pulled off my heels, stripped out of my dress, and changed into the uniform I had in my bag: black slacks, a gray button-up shirt, and an orange scarf I had to tie around my neck. As I was stuffing my banquet outfit into the bag, a question flew into my mind: "What if I don't hear from the Keets again? What if they start remembering how badly I hurt them and decide they don't want to reconnect with me after all?" My own internal voice had the clingy, panicky tone of an eleven-year-old.

I pushed that thought to the back of my mind, along with all of my other memories of the previous few hours. I had to face customers.

Even though I didn't say a word about what had happened to me, I knew I was glowing. When a woman pulled up to the drive-thru two minutes before closing and cursed at my window attendant for having shut down the milkshake machine, I was a model of patience. "I totally know that midnight milkshake craving," I said to her. "Really, I do. The thing is, it takes us forty-five minutes to take apart the machine and clean it, and we already started that process for the night. I'm so very sorry. We've got a variety of other dessert options though, and I'd love to get you one." She softened and ordered a vanilla cone. I gave her the biggest smile I could—and it wasn't fake.

They would call. In my heart, I knew that.

74
Patrice

I called Anne the next morning. She sounded out of breath as she said, “Patrice, I was thinking about Melissa all night. I was just telling my husband the whole story.” She described how she’d taken on a role somewhere between mother figure and cheerleader for Melissa, Heaven, and Trinity. “I call them my ‘little family,’” she said. Then she launched into a description of their living situation. “They’re all crammed in with her brother and his son in a small apartment.” She added that the building was surrounded by barbed wire fencing and located right in the middle of Watsonville’s gang territory. “I hold my breath every time I go to pick up my little Heaven. I worry about them every single day. Those girls are so beautiful and vulnerable.”

Although I dreaded hearing more details, I asked where they all slept. She told me that Melissa and the girls shared the one bedroom and slept in the same bed. Daniel and his four-year-old son had a mattress on the floor in the other room, which also served as the kitchen, living room, and common space. Anne said the girls didn’t have anywhere to do their homework. I glanced around my good-sized kitchen and thought about the extra rooms we had in the large Victorian house we’d moved to six years earlier.

“She’s raising those girls all on her own,” Anne continued. “I have no idea how she gets by, even with the low rent she’s paying.” We talked about how smart Melissa was, and Anne mentioned that Melissa wanted to go back to school. She'd taken a few courses here and there but couldn't get a foothold toward a degree with all she had going on.

Before we hung up, Anne said something that sent a charge down my spine. "I can't thank you enough for making plans to see my Missy again. You guys might be just what they need."

Bob had never been the social planner in our long marriage; yet, he had arranged for us to have lunch with Melissa at The Star of Siam. It was obvious that he couldn't wait to see her again. I was excited, but a sneaky little voice still cautioned me. What if she wasn't actually the way she presented herself during her speech? What if she resented me? I didn't want to think about what could go wrong, because I had, once again, been so taken with her.

With my heart pounding, I turned into the restaurant's crowded parking lot. I'd been worried that she might not show up, but, through the stenciled glass door at the entrance, I could see her and Bob seated at a round table next to a bank of three-foot-long fish tanks. They were already chatting away and sipping bright Thai iced teas.

"Hey, it's great to see you!" I bent down and gave Melissa a hug before joining Bob across the table. "I'm still so blown away. We have so much to catch up on. We have to hear more about your life and your girls."

The waitress appeared, and we quickly ordered. As she was walking away, I reached over and placed my hand over Melissa's. "I can't even imagine the schedule you keep and all that you balance raising kids on your own."

Her face flushed. "Thanks. Sometimes it's harder than others." She went on to tell us about her living situation, which corroborated what I'd heard from Anne. "I'm gone at work a lot of the time. Late nights closing the restaurant—and often early morning openings, too." She took a deep breath, reached for a spring roll, and then fidgeted with her flowing hair. She went on to say that the girls were used to it, and that Daniel helped out with them when he had the energy. She sat up straighter when she told us that she'd worked her way up to being a manager of Burger King, which, she said, was both good and bad. She had more flexibility with her schedule but was responsible for anything that went wrong. "I'm not sure all the grease in the air is good for my asthma, but it's better than some jobs I've had." She explained how she'd taken a part-time second job as a home health aide for a woman with disabilities. When she said that job might not be the best fit for her, she hung her head. We didn't ask why.

She fussed with the beaded necklace she was wearing and pulled out her compact to check her lipstick as our food arrived. After a couple of bites, she looked up, smiled, and said, "The girls are doing pretty well. I wish I had some new pictures of them to show you. They're special kids."

Ignoring our food, Bob and I bombarded her with questions about Trinity and Heaven. Her eyes widened. "Well, Heaven's so much like me. That kid is full of spunk and says what's on her mind. Talk about a handful! Trinity, though...I sometimes think she was born a grown-up. She's so responsible and seems to take life so seriously." She sat back in her chair and exhaled. "Not to brag, but they are both smart as can be." My pulse quickened as I felt the same electric current of excitement that had coursed through me when I met Melissa in 1993. Under the table, I reached for Bob's hand and felt him squeeze mine back.

When Melissa stopped to take a breath, Bob and I turned and looked at each other with cocked heads and faint smiles. Without missing a beat, she said, "What's up? Why are you guys looking at each other that way?"

"Um, well, we can't wait to meet your girls," Bob said. "Would that be okay? Can we make a date for all of us to get together?" He fidgeted with his chopsticks.

"I would love that. I've told them so much about you over the years." She had? I felt my stomach flutter. Maybe that meant we weren't just another home in the string of foster placements. After some discussion, we agreed that we'd all go out together on our sailboat.

As we got our check, I mentioned the weird coincidence I couldn't help but notice: Heaven, nine years old, was the same age Melissa had been when she came to live with us. Trinity, twelve, was close to the same age Melissa had been when she moved out of our house. "I was thinking the same thing," Melissa said. "I wonder if I was as challenging as they are sometimes." She looked down into her lap.

While we were paying the bill, I wondered if we might be moving a little too fast for her. Those worries evaporated with her profuse thanks. "I can't wait to see you again," she said, hooking arms with me as the three of us headed for the parking lot.

On the day we met, the weather was sunny and cloudless, and the collage of colorful sailboats on the bay looked like an Impressionist painting. I spotted Melissa pulling into the crowded parking lot and directed her to a free space. Both of her girls were waving from the back seat. Melissa jumped out of the car and rushed toward me with her arms outstretched. She wore a tight white t-shirt with silver-studded stars forming a heart across her chest. As the girls got out and gathered around their mom, I was stunned by how beautiful the three of them were together. Heaven looked like a model from a teen magazine. Long, straight, blonde hair hung loosely down her back, and her expansive smile showed perfect teeth. She had robin's-egg blue eyes that were set off by high cheekbones. Trinity was striking in a very different way. She had dark brown hair, hazel eyes, and chiseled features. She was only slightly taller than Heaven, although I knew she was three years older.

Melissa proudly introduced them. Heaven stepped forward and hugged me. "You're the one who taught my mom how to kayak, aren't you?" she said. I smiled and laughed. Trinity hung back by her mom's side but grinned as she reached out to shake my hand. After they grabbed their jackets and bags from the car, the four of us made our way down the metal ramp to the dock where Bob fiddled with the sail cover. He gave a big wave and jumped off the boat.

"So, what grades are you in? And how's school?" I asked, after everyone was settled on deck. They responded like typical pre-teens, focusing on which kids and teachers were mean and how much homework they got. Before I could ask anything else, Bob pulled out lifejackets and suggested we set sail. The girls asked question after question. Where did we work? What did we do for fun? Did we have kids and grandkids? Before we'd reached the first buoy, we'd started telling them stories about their mom as a child. They loved hearing that she was strong and opinionated and that she'd spent much of her time on the trampoline and in trees. We told them about the trips we had taken together to Seattle, the Grand Canyon, New York, and Lake Tahoe, and we watched their eyes widen. They nodded and leaned their heads against their mom when I said that she'd been a super smart kid who loved to read. Heaven said something like, "Yeah, I can believe that, but she never has time for reading anymore. We don't even get to see her very much." Melissa hugged them tighter and looked out across the bay.

As we sailed past the kelp beds, Bob and I talked about sailing trips we'd taken in different countries. The girls were like little sponges absorbing everything we said, and, for the rest of the time, they peppered us with questions about everything ranging from what our favorite foods were to whether we wished we had pets.

When we returned to the slip, Heaven asked about the fiberglass kayak tied up next to our boat. Bob told her it was ours and asked if she'd like to paddle around the harbor. She jumped up and down on her seat cushion clapping her hands together. "Yes, yes. Can we do it now, please, please?" Bob gestured to me with his thumb and told them that I was the kayak expert. Soon Heaven and I were scrunched into our cockpits. After I gave her a quick lesson on staying upright and paddling, she and I paddled from one end of the harbor to the other for the next half hour. Heaven squealed every time we came close to a harbor seal or pelican flashing open its pink-throated pouch to scoop up nearby fish. We were lost in conversation about all the ocean smells as we approached our dock and climbed back aboard the boat.

The mood had shifted in our absence. Bob's usual smile was gone, and his brow was furrowed. Melissa and Trinity sat quietly next to each other. The lively conversation going on earlier had been replaced by silence. Melissa took a deep breath when Bob suggested we go to lunch at a restaurant called The Crow's Nest next to the harbor mouth.

After we were seated, I saw the girls shoot questioning glances at their mother. "Hey, go ahead and order whatever you want," I said. "We've got a gift certificate we need to use."

"Really?" Trinity and Heaven said in unison, before ordering and wolfing down fried calamari and onion-smothered cheeseburgers. After they finished their molten chocolate cake slices, the girls trotted off to explore. That left a window for Bob and me to gush to Melissa about how curious, smart, and polite they were. As we finished our tea, I put my arm around Melissa and told her what a wonderful job she was doing. "How do you do it all by yourself? Do you get any help from their dad?"

Her next words were firm. "No. And that's the only way it can be. I can't let him back into our lives or near the girls." She had a look of intense resolve on her face. "He'll never mess with me; he's too ashamed."

Back at our cars, Bob and I hugged the kids. "Thank you so much," Melissa whispered in my ear as she squeezed me to her chest. After we finished our goodbyes, I watched the three of them, arms linked and swaying together from side-to-side, stride to Melissa's yellow car as if propelled by a shared strain of music. As they drove away, an uneasy feeling washed over me. A minute before, I'd been relieved and pleased that our time with them had gone so well, but, in that moment, something didn't feel right. As Bob and I stuffed our boat bag with the extra life jackets and loaded our cooler into the car, I asked Bob what had happened while Heaven and I had been gone. "You guys looked so somber when we got back."

Bob cleared his throat as he got into the driver's seat. In a halting voice, he told me that Trinity had let it slip that they were going to be evicted from their place in Watsonville. He'd just been trying to make conversation about where they were living when Trinity said, "Yeah, we won't be living there much longer. We're getting kicked out." Melissa had immediately whipped her head around and given Trinity a stern look. Then she stood up and grabbed one of the beers from the cooler. When she turned back, she had what Bob described as a "Hollywood smile" plastered on her face and said, "Hey, no worries. It will all work out. We'll be fine. We always are."

Images of Melissa and her girls living on the street or in her car flashed through my mind. She'd told us how close to the bone they lived. "What happened? Did they do something wrong? What are they going to do?"

As Bob reached for my hand, he started filling me in. The owner was involved in a property dispute with a relative and had asked them to leave. Bob was especially moved when Melissa had said, "I'm really worried about where my brother and his son will go."

"Yeah, but what about her and her girls?" I was focused on the three people I knew. Bob explained that their only available option seemed to be moving into a studio apartment with a friend who was fresh out of rehab—an environment that Melissa had confessed might not be a good idea for her. "Honey, this makes me feel sick. Can you even imagine those darling girls and Melissa being homeless again?"

Bob nodded and swallowed hard. "Let's see if we can have them over this week and talk about this some more."

"That sounds good. I'll call Anne again to see what she knows." We were quiet the rest of the way home.

75
Melissa

Bob and Patrice wanted to meet the girls, so just a few days after the dinner, the five of us went out sailing on the boat they kept in the Santa Cruz Harbor. I think I'd worked a seventy-two-hour week, and, once again, I was operating on three-and-a-half hours of sleep. But I was committed to making this happen.

As I watched Bob and Patrice with the girls, I felt like I was watching a movie of myself as a kid. Maybe my sleep-deprived state had something to do with it, but I couldn't get over the similarities. "I don't really want to wear this," Heaven said when Bob handed her a life jacket. "It looks uncomfortable."

Bob stopped what he was doing and sat down next to her. "It's not too bad, Heaven. It's an important piece of safety gear." Heaven scrunched up her nose. "I'm wearing one, and I'm a really good swimmer. And look over there at that boat." He pointed to a fancy yacht on the other side of the harbor. "Everyone on that boat is wearing one. And theirs are uglier, too!" He went on to explain how someone could get hit by the boom and knocked in the water and how, in that situation, the life jacket might save them. Of course, she ended up putting it on. I smiled. Before living with the Keets, I'd only ever heard people say, "Because I said so," when I asked them for explanations.

While Bob and Heaven were talking, Patrice had sat Trinity down and was looking right at her, asking questions. I couldn't hear what she was saying, but I remembered this characteristic of Patrice's, how she always wanted to get to know a person's essence. She was always so curious about what I thought, and that curiosity showed in her eyes. I saw that same look as she listened to Trinity. I could tell by the way Patrice moved her hands and the way wrinkles appeared around her eyes as she listened that she was one hundred percent invested in the conversation. I knew what it felt like to have the warmth of Patrice's full attention.

I spent a lot of the sail lying on the warm sandpapery surface of the boat deck in the heat of the sun, barely able to stay awake, praying that the Keets wouldn't think I was bored. While Patrice and Heaven went out on a kayak, Bob asked me a bunch of very normal questions like, "What are your coworkers like?" and "What's your apartment like?"—only, at that time, those simple questions opened up cans of worms for us.

I had just found out that we were going to be evicted. We hadn't done anything wrong; the landlord was in a legal dispute with his family, and he needed half of the tenants to leave in order to move forward with his court case. Daniel and I were both really stressed about moving because neither of us had any leads on housing options. I had already lowered my income by leaving Carl's Jr. I was planning on going back to school, and they couldn't accommodate my class hours, so I had shifted to working a forty-hour work week at Burger King and taken on a second twenty-five hour per week job as an in-home care aide. I had taken that second job in hopes of getting ahead before school started, but I was starting to face the reality that I might need to keep the job indefinitely to make rent. I wanted to quit so badly—not just because of the hours, but because there were drugs all over the woman's house. I wasn't tempted by them; I was afraid she'd get busted, and that I'd somehow be sucked down with her, after I'd come so far. All I was doing was cleaning up her messes, but those messes included meth pipes, bags of pot, coke, and crystal.

"Where are you going to go?" Bob asked.

"I don't know, we'll find a place." I was feeling touchy. I didn't want to portray myself as being in a position of need, but I didn't want to lie either. "We'll be okay, we always get by." Which was mostly true. I wasn't sure how that would happen this time, but the last thing I wanted was Bob and Patrice worrying about it. I'd caused them enough worry twenty years earlier.

76
Patrice

"Oh, my God, I'd recognize you anywhere—even though it's been twenty years!" Melissa yelped when Colin walked in with his family.

It had been a whirlwind week, but when I asked Melissa to come over for dinner to see Colin again, she'd jumped at the idea. While I had her on the phone, I got up the courage to ask her about their possible eviction. "Yep, we're going to have to move. Sorry that news leaked out when we were on the boat." She sighed. "Trinity is a worrier, and this is really eating her up. I try to reassure her by telling her that everything will be alright, but she knows that hasn't always been true for us." She took a quick breath. "Thanks for asking. I've gotta get back to work—see you on Friday."

Melissa's face lit up as she hugged Colin, then his wife, Meredith, then six-year-old Harper and four-year-old Alida. Melissa stepped back and ruffled up Colin's hair. "Still a tow-head." She grinned. "Oh my God, it's so good to see you."

Colin put his arm around her. "I've thought about you so many times. It seems like everything happened so fast when we were kids. Suddenly you were with us, and then, just as suddenly, you were gone." He shrugged. "I'm sorry I wasn't much of a big brother. I was always with my friends back then."

"I might have been a little stand-offish myself." Melissa flipped her hair back and chuckled. "I can't believe I already have a daughter close to being a teenager, and you've got a preschooler. How did that happen?" While she asked him questions about where they lived, what they did for work, and what the girls liked to do, Harper and Alida spirited Melissa's daughters away to give them a tour of the house and play in the backyard.

I brought a plate of cheese and crackers to a table outside and sat down with the other adults. From there, I could see the four girls—Trinity, Heaven, and my two granddaughters—doing gymnastics and playing ping pong in another section of the yard. They looked like old friends, laughing as they missed ball after ball. As I drifted in and out of the adult conversation, a vision of an expanded family took shape in front of me: loud family dinners and celebrations, mass trips up to Tahoe to play in the snow, backyard movie nights, and kids helping each other with homework. *Cheaper by the Dozen*, again—but a grandparents' version this time. Melissa and Colin had more in common as adults than they did when she was ten and he was fourteen. They both had daughters to raise, families to provide for, and all the other responsibilities that came along with being in their thirties. Maybe they could become friends, and their girls could grow up to be close. I knew that Melissa's girls had had fragmented relationships with their extended family, and I imagined that the stability of Colin's family could be healing for them.

Melissa took me aside before everyone departed. She clasped my shoulders and said, "That was the loveliest evening ever. Thank you so much for including us." Colin called the next day and said that Harper and Alida couldn't talk about anything besides when they could see Heaven again.

That Saturday, like most Saturdays, Bob and I went to the Santa Cruz Farmers Market. As we were driving there, I turned to Bob and said, "Do you realize how lucky we are to be able to go out and buy whatever food we want?" I felt even more aware than usual of the resources we had at our disposal, after having talked about the eviction Melissa and the girls were facing.

"I know." Bob shook his head. "I was up a lot of the night with their situation running through my mind." He kept shaking his head as we parked and gathered up our shopping bags.

After we stopped by our regular stands, we ordered breakfast from one of the Mexican food trucks and found a table out of the way. "I'm not sure I can eat," Bob said, poking at his tamale with a plastic fork. "I'm actually sick at the thought of them going to live with her friend in recovery—and, from the sounds of it, that might not even be a possibility." He shoved his plate across the table. "Who knows what's next for them? And here we are, living in a house that's way too big for us. No one has lived in our downstairs apartment for five years, and the three of them are barely making it. It feels wrong."

I, too, was picking at my food, pushing it around the plate like the thoughts I was trying to put in order. For both of us, this felt different from the homelessness we saw on the streets of Santa Cruz. This was deeply personal. Melissa and the girls weren't strangers who needed a place to live. Melissa was the girl we'd loved when she was nine. These were her daughters who had all the promise in the world, whom I'd had visions of incorporating into our lives just the other night at dinner.

Bob put his hands over his face. "Let's get out of here. I'm going to the car." I grabbed some takeout containers and walked over to the parking lot where I found him staring off in space. "Sweetie." I pulled him towards me and rubbed his back. "Let's go walk on the beach and talk about how we could help them—what we could do, okay?"

"Well, I think I know what we could and *should* do, and also what I think I *want* to do." We were both silent for the drive across town to the beach in front of the yacht harbor, the place where we'd met Melissa's girls just a few days before. The sun broke through the clouds as we started walking, slowing our gait to watch families gathered around the metal burn barrels that dotted the beach. Fit young men kicked soccer balls to kids, creating curtains of sand. Elderly men and women hunched over game boards at picnic tables. As we reached the water's edge, we sat down on a mound of packed sand where we could feel an occasional wave lap over our toes. I turned around at the faint sound of the "Happy Birthday" song rising from a boisterous group behind us. "Melissa and her girls sure seemed to fit in seamlessly with our Keet family get-together," I said.

"I know." Bob mounded damp sand into a primitive sandcastle and started carving away at its walls. I dragged my fingers across those walls to add some flair and stuck some pebbles into the ridges. Then I grabbed a couple of clumps of wet sand to add more rooms. I could see the beginning of a smile forming on his face. Rubbing elbows, we both worked in silence for a few minutes. "You know, if we asked them to move in with us, it wouldn't just be for them. It would be fun for us, too—and rewarding—watching them grow up and being a part of their lives." He stopped building and looked up at me. "Don't you think?"

I brushed the wet sand off of my hands and threw my arms around him. Once again, in this relationship of over four and a half decades, we'd independently arrived at the same conclusion. I looked into his eyes and saw the same expression that he'd had when we'd agreed to take Melissa in twenty years earlier. "This generosity is one of the reasons I love this man," I thought, holding his gaze and squeezing his shoulder tighter. "So, should we invite Melissa and the girls over to talk about them living in our apartment?" I knew there'd be details to work out, but I figured we might as well get the conversation started.

Bob leaned into me and kissed my forehead. "Yep. Let's do it." We both lay back in the sand with our arms looped together and watched the seagulls overhead.

The next day, I picked up the phone with my hands shaking. As soon as I heard Melissa's voice, a feeling of pent-up energy coursed through my body. "Bob and I were wondering if you and the girls could come over for a spaghetti dinner on Wednesday evening." I chose my next words carefully: "We have something we'd like to talk to you about in person." I was afraid that, in my excitement, I might just go ahead and ask her the big question.

"Um, okay." I could hear Melissa take a gulp of air before she continued. "That's very nice of you. I'm sure the girls would love it." She went on to ask what she could bring and when they should arrive. Before we hung up, she asked, "About our talk, is everything okay?" As soon as she asked this, it occurred to me that probably many "talks" that she had been summoned to hadn't spelled good things to come.

"Oh, yes; yes, really." I made sure to use my most reassuring voice. "Everything is just fine, and we're looking forward to sitting down with you."

After hanging up, I made myself a cup of tea and sat in the sunroom overlooking the backyard. Autumn flowers were blooming in pockets, and the last of the persimmons were hanging like Japanese lanterns on the tree by the fence. Who could say no to an offer of a free apartment and a setting as beautiful as this? Even though her other option might be homelessness, I wondered if Melissa might cling to her independence. It was probably one of the main pillars holding her up, and who were we to interfere with that? I made my way down the outside stairs to wander among the many fruit trees I had nurtured from infancy.

Clearly, she'd want to move in. I opened the French doors to the ground floor apartment we would offer them. I looked at the oak bookshelves lining the living room with their colorful collections—windows into Bob's and my interests and hobbies. We'd have a lot of stuff to move out to let Melissa make it her own, but we'd make it work. And it would be fun to see what the grown-up Melissa would do to personalize the space. I walked into the apartment's kitchen area and envisioned Melissa making healthy meals for her girls. Maybe I could teach them how to make some of the exotic international dishes I loved preparing, like Moroccan chicken bastilla or tofu tikka masala. The girls had told me they liked very spicy foods, so I'd have to kick the seasonings up a notch. My reverie was cut short by what felt like an emotional rain shower of doubt. What if Melissa said no to us now, just as she had when she was eleven?

Bob and I had talked over her possible reactions the night before after dinner. "It's her decision, after all," he'd said while putting away the leftovers. "I wouldn't think of pushing the idea on her. Just like when she was eleven, when we found out that all we could do was offer her a home. We couldn't make her stay."

I nodded vigorously in agreement even though a big part of me wished I had made a different decision back then. I would probably never know if leaving it up to her was the right call, and I still ached with regret over not having taken the reins and brought her back into our family. I avoided sinking into that well-worn emotional rut by running through more logistics: If she did say yes, we'd have a slew of other things to figure out, like whether there should be a contract with her about our expectations, and whether or not there should be an "out" for Bob and me as well as for them. I voiced these concerns to Bob.

He rubbed his chin and tilted his head, "I'm not sure about that. I guess we have to have a set of expectations—although, I don't know. Maybe any issues will just work themselves out. She's a good person who's at a rough patch in her life. And the girls are darling." The non-emotional part of me knew we would need some ground rules. However, at that moment, it seemed like a monumental task to figure out what they'd be. Their needs were obvious; ours weren't. The next night, Melissa, Heaven, and Trinity arrived right on time with a small basil plant wrapped in silver foil. "Perfect for our pasta pomodoro," I said, greeting them at the front door. "Thank you, my dears." After hugs all around, the girls made their way out to the lawn. They looked like they already belonged in the space as they tossed around a volleyball. Melissa, Bob, and I sat out in our sunroom with glasses of chardonnay. After some small talk, I said, "Melissa, I hope you know how happy Bob and I are that you've come back into our lives. It feels like we were meant to meet again."

"Yep, it feels that way to me, too." Melissa put her arm around my shoulder.

"We've been pretty concerned about you and the girls and where you'll go after you have to move out of your place," Bob said, with his voice catching. "Patrice and I have talked and talked about how we could help you. The thought of you being homeless or in a bad living situation makes both of us sick."

Melissa had put her head in her hands while Bob was talking. From that position, she mumbled, "Thanks, but we'll manage. I hate for you to worry."

I jumped in. "What we're thinking is that we could help you out with a place to live."

Melissa lifted her head. "Um, what do you mean?"

"Well, we could help you out with money for a place." I

quickly presented some ways that might work, but really, I was anxious to get on to the option Bob and I wanted. I struggled to present it as respectfully as possible. "We don't know if it's important to you to have your very own separate place or not, but you've seen the apartment we have downstairs. It's empty, and Bob and I wondered if you and the girls would like to move in there."

Bob jumped in before I could take a breath. We were both so excited about this offer—about the chance to make things right after what had happened all those years ago—that we were tripping over each other trying to talk. "We'd make some changes to it. Like, create some privacy for you from the girls. Put up a wall and make a bedroom for you. It already has its own full kitchen and separate entrance."

Melissa's face flushed to nearly the color of the roses in the vase next to her, and her eyes widened. She reared her head back and hunched up her shoulders. "Oh my god, I'm, uh, overwhelmed." I could see her chest heaving up and down as she put her right hand over her heart. She got up and leaned against the kitchen island as she rubbed her forehead. "Can I get some water please?"

"Of course. Let me get some ice." I walked over to the sink.

She took the glass and stood up taller. After several deep breaths, she exhaled and put it down with shaking hands. "You don't know how I've struggled to be independent over the last few years. Getting away from Greg was so hard. I finally got on my feet living with Daniel, and now this fucking eviction." She pounded her fists on the counter. "I'm sorry. I'm so bad at taking help." She looked back and forth between Bob and me and clasped her hands together until her knuckles started turning white. "I couldn't impose on you in that way. But you're so kind to offer." With those words, she started to reach toward me then quickly pulled back. She backed up to the bench seat, sat down, and drummed her fingers against the cushion.

Bob and I stood at the kitchen island looking at each other. I waited a few seconds to see if she was going to go on. Then, I sat down a foot or so away from her. "I get that. I really do. But, you know, Melissa, most young people get some help and support from their families. We were family back then. Maybe we could be family again." I put my hand on her arm.

I saw tears on her face, but she pulled away—almost imperceptibly—like I'd seen her do as a child. Then, she quickly composed herself. I'd seen her do that as well, even a couple of times since we'd re-met each other. "I just couldn't think of inconveniencing you, and I don't think I could afford the rent downstairs."

"Melissa, we're not talking about renting it to you." Bob's voice came out harsher than he'd expected. I could tell because he softened his tone when he pulled up a chair next to Melissa, put his hands on his knees, looked straight into her eyes and said, "It's extra space we have, and we'd like the three of you to have a secure place to settle into—here, with us. We know you didn't expect to be kicked out of your current place. We want to help you and the girls, give you a little safety net." By the time he'd finished, I could see his chest expanding as he refilled himself with breath.

Melissa leaned her head back against the cushion, looking like she was going to melt into it. Then, she sat forward again and rested one hand on Bob's forearm and one on mine. "Thank you so much. I can't believe you're offering this. I just...I just need to think things through. Is that okay?"

"Of course," Bob and I said at the exact same time.

Just then, the girls ran up the back stairs as if summoned by an invisible whistle. "Is that spaghetti I smell?" Heaven asked, as she nestled into the narrow space between her mother and me.

"Yep, and it's time for me to get this dinner served." I

stroked the back of her hair, stood up, and made my way towards the cabinets that held our dishes. Pulling out pasta bowls, I glanced at the girls and asked, "Will you two help me set the table, please?" They jumped up and followed me to the dining room. The rest of the evening consisted of easygoing laughter and a frenzy of questions about each other's lives.

Later that night, steeped in a bubble bath, I wondered if we'd get a second chance to help Melissa out of a tight spot—and whether she'd come back this time.

77
Melissa

After sailing, we went out to lunch. It was clear that the Keets had fallen in love with the girls, and they invited all of us to dinner a few days later. It was at that dinner that they offered us their assistance.

I think the way they phrased it was, "We want to help you with your living situation." They brought up a couple of options. The first was to help me pay for an apartment of my own, which made me really uncomfortable. "Really?" I thought. "They're going to pay their hard-earned money out of their own pockets to help support me and my kids? I should be able to support my own kids, even though I can't. Who does this? We're basically strangers! Strangers in love, yes; but still!" The whole idea made me feel uneasy.

Bob explained the other option, that we could live with him and Patrice. I didn't know how to react to it. I felt incredibly guilty, like I should never have said anything, because they now felt obligated to help me. It was such a generous offer, and it made me so uncomfortable. I felt this powerful pressure in my chest, like a weight had fallen onto it and caused my heart to race and my skin to flush. I burst into tears.

I grew up feeling—or maybe knowing—that I was a burden on everybody. I had finally gotten so close to being self-sufficient. Right before I gave the speech, I could say that no one was paying my rent, no one was paying my childcare, and no one was giving me assistance. Yes, I was poor; but, for a change, I was getting by on my own. Once Daniel and I were faced with losing our cheap housing situation, however, I was slipping backwards. "Here I am again," I thought in that moment. "I just can't get out of this cycle of being dependent on other people." It had been my goal for so many years, and I just could not make it happen.

I took a deep breath and said, "Thank you so much, but this is not your responsibility."

"We don't have to do this," Patrice replied. "We *want* to do it because we love you."

I was crying and breathing hard and trying like mad to quickly calculate what would be less of a financial burden on them. With the apartment option, they said they'd pay the difference between what I could pay and what the total rent came out to, but given my situation at the time, that meant they'd basically be paying all of it. If we lived in their in-law unit, they wouldn't really be paying any of my rent, so I started to consider that option.

"We've had people live with us before, like family and friends—even an intern from the university," Patrice said. I felt a little better knowing that at least I wouldn't be the first person to move in with them. "We own our home, so we wouldn't feel comfortable with you paying us anything. We don't want your money, and we don't need it."

It also seemed like they actually wanted us around. I remember Patrice saying, "We could do dinners together—it'll be so much fun!" with such excitement in her voice that I thought we might somehow contribute to their lives.

I left the conversation feeling so guilty. But, in reality, I didn't have any other option.

I agreed to move in with them, but it didn't feel real. I have to admit, I just assumed they'd take back their offer. In fact, I kept operating under that assumption up until the day we were moving in—and for several months afterwards as well. I was squirreling away extra money for when they'd get sick of us. That had always been my experience with generosity in the past. People were generous until it inconvenienced them.

Daniel was very supportive of the move, but the rest of my family was not. "Sure, we're really happy for you and all," they said. "But you be careful now, Melissa, be very careful." I waited for the catch for months. I know I'd said things to a couple friends, like, "I don't know what role I'm supposed to be playing here," and "I'm afraid to be spending any money, because I don't know what might happen tomorrow." I was in survival mode, as I had always been.

78
Patrice

Melissa called me the next day. “I’ve been thinking a lot about your offer for us to move into your apartment.” I could hear her voice waver. “It totally caught me by surprise, as you saw. I have a lot of pride, and I get afraid when I don’t handle everything myself.” She paused to inhale deeply. “Patrice, I can’t tell you what a kind offer this is,” she said, and then she nearly whispered, “and I’d love to try it, if you still want us there.”

I wanted to cheer into the phone, but I didn’t want to scare her with my enthusiasm. It was really going to happen. We were going to get that second chance.

After she’d expressed her gratitude multiple times, her tone got lighter as she said, “By the way, could I come by and visit the children’s museum you’re starting?”

I wasn’t sure that I’d heard her right. I knew I’d talked about the challenges and rewards of my latest undertaking—starting a museum from scratch with my niece, Bonnie—but I couldn’t remember what I’d told Melissa about it. “Um, sure, I’d love that. I’m there all the time since we’re finally getting ready to open.” I was flattered that, even in the midst of our emotional conversation the night before, she’d picked up on how important the museum was to me.

The next day, I was sitting at a table covered with architectural sketches, miniature exhibit prototypes, and stacks of membership forms. We’d set up a temporary office space in an empty store in the Capitola Mall, down the hall from where the museum was being built out. In the middle of an intense phone call with a prospective donor, I looked up and saw Melissa saunter in the door with a big smile on her face. My heart skipped a beat as I waved to her. By the time I got off the phone, she was already chatting with two or three people. Bending over a diorama, she exuded the same confidence I'd seen when she'd spoken at the CASA event a few weeks earlier.

I gave her a quick hug and started introducing her around. I stuttered because I wasn't sure how to identify her—my foster daughter? My friend? The two of us walked through the shopping mall to the eight-thousand square foot former Abercrombie and Fitch store where construction workers were putting up sheetrock. Our museum office manager and two other employees looked like they were swimming in a sea of cardboard boxes. With their hands on their hips, they stood shaking their heads. "Patrice, what are we going to do with all this stuff for the gift shop?" one asked. "We're having a heck of time figuring out the point-of-sale system."

Before I could open my mouth, Melissa stepped up to the computer console, leaned over, and said, "What do you need to do? I've worked on this kind of system at every fast-food restaurant in the county."

After I introduced Melissa to the group, I shrugged my shoulders and raised my outstretched palms. "Well, okay, Melissa, have at it. Katie and Rachel can explain what they're up against. I've got to run." I gave Melissa a pat on the back. "Good luck."

"Yep, I'll check in with you in a bit." Melissa squinted at the screen.

Two hours later, my operations manager rushed in and asked me to meet her outside by the fountain. "Patrice, where did you find that Melissa? She's incredible. She taught all of us how to use our new system." She added that Melissa was an excellent teacher and had been patient with everyone as they learned. "I've got to know more about her."

"Well, I'd love to fill you in, but it's a long story." Would I even want to tell it if I had the time?

Melissa came back the next day, after she finished her home health aide job, and she kept coming back after that. After about a week, our operations manager asked if she could hire Melissa to help with the gift shop and run the front desk. I raised my eyebrows and told her that *I* couldn't hire or supervise Melissa because she was about to become a member of our family, but that *she* could. By then, I'd realized that I had to tell her about my connection with Melissa, so I gave her the bare bones version of our history, including the news that she and her daughters were moving in with us.

Walking out to my car, I was stunned by the way things were unfolding. On the one hand, I felt a wave of relief that Melissa had this great opportunity to be in a job in a safe and fun environment where she could shine. My heart warmed with the idea that Melissa and I could share the adventure of making a valuable community asset together. And, that excitement gave way to scary questions: What if she didn't work out at the museum, and we were living together at the same time?

That evening, I told Bob that our office manager wanted to offer Melissa a job. He pumped his fist in the air. "Does that mean she'll be able to leave her job as a home health aide?"

"Yeah, I guess so. But it does feel like I'm doubling down on her—with both the job and the apartment. Don't you think? What if one doesn't work out?" Twenty years before, Bob had asked that same question while we were deciding whether to bring Melissa into our family.

Bob hugged me close. "Honey, it all calls for a leap of faith, right?"

We hadn't changed much. We were still the optimists leading with our hearts and holding onto the belief that people could thrive with some help. This time, though, we had a few more tools. And a lot more information—about everyone involved.

79
Melissa

When I told Bob and Patrice why I wanted to quit my in-home care job, they encouraged me to resign immediately, which I did. Somehow, I started volunteering at the Santa Cruz Children's Museum of Discovery, Bob and Patrice's monumental undertaking, instead. Patrice is like that—she has such amazing enthusiasm, and she manages to suck you into things, always.

Even though I barely had the time to be volunteering, I was glad to be doing it. It made me feel like I could still make a contribution to the world in some way, even though in so many other ways I felt useless as a mother who couldn't provide a roof for her children or herself.

I'd only been volunteering there for a week when the Director of Operations offered me a job. She must have liked how I just jumped in and took the reins. No one had ever really told me what to do when I was volunteering, so I just came up with tasks on my own. I got on the phone. I wrote some scripts for what to say when callers had certain questions. I cleaned up the office. I figured that if they didn't like what I was doing, they'd tell me, and we'd fix it. It was a part-time job, and it paid less than what I was used to getting, but I wasn't going to be paying rent. For a change, I would be going to school and planning for my future, so I took the position.

My name tag at work said, "THE Melissa." Patrice had told everybody about me and about our amazing reunification, so people would come up to me and say, "Oh my gosh, you're THE Melissa!" and I'd have to say, "Why, yes, I am THE Melissa," as though there were no other Melissas in the world that mattered. It became a joke around the museum. And, at the same time, I felt a little awkward. I was afraid that the other employees would assume that I'd gotten the job because I knew Patrice, even though it wasn't her idea to hire me.

All of this happened so fast and seemed so positive; and yet, I questioned whether I was making a mistake. Not only was I living in the Keets' home, but I would also be working in the museum they helped build. I'd be dependent upon them for both my housing and my income. I had no reason to believe that they'd ever do anything to harm me. But I was uncomfortable with the uncertainty of it. I didn't know how long this was supposed to last. I didn't know if there was an expiration date to our arrangement. I didn't even know what their expectations of me were.

I guess I just came to accept it, though. I know that I love doing things for other people. When I'm helping others, I feel like I'm being the person I am supposed to be. I think about how I would feel if somebody took those opportunities away from me, and I imagine that for Bob and Patrice, the feeling is similar.

And, if the Keets hadn't offered their home to us, we would have been in a rough spot. I had already called two shelters, and they had no available rooms, so we might have ended up on the street. I never told Bob and Patrice how dire the situation was, and I didn't plan to.

80
Patrice

We had six weeks to get the apartment downstairs ready for Melissa and the girls.

When we first bought our house in 2006, our ground floor, low-ceilinged, spider-ridden basement was a scary and unusable space. As part of shoring up the foundation of the house, we decided to remodel the basement into a full apartment with its own entrance and kitchen. It had worked out well when one person lived there—first my father, and then Bob's mother. Neither of us could see Melissa and her two girls crowded into the one small bedroom in the otherwise good-sized apartment, however, so we had a friend enclose a large alcove to make another bedroom. Within a month, the room was ready to be painted. Melissa twirled with delight when we asked her to pick out the color.

When she and the girls came over for dinner a couple of weeks before their move in, Melissa told us she was worried about how they were going to furnish their bedrooms since the furniture and bedding they'd been using belonged to Daniel. "I'm thinking we could sleep on the couches in the living room for now," she said. I called Melissa the next day and told her that we wanted to take the three of them on a surprise field trip. That Sunday, the five of us packed into our minivan and headed to the IKEA down the highway. On the way, we told them that they could pick out whatever bedding they wanted. I remember hearing Heaven and Trinity in the back seat whispering to each other. "Do they mean us or just Mom?"

The whispering continued as Melissa answered. "I don't know. Just go with it. And, whatever you do, don't break anything."

When we walked into the huge store, the three of them stopped in their tracks. They squinted from the bright lights and jostled each other to be first on the escalator. "What the heck *is* this place?" Heaven asked, as she ran to the closest king-sized bed and started bouncing on it. "Look Trin, it has orange sheets!" Melissa rushed over and grabbed her, but there was no containing Heaven's exuberance as she tried out every chair we passed. We wound our way through the maze of couples and families filling their carts until we got to the bedding section. "Go for it. Just don't buy out the whole store, okay?" Bob said, winking at Melissa. Bob and I stood back holding hands and smiling as the three of them dashed from one aisle to the next.

"I think that it was the best few hundred dollars we've spent in a long time," Bob said, as we soaked in our hot tub that night.

Six weeks later, I sat in our sunroom staring at my day planner. It was opened to a section of November 2014 filled with so much writing I could barely read my notes. The Museum's Grand Opening celebration was scheduled for the next day, a Saturday, and Melissa and her daughters were moving in on Sunday. Since the museum opening had been on the calendar for six months, and Melissa's landlord had given her a fixed move out date, neither event had a negotiable timeline. I leaned back against the bench and marveled at the way these two parts of my life had come together. The fact that Melissa was working on the project that had consumed my life for two years *and* was moving in with us was almost overwhelming.

I thought about this unusual intentional family we were forming. We weren't just "letting them live downstairs;" we were blending our families and building a future together. It looked like a win-win on paper: Melissa and her kids needed a place to live and emotional support. Bob and I would get a chance to add grandchildren, manifest our belief in helping others, and have a second chance with someone we'd loved and hoped to adopt as a child. But lives don't take place on paper, and, of course, we had only the slightest inkling of what we were getting into—again.

That night at the museum, Melissa, Bob, and I worked side-by-side like synchronized swimmers. We weaved in and out of each other's paths, putting the last coats of paint on the car ramp exhibit Bob had built and hanging additional spotlights above the children's stage. When I stopped for a moment to look at my checklist, I'd see Melissa unpacking boxes and smile. I loved that the tables were turned, and she was helping us.

An hour before our ten o'clock opening, crowds started swarming our doors. Mothers holding infants and fathers being tugged by their toddlers pressed their noses up against our giant picture windows and jostled one another for a peek inside. The mall's corridors became so congested that the security guards came to help waiting guests form orderly lines. As we opened the doors, families flocked toward our registration desk to purchase annual memberships. When the final tally came in, it showed we'd had over two thousand visitors. We'd pulled it off.

At 7 am the next day, I was at the museum again. Bob, too, was up bright and early, cleaning out the truck he had borrowed to go down to Watsonville. I'm not sure if I was conscious of it at the time, but I clearly didn't want to be a part of Melissa's move. I didn't want to see the neighborhood the girls described as "scary" or the quarters they'd called "cramped." I suspect my reluctance was another version of the self-protection mechanism that had cropped up back when Melissa was moving in with us for the first time, when I went to great lengths to avoid reading Melissa's file. Back then, I wanted to be done with the messiness of her past and move on to the fresh start we were offering her. And here I was, wanting that same thing again for her and her girls. Apparently, I hadn't noticed that my avoidance of messiness didn't work out very well the first time. This time, however, I had a compelling excuse to avoid the task: it was the museum's second day of being open to the public, and it promised to be just as busy as the first. And, although I wouldn't see the apartment, I knew all about it. More importantly, I knew Melissa's whole history this time. There were huge differences in our backgrounds, upbringings, and priorities. While I wasn't sure how we'd transcend them, at least I knew what they were, and I was ready to talk about them.

For me, the day at the museum was such a happy and hectic blur that I didn't even have time to check in with Bob. As I drove home from the mall that evening, it dawned on me that I'd be arriving to a bigger family. I noticed myself driving faster than I normally would have—until I was stopped at the traffic light in front of the newest homeless encampment. For the two minutes I sat there, I looked at the faces of men and women pushing bicycles, shaking out sleeping bags, playing guitar, and lighting pipes. Any one of them might have had housing a year ago, or even a week ago, until a medical bill or a missed rent payment—or a landlord with a property dispute—put them over the edge and landed them there, on a grassy patch of land between the freeway and the river. There were probably twenty sagging tents in my sight, each with piles of possessions surrounding its nylon walls. I knew this scene repeated itself at multiple other spots in town—parks, beaches, along the railroad tracks; the locations varied depending on the city's statutes and their level of commitment to enforcing them that month. Every time I sat at that light, I was overwhelmed by the sheer number of people that needed shelter. I sat with my empty feeling, then I steered my thoughts back to Melissa and the girls. I would see them just as soon as I got home.

A few minutes later, when I pulled into our driveway, I smiled at the brightly lit windows glowing behind the decades-old Cecil Brunner rose bush. Laughter drifted out from a partially open door. I paused on the patio and spied on a scene of vibrant chaos. Inside, Heaven and Trinity were having a "snowball" fight with scrunched up packing paper, and Melissa was halfheartedly shouting at them to get back to unpacking. I saw the desk that Bob had set up for the girls in the family room and the baby grand piano, passed down from Bob's brother, that we'd left in the space, tuned and ready for the girls to take lessons.

I closed my eyes for a moment, trying to picture how the next chapter of our communal living would unfold.

81

Melissa

Four Years Later

Everyone always wants to know how I did it. How did I escape the cycle of poverty and abuse when so few others do?

The reality is, I don't really know. I think about it all the time, though. I have to remind people that things in my life went wrong so many times before they went right. Look at how many times I went back to Greg thinking that he could change, that we could be the Brady Bunch family I'd always dreamed of. Look how many times I was at the end of my rope: I tried to commit suicide twice. I was homeless in multiple cities. I was on and off public assistance constantly. I know I am not superior to anyone, and I'm not any "better" than someone who is still stuck in the cycle. I didn't come through all of this because I was somehow "worthy." There's a certain amount of dumb luck involved. Some secret combination of how events unfolded for me, in what sequence, and with what timing to put me in a position to sneak through a little crack in the wall. My life could have turned out so differently.

But we've been here in Patrice and Bob's downstairs apartment for over four years now. I'm working on applications to schools with master's in social work programs, writing another essay about our nation's need for wraparound services. I'm trying to describe the conversation I had with a well-meaning fellow student in my sociology class at UCSC last week. She's a super nice woman, but she just may never get what it's like to have all the shit in your life so twisted up that every movement makes the entanglement worse. "We just need to house everyone," she said. "It's expensive but simple. Make sure everyone has safe and reliable shelter, and everything else falls into place." I hear this a lot these days. I'm not denying that housing is fundamental. It is a basic human right, and there's no way you can deal with a job or school or a health problem while living on the street. But you can't just give someone a place to live and assume they will take it from there. I was deposited into the nicest house imaginable, with generous, caring people and all the resources in the world. Being in that house didn't help me deal with my trauma. It didn't help me fill the holes left by my biological family. All of the housing opportunities I was given as an adult provided me with huge boosts, but they didn't stop me from letting Greg back into my life. They didn't stop me from getting sucked back into the gravitational pull of Greg's family again and again—from choosing the dysfunctional but known over the healthy but uncertain. They didn't stop me from having suicidal thoughts. They didn't fix my health issues, and they didn't get my kids back.

"Poverty is a lifestyle," I told the young woman. "To fight it, you need a multi-pronged attack—housing, mental health, physical health, communication, education, job skills, money management, self-esteem..." I tried to explain to her how people who grew up in my circumstances need support in all these ways, all at once. To do so, I ended up telling her a shortened version of my life story—of Patrice trying to save me, of me trying to save Greg, of all of us trying to pull each other out of cycles that are far too strong for any one person to overcome. As I spoke, I saw the confusion on her face. I could tell she wanted one logical explanation for everything I did, as though by landing on that one logical explanation, we could come up with one logical solution and dismantle the alarmingly complex cycles of poverty, domestic violence, substance abuse, and homelessness. It's not that easy. I only know this because I lived it.

Maybe I am right where I need to be, still.

82

Patrice

Four Years Later

"Can I talk to you for a minute?" Melissa asks, after rapping gently on the upstairs door. I never say no; at least, I haven't so far in this second chance relationship. Believe it or not, it's been going on long enough for Trinity to have started at the high school down the street. Heaven is at the nearby junior high. Melissa and I are both still working at the museum, and she's about to graduate from UC Santa Cruz, after a few years at the community college down in Aptos.

I'm dressed in my bathrobe and about to turn out the kitchen lights, looking forward to crawling under the sheets with Bob after a hectic day. I have a feeling Melissa wants to talk over some issues with Heaven. She's been getting caught in lies lately—silly ones that are easily detectable—just like Melissa did when she was young. Or it could be about Trinity who, uncharacteristically, got herself grounded earlier in the week. Either way, I'm not sure if I have the energy for it, and I wonder how many other women my age—sixty-eight at this point—are still having these kinds of conversations. Regardless, I say yes.

I pull the crocheted blanket I've been carrying up over my shoulders, and the two of us make our way to the sunroom. I tuck my legs under me and settle in. "Have we done something to upset you?" Melissa asks. "Me and the girls? Have we worn out our welcome here? You seem angry with us."

I scrunch up my eyes and lean on the table with both elbows. I replay our family dinner from earlier in the evening. Trinity, Heaven, Bob, and I—along with Colin's two daughters, Harper and Alida—just enjoyed a sweet family meal together while Melissa was at one of her final college classes. I thought everything was fine. Trinity lingered around the table after dinner, and, by the time she was ready to head downstairs for homework, I felt closer to her than ever. "I love you, Trinity," I said, as we hugged.

When did I start telling them that I love them? I felt it as soon as I met them, but I only started getting more expressive as they turned toward us more and took down some of their barriers. Trinity blushed and started towards the door to their downstairs apartment. Then she stopped and said, "You know how you asked us to not spray hairspray a few weeks ago? Well, we stopped doing that, and I'm wondering if it's gotten better." I told her it was a lot better and thanked her. It has been better; the smell that wafted upstairs every morning had me on the verge of a migraine several times. But it still bothers me some, as does the music after 9 pm and the fact that they often forget to take out the garbage. As I watched Trinity disappear down the stairs, I realized that I'd stretched the truth to avoid a confrontation—not for the first time. But it's not 1994; it's 2019, and Melissa is fully capable of identifying her emotions and expressing them to me.

Clutching an embroidered throw pillow on the sunroom couch, she turns to me. "Sometimes people say one thing, but it's a cover for something else. They don't always say all of what they mean." She pauses. "Have we done something to offend you?" Her face is contorted as she looks into my eyes. "You know how you asked the girls and me to stop spraying hairspray? Well, we did that, but it still seems like you are still bothered. I'm worried we've done something to you, and we don't know how to fix it." She can't sustain our gaze and looks down to the floor. Her normal hand tremor has become so strong that she grabs the table to steady herself. "Would you rather have us gone?"

I fumble with my blanket as I reach for her hands. Of course, I don't want them gone. In all honesty, there are *moments* when I do—when I wish I could use the washing machine, which is in their apartment, on my own schedule instead of having to wait hours while they do laundry marathons. Or when Melissa blocks in my car and I have to be at work before she leaves for school. Or when I see people coming and going from their apartment whom I don't know. But these are just moments. I really do want them here, and I know I need to provide the kind of unwavering stability that Melissa never really felt as a child. "No, no. Melissa, we love you. We love *all three* of you. We want you here. We love having you here. In fact, when you talked about moving to campus last year, I called both Ellie and Colin to tell them how sad I was that you might do that."

I see that her whole body is trembling. "Oh God, really? I'm so glad to hear that." It takes a few moments for her to steady her breathing and wipe her wet face. "We love being here with you. We *want* to be here with you. It's just..." She pauses and looks up before jumping back in. "We just don't want to be a burden to you. And Bob might want to retire in a year or so, and, and...you might not want to have this big house. We don't want to overstay our welcome."

"What? Overstay your welcome?" I've been thinking that they're finally really family, but she's making it sound like they're just another set of overnight guests. I've probably said something recently that triggered her to think that. I've tried to be less critical, but I am who I am, and my judgments just come out. "That's not how families work. Melissa. Just because we annoy each other sometimes...you know that's only human and natural, right? Living so close to each other and having our lives intersect in so many ways is intense, and we're bound to rub up against each other in this kind of a situation."

And, in truth, living with Melissa and the girls is not as easy as living with Ellie and Colin was. Our cultural differences are still very real, and the fact that our relationship is not well-defined and not at all typical doesn't help.

But we're committed to making it work, and I need to make that clear in whatever way I can. I reach up, turn to her so we're eye-to-eye, and hold her face in my hands. "I'm so sorry that I haven't told you more how much we love you, *and* how much we love having you right here, in the middle of our lives."

My tears start flowing as I accept what a gift it is to have a second chance at being less critical with Melissa. I don't want to mess it up. "Melissa, I want to do better this time than I did before." These words come out of my mouth before I even think them. They are so true that they take my breath away. It pains me to think that I haven't shown enough love and acceptance to foster their sense of security. I have a flash of that same feeling of failure I had when she moved out as a child. Now, however, I'm strong enough to stay with those feelings. I can talk them through with her and get to the other side. I know I won't crumble because of this conversation. "Melissa, I know we haven't done anything to formalize our relationship, like go through an adoption or something, but you are family. You and the girls are part of our family, and we are here for you—emotionally and financially, to help all three of you realize your dreams." I pull her head close to mine and stroke her hair. "There's no expiration date on our commitment to you." The words keep tumbling out of me from a deep place. "We are here for you for the long haul—whatever that is."

She leans back, then grabs me in a bear hug like she did when we re-met after her speech. "I love you, Patrice, and so do the girls. I've always loved you and felt like part of your family, even when I ran away." I grimace and shudder against her chest. Apparently, this pain is never going to go away, no matter how much I talk about it, think about it, or cry about it. "The two years I spent with you were the only happy part of my childhood. Every single good and happy memory I have of childhood happened with you. I took those memories and the praise you offered with me. Your positive feedback literally kept me alive in the face of a failing marriage, drug abuse, and challenging court cases."

I let her words wash over me like a warm shower on aching muscles. I couldn't ask for any more validation. It allows me to open up my big box of guilt and confusion. "I don't know why I didn't come after you. I'm still struggling to figure that out. It was so out of character for me. I was so hurt and felt like such a failure." The reality of speaking these words to her hits me. I am really saying them to her, not just to my therapist. I might as well admit it all. "I don't think I could have handled any more rejection. I just wasn't up to it." I close my eyes and squeeze out the air that's filled my lungs like a balloon.

Melissa nods. "I never thought about adults' feelings then. I was so busy trying to survive and was so involved with my own feelings—there was no room for anyone else's. I only started understanding how much I had hurt you sometime after I had my girls."

For the hundredth time, I realize that this isn't an easy thing we're doing—coming back together after all these years and being family—and I tell her this. I tell her that I want to remember and celebrate our successes in creating an alternate, non-traditional family. As we have this conversation, she's a month away from becoming a graduate of UC Santa Cruz at age thirty-two—the first person in her family to complete college, and a prestigious one at that. This is clearly one of those successes.

"Yeah, I guess this is groundbreaking." Her face lights up with a grin. "Nobody else has ever done this, have they? I never thought of that." She leans over before heading downstairs to her apartment and puts her arm around me. "Hey, would it be okay with you if I put up some quotes on the walls going down the stairs to our place? Inspirational quotes, maybe, with pictures like the first man stepping on the moon and saying, 'going into new territory' or something like that?"

"Of course. I love that idea." And I really do love that idea, although it's been more like their threesome and our twosome landing on the moon from different planets. We are each trying to figure out the other's languages, customs, and habits. Our willingness to struggle through getting to know each other deeply comes from our belief that it's possible to bridge the chasm of our vastly different experiences.

After I close the door to the downstairs apartment, I slide down to the floor, lean against it, and draw my knees into my chest. I'm exhausted. My mind drifts back to other times I've been exhausted after a conversation with Melissa—after that scare at the Grand Canyon, after the wallet stealing incident, after the horrible session with Olga. I smile and think how grateful I am that this version of exhaustion feels much healthier.

We're still not quite on totally solid ground; I worry when I don't see Melissa around for a few days. I wonder what she's doing, and I have to stop myself from giving her parenting advice. Both Trinity and Heaven are doing well in school, but it wasn't long ago that I worried about twelve-year-old Heaven not taking school seriously and her believing she wasn't smart. When I see Trinity with boys, I want to ask Melissa if she's talked to her daughters about birth control. I'm too scared to ask her, but I'm also scared that one of the girls will end up pregnant and slide back into the cycle from which their family may have finally escaped. These fears might be unfounded, but I can't quite make them disappear. By the same token, I know Melissa still thinks about back-up plans. Given her history, she has to.

Still, we're absolutely on a positive trajectory this time around.

I slowly get up, knowing that I have another flight of steps to climb before I can collapse into bed with Bob. I make my way to the sunroom to turn out the lights. As I do, I see that the outside lights are on, illuminating the garden. The lemons are producing fruit like crazy, and I make a mental note to tell Trinity and Heaven to take some to their teachers. The lime isn't doing as well, but it had a big year last year. Maybe it just needs a break. I haven't tended to my roses in weeks, and it shows. I should probably trim them tomorrow, along with mulching the beds of irises and daisies that have finished blooming for the spring.

Then again, if I don't get to those tasks tomorrow, they'll all still be fine. I think what I want to do tomorrow is sit out there on the patio and admire them as they grow, however they grow.

AFTERWORD
Melissa

I understood from a young age that someday I'd share my story with the world. I didn't quite understand how or when, but the drive to connect with others through shared lived experience gave me strength. It gave meaning to the horrific events I'd survived, and that meaning helped me to trudge forward through many of the low points in my life. I hope this book will touch those who can relate to my life experience and give them a sense of connectedness. I also hope it will inspire an evolved perspective in those who wish to understand the cycles of abuse and systems that maintain poverty, educate those who stand dumbfounded in the face of a loved one's illogical life decisions, and motivate those who wish to make lasting systemic change.

My relationship to this book has shifted many times over the years, and I'd be lying if I said it was a walk in the park to get it out into the world. Developing this work forced me to relive trauma and come face to face with the lingering regrets and shame of my early life decisions. Yet, the process also helped me to grow—as a mother, as a survivor, and as a daughter. Today, I know what it feels like to have an amazing support system of loving parents, caring children, and loyal friends. It is because of their collective support that my lifelong desire and dedication to ending the cycles of violence and poverty that I was born into has largely come to fruition. I no longer work purely out of the necessity of scraping by to pay the next bill. I now have a career path that fills me with intrinsic reward: As a social worker for the county of Santa Cruz, I help shelter people who are working to overcome many of the same obstacles I did. I feel a sense of pride to be the first person in my biological family to hold a college degree. I understand that the pathway I took isn't a one-size-fits-all solution, and education isn't the answer for everyone growing up in a situation like mine. Still, I'm grateful that it has worked out well for me. I have an amazing relationship with both of my girls, and I'm so proud of the intelligent, compassionate, and driven women they are blossoming into. Although our story is far from over, the fact that I supported my girls in avoiding many of the mistakes I made so blindly in my youth gives me a great sense of accomplishment.

I think that if I were still that nine-year-old girl sitting in her school counselor's office, I'd view this phase of my life as the satisfying "happily ever after." But the truth is, I don't need that kind of ending anymore. Through the steadfast love that Patrice and Bob—my parents—have shown me, I now allow myself to be whatever I am at any given moment. It's because of them that I know I'll be loved in any version of me to come, and they inspire me to be the best version of me that I can imagine. I remember so many moments in my life where I couldn't help but ask myself, "Why me? What have I done to deserve this?" And, ironically, I still ask myself those same questions today—but in quite a different context. Now, I wonder, "Why me? Why am I so lucky? What have I done to deserve this when so many others never get to?"

I really do have the family I longed for all those years as a child, and it's one that's complicated and quirky and perfectly flawed.

AFTERWORD
Patrice

Melissa and her girls have lived with us for seven and a half years—almost half of Heaven's life.

During that time, Melissa graduated with honors from the University of California at Santa Cruz. Her degree in psychology enabled her to get two different jobs working with unsheltered people in our town, and she is currently applying for master's in social work graduate programs. While Melissa's commitments keep her very busy, we do occasionally get time alone. When we're lucky enough to spend a handful of hours together, we often talk about parenting and psychology. In addition to Heaven and Trinity, mental health and social issues are two of our main overlapping interests. We speak the same language when we talk about how best to tackle these problems and, in doing so, create common ground and gain a deeper understanding of each other's perspectives. I love the same qualities in Melissa that I was drawn to when I met her as a child—her strong spirit, her intelligence, her resilience, her straightforwardness, and the depth of her caring about others. From our first meeting, Melissa has activated and highlighted in neon colors parts of me that have been both hard and joyful to look at. I know that my worry about her always got in the way of my full, unabashed acceptance and embrace of her. With that worry now relegated to the typical parental worry pile, I have been able to be the fully loving, proud, and accepting parent I hoped to be when I met her.

Both girls finished high school with flying colors and

earned scholarships to excellent colleges in Southern California. Trinity plays in the marching band, works in the arts as an usher, and is considering a career in psychology. This fall, Heaven will begin a nursing degree while pursuing her passions for dance and meeting new people. Both girls are kind, generous, diligent, respectful, polite, and attentive to their mother. We keep showing up as grandparents to them—attending their performances, listening to all they are willing to share, and providing support as they negotiate the process of leaving home. The real success is that we like to be around them.

It hasn't all been easy since we joined our families. We've had to manage issues of all types and sizes, from how to fit four cars into the driveway to expectations around finances and overnight visitors to deeper issues of emotional support and fostering independence. Sometimes, I still feel like I'm tiptoeing around them, hoping not to trigger an event that puts up a wall between us. Other times, I feel really close to them, and our communication is straightforward and easy. No matter how things are going, however, I embrace my role with Melissa and the girls. Age, wisdom, and a constant awareness of their pasts (which Bob does a great job of keeping in our sights) helps me to do this, as do the countless hours we have all spent trying to bridge the cultural and life experience gap between us—the one I once envisioned as an uncrossable chasm. These days, I feel closer to Melissa and the girls than I ever have, even though all three of them are in the process of slowly moving out from underneath our protective roof, but not our parental orbit.

I've stepped down from my position at the local children's museum, and Bob is closing in on retirement as well. When Melissa, Heaven, and Trinity all leave, we'll finally be true empty nesters- well into our 70s. When I look back on our *Cheaper by the Dozen* fantasy, I see that, even though we didn't have twelve children under our roof, we did get the love and liveliness we were looking for. We got some challenges as well, and we learned more than we could have ever anticipated about the obstacles our society faces in coming to terms with issues like abuse, addiction, and income inequality.

Bob and I have the privilege of having another daughter and two more granddaughters, which, as they say, is priceless.

Acknowledgments

Melissa LaHommedieu

To my amazing daughters, for giving me the strength and motivation to move forward when all of my being yearned to give up. I am forever proud of you.

To my brother, for being a consistent source of support throughout my life, for all the ways in which you have sacrificed your own needs to help me meet my own, and most of all for your forgiveness.

To Anne Young, I couldn't have come so far without your steadfast friendship.

To Luz Miranda, for your mentorship.

To CASA of Santa Cruz, for providing foster youth with a community of support.

To Camp Opportunity, for creating a space of acceptance.

To Bridget Lyons, for your ability to listen and allow my voice to be heard.

To my closest friends, A.K.A. my Coven, for loving me in all of my strengths and weaknesses. Your collective friendships have allowed me to grow as a woman, a mother, and a friend.

Lastly, to my parents, Bob and Patrice Keet, for your patience, love and acceptance. It may have taken 30 years, but you were both worth waiting for.

Patrice Keet

First, I would like to thank Melissa for stealing my heart and leading me on a journey of self-discovery and enrichment. Her spontaneous and enthusiastic "yes" when I proposed the book idea propelled me through years of writing. I remain in awe of the courage and persistence Melissa brought to this project and to the challenges in her life. Many thanks, as well, to Melissa's daughters—beautiful young women both inside and out who have allowed my husband, Bob, and me to share their lives.

Bridget A. Lyons, my editor and coach, champion, and friend, deserves huge thanks for helping me through the process of putting my personal story into words. Her wisdom, talent and ability to help me take a tangled ball of complexities and create a coherent story from its threads enabled me to get to the finish line. I will always be in her debt.

While writing this book, I sometimes lost faith in the value of my story. I want to thank the following people for shoring me up and helping me to dig deeper and write better. They have been early readers, gracious critics, enthusiastic supporters, and believers in me.

Heartfelt thanks to: Andy Couturier of The Opening, Cynthia Druley; Olof Einarsdottir; Terry Grove; Julie Jaffe; Bonnie Keet; Janice Manabe; Mary and Henry Reath; Patrick Sullivan; my niece, Amanda; Jill Tardif; Anne Young; and to Quinn Cormier and her book group for offering me my first book club appearance.

Lifelong thanks to my kind, loving, clever, hilarious sister, Kathy Schneck. You've always believed in me. Pack the sandwiches for the tour!

Deep thanks to Virginia Scott for decades of helping me accept myself and for her insightful comments about how to improve this book. Thanks also to Patricia Noel for her emotional support and psychological insights as well as to Faye

Crosby for her detailed edits.

Thanks to my editors at Atmosphere Press, Tammy Letherer and Alex Kale, for getting this important story out into the world.

A very special thanks to Louis Jemison who left us way too soon and was an unabashed supporter of me, this book, and Melissa and her girls. Lou read the manuscript twice in one sitting and, never one short on advice, called me and said, "Write more." Lou's wisdom about living and dying and his steady presence and encouragement were invaluable.

Unfailing thanks to Corie and Kevin for being bright stars in my life and for opening their hearts to increasing our family.

"Thanks" is a paltry word for the constant, loving, and encouraging presence of my husband, Bob. He has been my rock and my wings for the past fifty-eight years. I particularly appreciate that he has never judged the blind spots in my parenting. He enabled us to take Melissa and her girls into our lives and continues to be the biggest cheerleader for them.

About the Authors

Patrice Keet was a marriage and family therapist for thirty years, with experience in private practice and school settings. She has hosted a radio show, started and ran a children's museum in Santa Cruz, CA, served on numerous non-profit boards of directors and raised two of her own children—in addition to being a non-traditional mother to Melissa and her daughters. This is her first book.

Melissa LaHommedieu is a social worker for the County of Santa Cruz where she specializes in matching individuals and families with stable housing solutions. She is the proud mother of two college-aged daughters and a star performer in her local karaoke scene. In addition to sharing her story through this book, Melissa is a regular speaker at events supporting foster care programs. She is a proud member of the Board of Directors of CASA of Santa Cruz County.

About Atmosphere Press

Atmosphere Press is an independent, full-service publisher for excellent books in all genres and for all audiences. Learn more about what we do at atmospherepress.com.

We encourage you to check out some of Atmosphere's latest releases, which are available at Amazon.com and via order from your local bookstore:

Finding Us, by Kristin Rehkamp

The Ideological and Political System of Banselism, by Royard Halmonet Vantion (Ancheng Wang)

Unconditional: Loving and Losing an Addict, by Lizzy and Adam

Telling Tales and Sharing Secrets, by Jackie Collins, Diana Kinared, and Sally Showalter

Nursing Homes: A Missionary's Journey Through Heaven's Waiting Room, by Tim Eatman Ph.D.

Timeline of Stars, by Joe Adcock

A Boy Who Loved Me, by Wilson Semitti

The Injustice in Justice, by Charmaine Loverin

Living in the Gray, by Katie Weber

Living with Veracity, Dying with Dignity, by Alison Clay-Duboff

Noah's Rejects, by Rob Kagan

A lot of Questions (with no answers)?, by Jordan Neben

Cowboy from Prague: An Immigrant's Pursuit of the American Dream, by Charles Ota Heller

Sleeping Under the Bridge, by Melissa Baker

The Only Prayer I Ever Have to Say Is Thank You, by M. Kaya Hill

Amygdala Blue, by Paul Lomax

A Caregiver's Love Story, by Nancie Wiseman Attwater